STREET ART AND GRAFFITI

A dissertation by street artist John D'oh

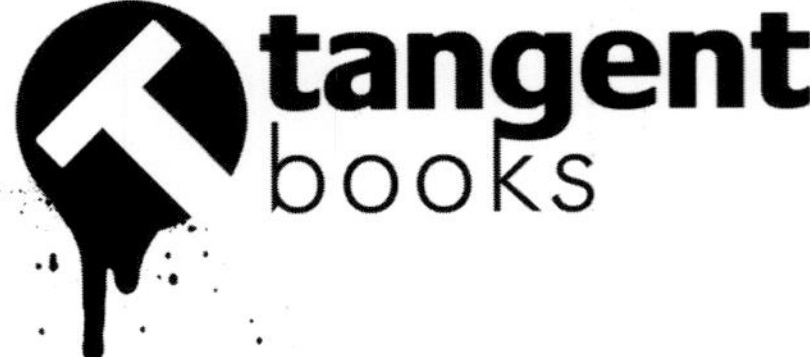

First published 2018 by Tangent Books
Unit 5.16 Paintworks, Arnos Vale, Bristol, BS4 3EH
Tel 0117 972 0645
www.tangentbooks.co.uk

ISBN 978-1-910089-76-7

Cover Photo: Shaun Brittain

Design: Joe Burt

Printed in Poland
www.lfbookservices.co.uk

A CIP record of this book is available at the British Library.

Printed on paper from a sustainable source

Contents

ACKNOWLEDGEMENTS

This book is inspired by the many questions I get asked about art by inquisitive students, members of the public and journalists. It is dedicated to all those who are engaged with and curious about art and culture in modern Britain.

I would like to take this opportunity to gratefully acknowledge the photographers who have supplied images for this publication and have allowed me to include their photographs free of charge. Without ongoing documentation, a lot of graffiti and street art would go largely unseen and forgotten because it is removed or painted over. So many thanks Paul Green, Jeremy Mosley and Rebecca Holmes.

I'd like to thank every festival that has given me a wall to paint on, as there are a lot of really talented artists and the selection process must be daunting. I appreciate having each opportunity.

I'd also like to take this chance to show my appreciation to Stik and Bambi for letting me use their images in this book.

I'd also like to express my gratitude to Mr. B for all the posters, prints and banknotes he's given me over the years – and I very much appreciate the crate of cider!

To everyone who has purchased this book, I can't thank you all enough. It is my first publication and has proved a bit of a challenge. Hopefully, it has inspired or provoked you in some meaningful way.

This book does not condone vandalism or the defacement of private or public property in any way.

Finally I would like to acknowledge my parents. I love you Mum. RIP Dad, I miss you every day. I know you said I can't change the world Dad, but hopefully I am making a difference in my own little way.

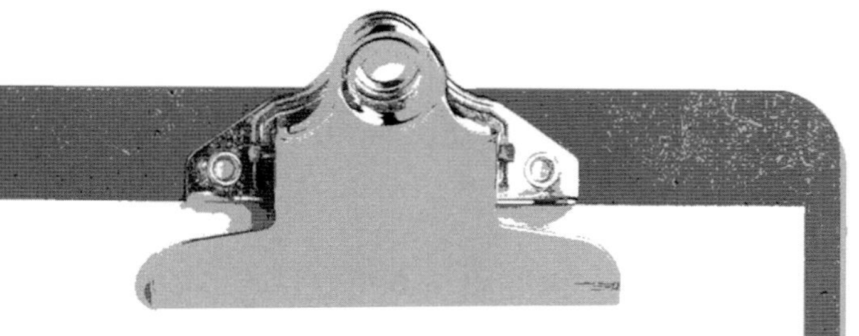

Introduction

I am honoured, humbled and feel more than a little privileged to have written this book. As with everything I do, some may find it a little controversial but I didn't want to just manufacture a generic picture book for coffee tables. As street art is slowly becoming part of the mainstream curriculum, I have been helping more and more students with their dissertations by answering their questions and providing personal insight into the world of urban art. I wanted to produce something that was thought provoking and covers topics that I regularly encounter from those wishing to learn both theoretically and practically. The views expressed are my own and hopefully at the end of this book you will see street art and graffiti more than just vandalism. My art is a little different than most and some see me as an activist or a humanitarian with a spray can. Take a look and make up your own mind.

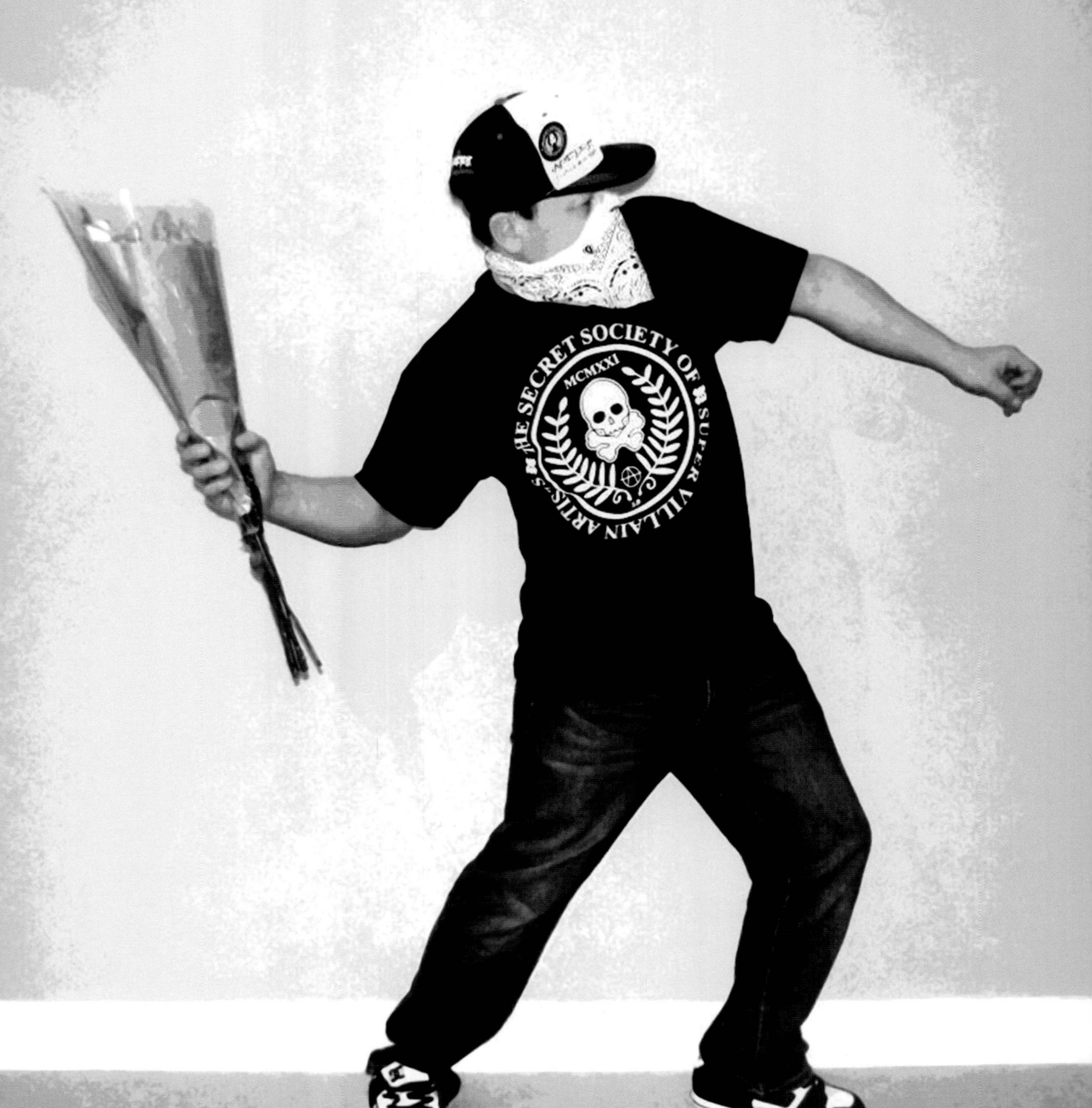
THE SECRET SOCIETY OF SUPER VILLAIN ARTISTS
MCMXXI

Who is John D'oh?

Persona, biography and the changing face of the Bristol graffiti scene

John D'oh?

Historically, "John Doe" was the fictional name given to a hypothetical individual who had the legal right to use a building, land or some other valuable property. In a similar way, my street art demonstrates that we all have the right to use and enjoy the public space that has often been privatised or sold-off to just a few wealthy individuals.

More generally, "John Doe" is a placeholder for a person who is either legally unidentified or whose identity is being officially withheld. So my borrowing of this title is not simply a reflection of the anonymity necessitated by the illegality of street art or the facelessness of the crowded urban environment, it is also an attempt to reclaim and re-appropriate this anonymity from bureaucratic and state power, showing that individuals have the right to control their own identities and the right not to be explicitly identified by the authorities.

"John Doe", like "Joe Public" or "John Smith", can also refer to an imagined "everyman" in certain situations. On the one hand, this generic name suggests a sense of "sameness" reflecting the conformity, depersonalisation and superficiality of investing in our metropolitan

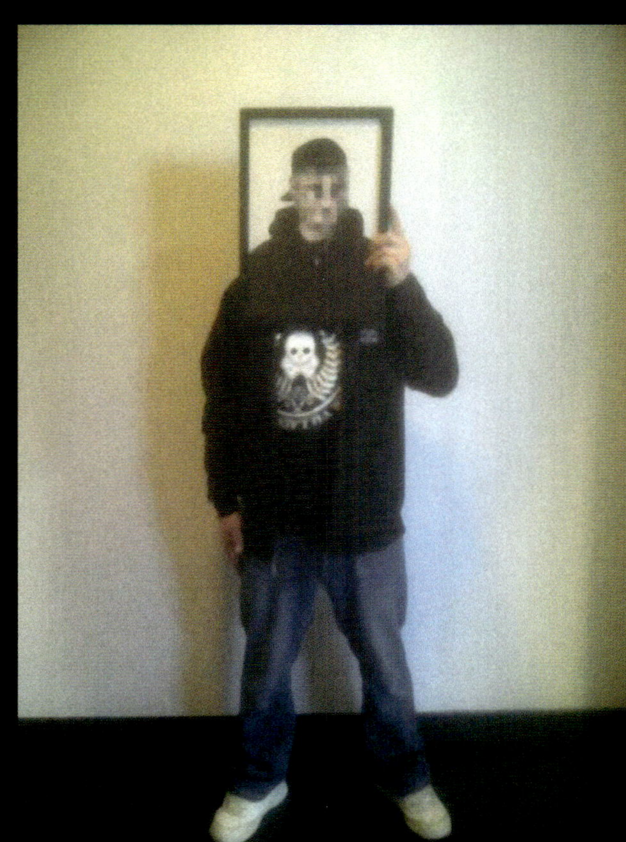

Self portrait of an anonymous street artist

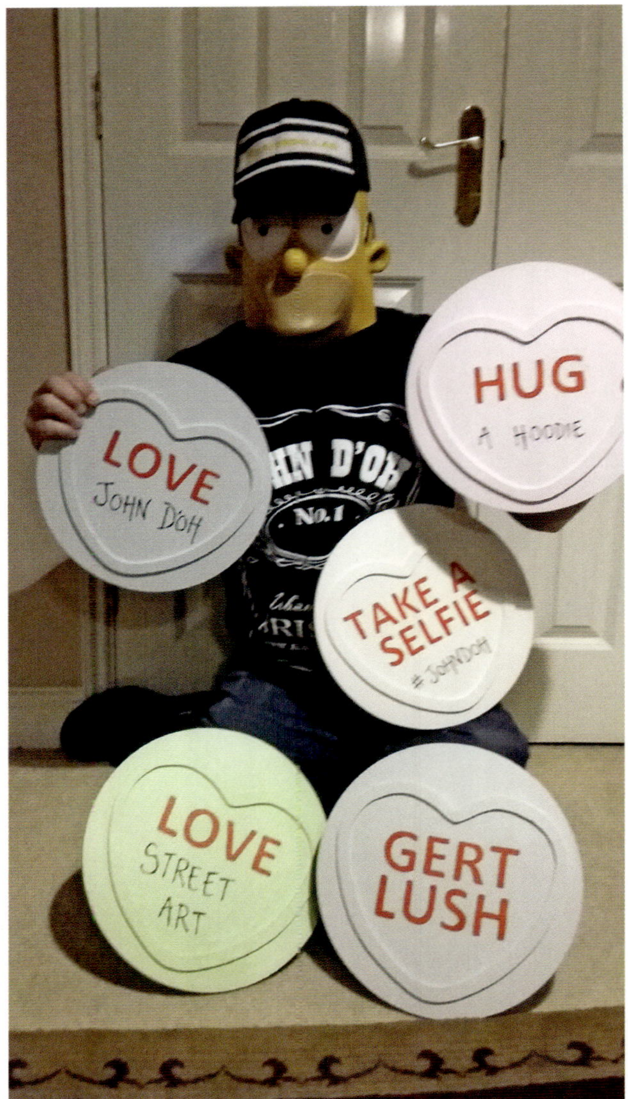

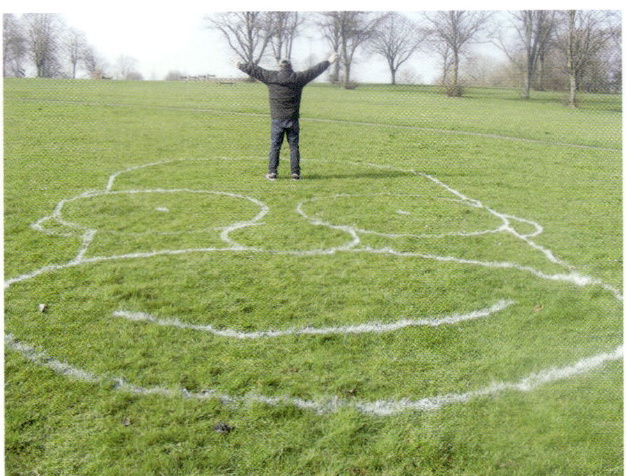

increasingly commercialised, citified world.

And this desire to provide humour and vibrancy to as many people as possible is partially why I changed the "Doe" to "D'oh" in my name. "D'oh" is an immediately recognisable catchphrase used by the fictional character Homer Simpson, especially when he realises that he has made a mistake or done an idiotic act. Using a pop cultural figure or phrase can be a way of grabbing a person's attention. Often, my work highlights the errors and idiocies of prominent public icons and politicians, making these authority figures seem just as cartoonish and fallible as Homer Simpson. I should say that he Homer mask which I occasionally wear is generally used to humorously conceal my identity. Contrary to some articles, I do not paint in the mask as it can be extremely claustrophobic and visibility is minimal.

About me

I was raised on the north side of Bristol during a relatively hard time. Unemployment was at over 10% – the highest rate in Britain since the Great Depression. I attended the local comprehensive school where my favourite lesson was art, although my drawing wasn't contained just within the session. After every lesson we would change classrooms for the next subject, giving me a new wooden desk to sit at and simultaneously a fresh canvas to doodle on. This schoolboy scribbling was often done over and alongside a previous child's

consumer culture. On the other hand, this "everyman" quality is inherent to street art, where painting is made readily available and accessible to the ordinary working people of the city. And, while I do not claim to speak for everyone, the artwork can provide humour and meaning to the average person as they go around their daily life, generating debate, conversation and a smile. This can act as a counterforce to the pervasive sense of invisibility, insecurity and rootlessness felt amongst people in our scrawls, creating a kind of competitive and illicit overlapping of words and images that is not dissimilar to the palimpsest of street art in the city. Inevitably, I was caught quite a few times and had to sand-down desks for what seemed like hours in detention. But this never put me off, it just made me more cautious. In fact, this could even be where my love of woodwork stems from. Who knows?

As with most teenagers music was a big part of my life and even during my time at school it changed from ska to hip-hop.

My art teacher was amazing, although we would cover topics in a much more practical and experiential way than in today's more theory-based education system. The school even had a kiln, although I never actually remember seeing it working. I imagine the clay was probably just recycled form the previous classes each time to save money. I can even remember learning how to create stencils in class, which the teacher demonstrated by making "revolutionary" posters. Looking back, I guess she was a bit of a hippy, but her classes were always fun and passionately executed. The stencils painted in school were done with poster paints but my first street stencil was done with spray paint shortly after.

I first started painting in 1983 and I would hardly call it an instant success. The stencil was roughly cut out from a cereal box with a Stanley knife blade and was sprayed in a shade of Ford Escort red in the same underpass that I walked through on my way to school. It was done in order to impress a girl and was a reproduction of a musician's logo that she had all over her text book. With a couple of friends on each side of the underpass you could practice to your heart's content. There was no specialist graffiti paint back then so I used to get my paint from the local cycle shop or car accessories shop. The paints were all cellulose based so would stink and were highly toxic.

At school everyone had similar canvas bags and rucksacks they wanted decorated in order to stand out, express themselves or simply increase their schoolyard popularity. So I became increasingly in-demand because,

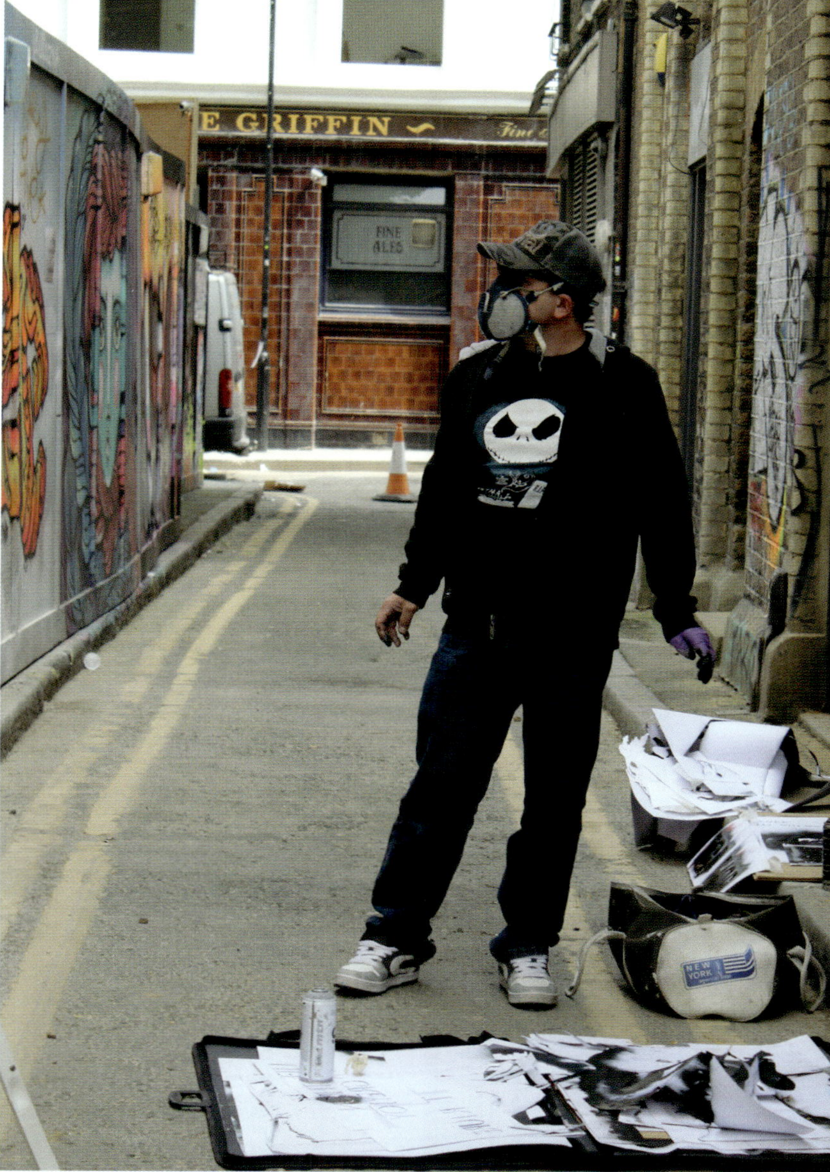

Blackhall Street on 28/05/2016

for the price of gravy and chips, I would take their bag home and bring it back the next day with its customised and requested design. The smell of correction fluid still stays with me today as normally Tipp-Ex and Biro were the media of choice when recreating the logos of groups like Madness and the Specials amongst others. As time went on and music genres changed, I also replicated things such as hip-hop album art and Rock Steady Crew cartoon figures. Occasionally I would also strip down and spay the odd push bike or BMX which had become

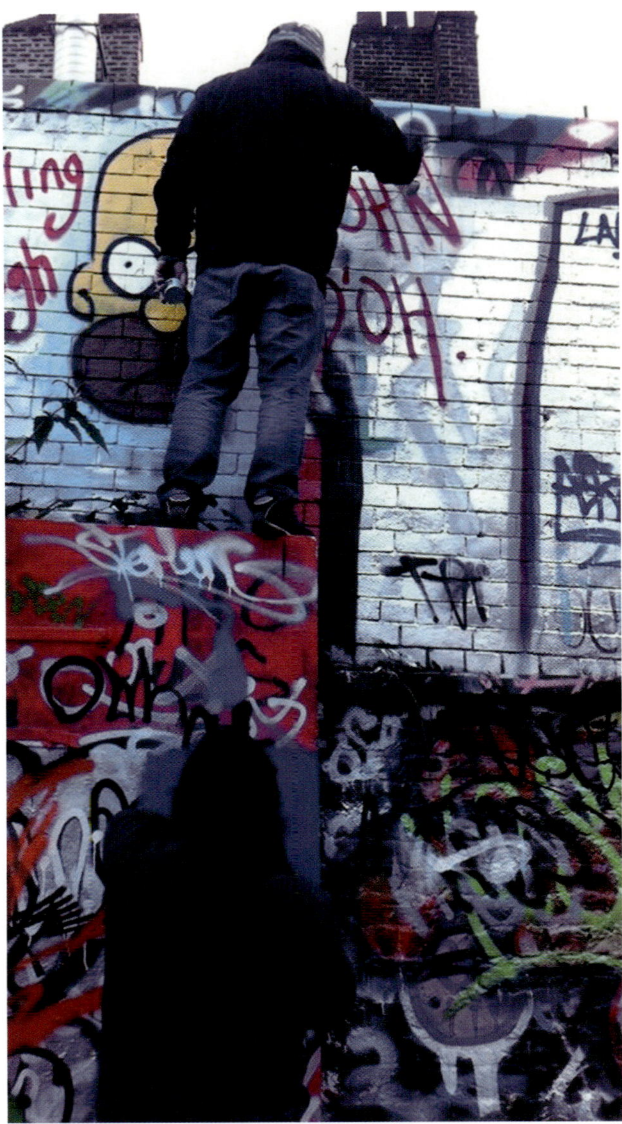

culture and anti-consumerism in street art culture today.

My painting was sporadic at the time as paint wasn't cheap. I often had to rely on my friends, who would break-dance for money at various locations around Bristol. Personally, I was never really that good at break-dancing and was generally quite a shy teenager, so I would hide at the back and do some mediocre body-popping. But here we see how other street activities, such as busking or dancing, form part of the overall context or culture that allows street art to function or flourish.

I grew up close to a railway track and coal yard, so occasionally we would go over there and mess around, throw bits of coal at each other and paint the odd coal carriage. You had to look out for the transport police though, as they were determined to catch you and would run after you for ages without stopping like a Terminator. However, if you managed to get under a carriage you could wedge yourself between the two axles and keep your feet off of the floor, thus hiding completely out of sight. Even now as a street artist, it is still much easier and more effective to quickly disappear or hide amongst the crowd rather than to frantically run away.

So, did you attend John Nation's Barton Hill Youth Centre in the 80s?
John Nation was a youth worker at the Barton Hill Youth Centre during the 1980s who encouraged many of the young but now well-known names and faces of Bristol graffiti that are still around today including Banksy, Inkie, Cheo, Jody, Nick Walker and lots more.

Unfortunately though for me I grew up on the opposite side of the city. There was no internet or social media back then but gradually you realise you aren't the only one who's doing it locally when you notice more and more art springing up around town. By suddenly appearing in the city all at once, the art made the streets feel spontaneous, organic and more connected. However, I did know Andy Burns Colwill at the time and he is still successfully painting today. Looking at the dates, I had got married and finished painting around the same time that most of John Nation's kids started their artistic

a bit of a hobby. And just in case you already have a bad impression of me, these bikes were not stolen. The new paint job was often done to make a cheap import resemble a more expensive, impressive and branded bike like a Diamondback. Cycle shops would also stock loads of different stickers and accessories to help pimp your ride. Instead of purchasing social capital directly, we reused already existing materials and cheaply imitated expensive brands in a way that prefigures the remix

Painted with
a paint brush
at the City
of Colours
festival,
Birmingham on
06/09/2014

"careers". Simultaneously, the state launched Operation Anderson in which 72 artists were arrested in a national operation. They were mainly from Bristol and from the club. So it is possible that "settling down" may have helped me avoid any personal incrimination. However, I would love to see some of the photos from that investigation to see if any of my old art is among the evidence. I used a different name and style back then, and even left work unsigned, which helps avoid these issues of liability, responsibility and alleged criminality. If a company can change its trading name and branding in order to avoid paying the debts it is morally responsible for, why can't your average citizen or artist?

The fact that there were other individuals and groups operating back then in the north side of the city outside of John Nation's now famous group of artists is a necessary corrective to the popularised narrative of street art history in Bristol.

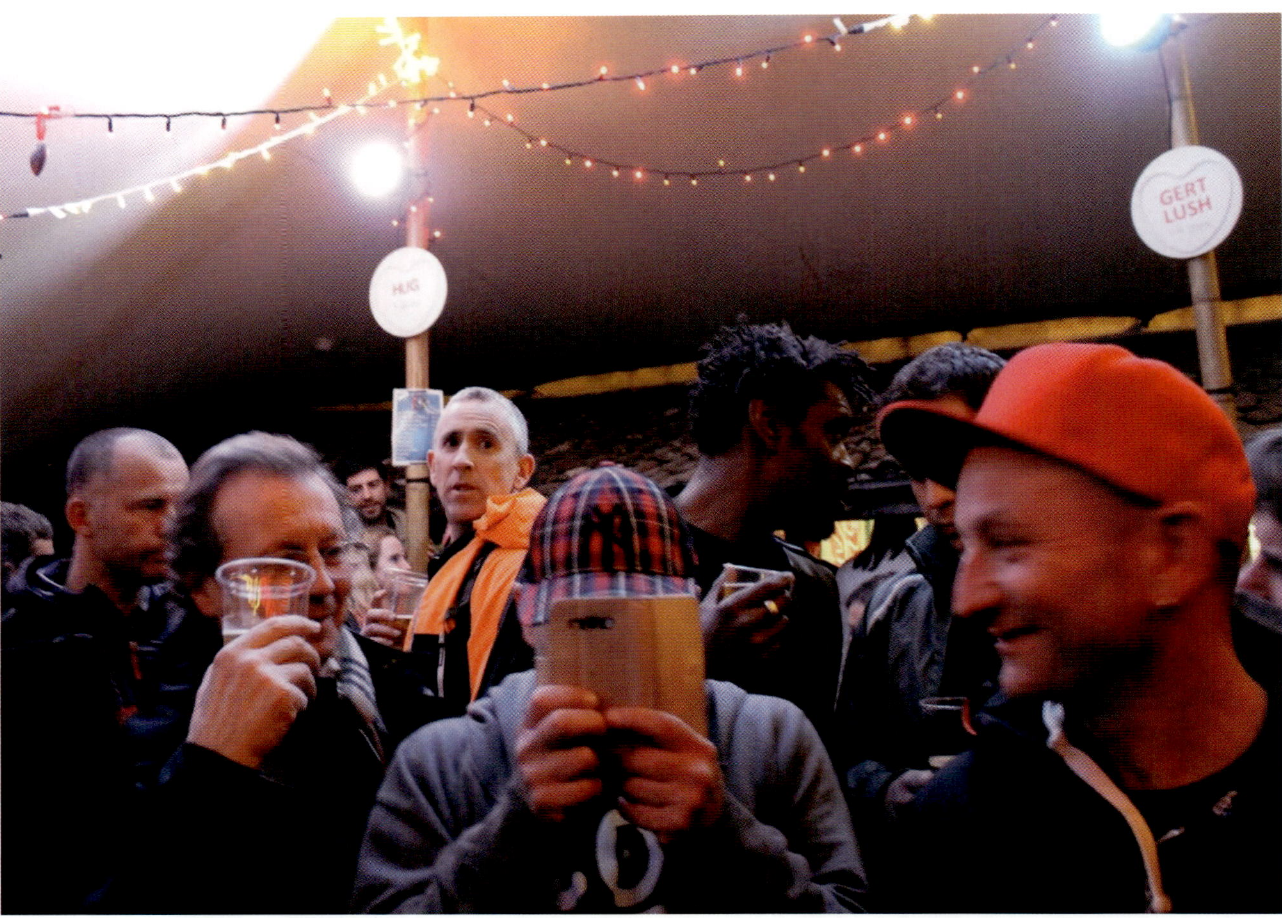

Has street art and graffiti changed since then?

In many ways, street art has become more acceptable within the Bristol community and has helped form a local and slightly anarchic identity for the city. However, we still have no recognised legal walls that I am aware of and artists still risk arrest whenever they paint. While Operation Anderson has generally been forgotten by the local street art scene, in 2015 a new investigation was implemented called Operation Block. This crackdown by Bristol City Council and the Avon and Somerset Police was much more narrowly targeted on restricting and removing tagging while retaining the more popular and pictorial forms of street art.

While opposing tagging, Bristol City Council's Assistant Mayor Daniella Radice was hoping to rewrite the local authority's approach to urban art by recognising the economic and cultural contribution it can make to the city. To this day there has not been any further development. With this unresolved, most artists will not openly paint and risk the chance of arrest. In response to this, Bristol has now seen an increasing amount of throw-ups or "throwies" on its walls. Unlike traditional tags throw-ups generally consist of two colours, one colour for the outline and one for the infill. These are quick to execute and therefore reduce the suspicion or attention given to the writer, preventing them from getting caught by the police.

Paint technology has also moved on immensely as there are now specialist low-pressure paints which are fair less toxic and an array of nozzles that can produce fantastic effects. The range of colours are improving constantly and they continue to get more environmentally friendly. I would still recommend always wearing a mask though.

Early documentation was not easy as digital cameras did not exist and developing photos was a bit of a luxury because the processing costs were very expensive. Cameras were generally large and bulky and would not fit easily into your pocket like modern phones do. Taking footage and photos was a much more conspicuous act. Developing was always a bit of a lottery because with cheap 35mm you never knew how many images would come out correctly exposed and the quality was often hit and miss. Also to develop images from rolls of film you would have to take them into a chemist such as Boots or stores such as Truprint which were on every high street and have since disappeared. Consequently, if you brought images of your art to be developed, the developer screening the roll of film could consider it as direct evidence of vandalism and contact the police. In fact, policing was a lot more proactive and local community police officers were the norm. The processors had to follow moral and censorious guidelines, with nudity, violence and any hint of criminality often being investigated. So the earlier unrecorded and ephemeral nature of graffiti can be seen as a response to the legal and sometimes technical inability to create photographs. However, I should add that some processors did have a sense of humour, positioning peelable "overexposure" stickers on top of exposed body parts and bits of nudity, which sarcastically drew attention to the very things they were supposed to be hiding.

Anonymity

Anonymity is one of the first things you need to consider. It can depend on where you paint, because some towns are more tolerant or simply less proactive in prosecuting street art. The content of your art is important when considering the degree of anonymity taken, because political imagery or commentary on sensitive public issues can cause offence in certain locations and thus increase the pressure to find and prosecute street artists.

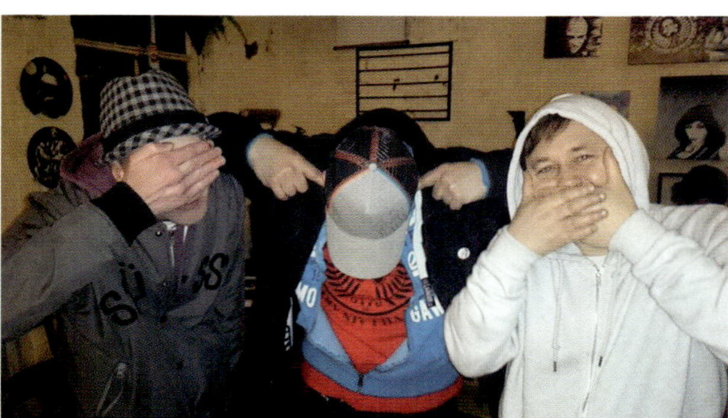

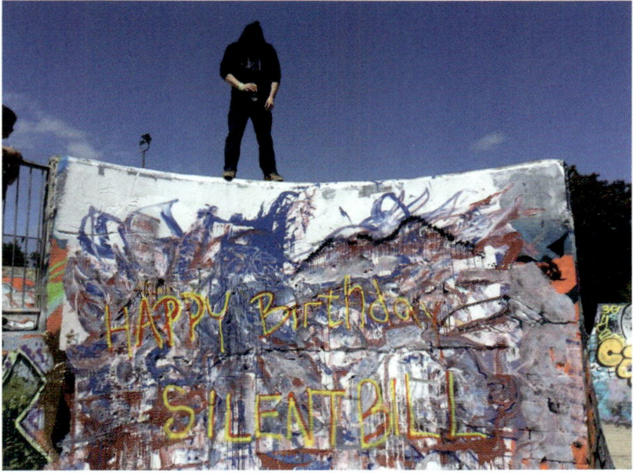

Anonymity may not even be entirely necessary if you are going to paint all of your art entirely legally. In fact, when it comes to profiting from street art a lot of clients want to physically meet the artist in-person and complete anonymity often makes exhibitions, shows and autographs a little difficult. I have had to refuse quite a few opportunities in order to maintain my anonymity, including spots on the *One Show*, *Made in Bristol TV* and *NTR television* (Netherlands) to give just a few examples from the last year alone. I have even rebuffed radio opportunities as my voice is instantly recognisable.

For some, incorporating a character-based mask or persona into your artwork allows you to remain both hidden and in public at the same time. Painting with a respirator doubles as both a health-and-safety tool while hiding your face. It is particularly useful all day at festivals and while not enjoyable it is often necessary.

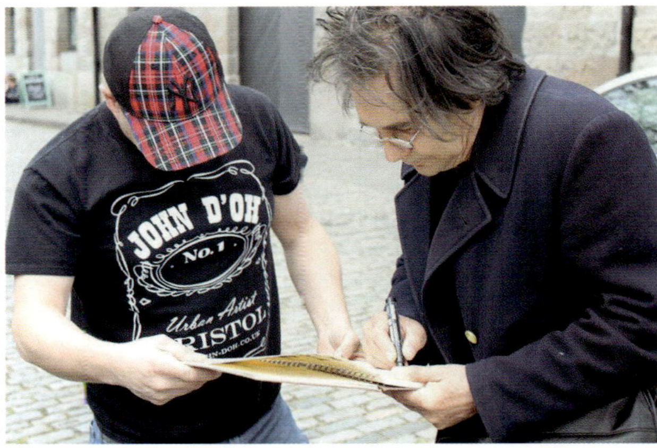

Me and Blek
Le Rat at the
Arnolfini,
Bristol on
04/2017

I have a fairly well-paid and responsible day job that I would like to keep and I am pretty sure my employer would disapprove of my creative streak. So, if you have a certain kind of employer, you will probably have to go to considerable lengths in order to hide your identity like I do. Being a part-time artist also limits the projects you can accept because, due to time constraints, conflicting schedules and far away locations, you may not be able to complete a work in a satisfactory manner. Arguably, if you are serious about becoming an artist and attempting to make an income from it, then part-time and anonymous is probably not the best way to achieve this goal.

Personally, I don't think my bad boy reputation is justified as the majority of what I paint is done legally and on builders' hoardings at festivals. I have often thought about the issues of legality and damage beforehand, so often my art is attached with screws and high-powered magnets that can be removed without any destruction.

To a certain extent, anonymity, by removing the biographical details, can allow people to focus more on the artwork itself and the messages that it is attempting to convey. On the other hand, anonymity can cultivate an aura of mystery and intrigue that turns the street artist into a kind of reclusive celebrity figure that the public constantly want to find out about.

I have found that there is generally some honour amongst thieves in the street art scene. In general, most artists won't "out" each other to the police or spread an artist's real name to others. Although violating graffiti etiquette and getting involved in the tribal politics between competing local artists can encourage this kind of behaviour. In fact, there is a very small percentage that does like to name-drop real identities in order to elevate themselves and gain popularity by appearing to be more connected and in-the-know.

Graffiti etiquette and tagging

Graffiti etiquette is generally followed by taggers and graffiti writers. There are many rules but the main ones are that you never paint over another artist's work unless you can do better and then it is courtesy to take out the whole piece. One particularly notorious example of the offence caused by an infringement of these casual guidelines is evident in the feud between King Robbo and Banksy. In 2009 Banksy partially painted over a 1985 King Robbo mural next to Regent's Canal in Camden, sparking an ongoing confrontation between the two differing styles of and attitudes towards graffiti.

It is considered a sign of disrespect to cross out or paint over somebody else's tag. These days, in the age of social media, it is much easier to contact a fellow artist and resolve any such conflict by occasionally asking permission to paint over a piece of work which has become heavily defaced. I have personally been contacted by other artists who have asked whether it is permissible to paint over my work, ironically changing a potential act of disregard into a mark of respect, which is nice. This is perhaps a necessary development, as it is a small community where everybody tends to know one another and any small disagreement could become quite fractious for everybody. I have many friends who are writers and taggers and theses days in Bristol most of us get along.

Historically speaking, notions of "politeness" have played an important role in distinguishing between and keeping separate the working and middle classes. These invented codes of self-consciously polite behaviour promoted cosmopolitan and educated values over the everyday practices of the lower classes. Arguably, the development of a self-aware decorum amongst artists

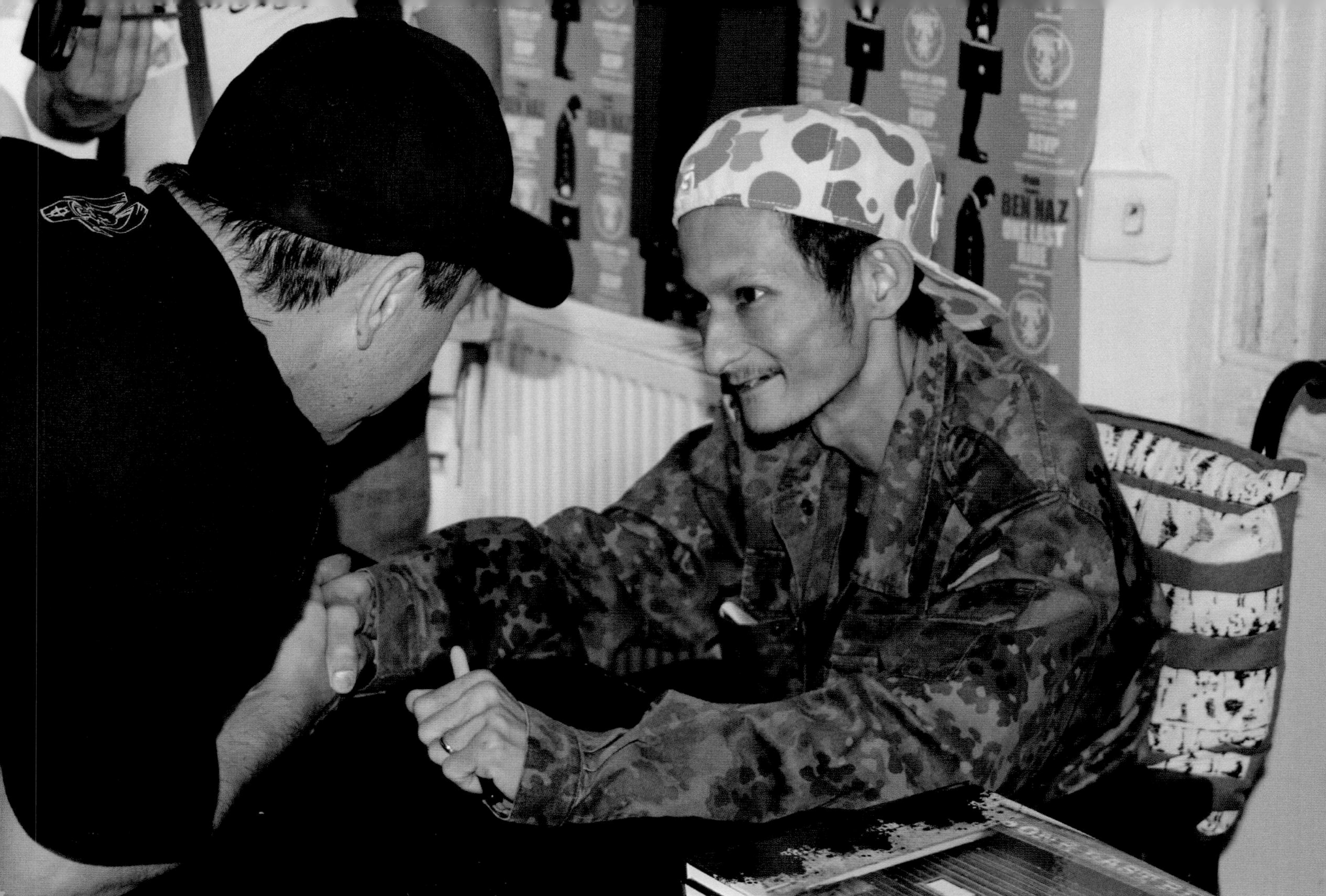

may reflect the increasing involvement of the middle-classes in street art and the gentrification of the urban art scene. At the same time, this "propriety" also works as a way of distinguishing "morally good" artists from the "bad" and thus creates a hierarchy of art that suits their social and political tastes, such as the prioritisation of property rights.

Artists of the early Renaissance and the Middle Ages were considered as simple craftsmen of no high importance. Consequently, they used the self-portrait as a kind of sneaky signature, often inserting their face in amongst the peripheral figures and anonymous crowds in their commissioned paintings. Later, when artists became highly-prized figures by giving princes, popes and bankers social prestige through their art, signing their work became an essential – and arguably narcissistic – part of the artist's brand. Tagging could be said to take a minimalistic approach to art, removing the representational content of an image and using only what is relevant in our celebrity and consumerist culture; the social capital of the artistic signature. On the other hand, tagging could be seen as a reversal of the specialisation and professionalisation of the deified artist. Here, the tagged "signature" becomes a

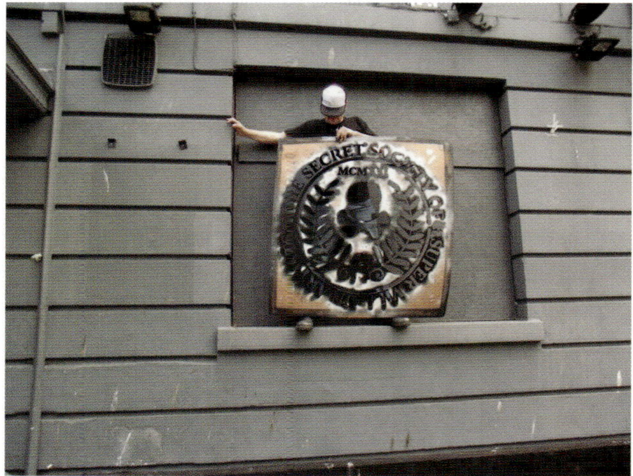

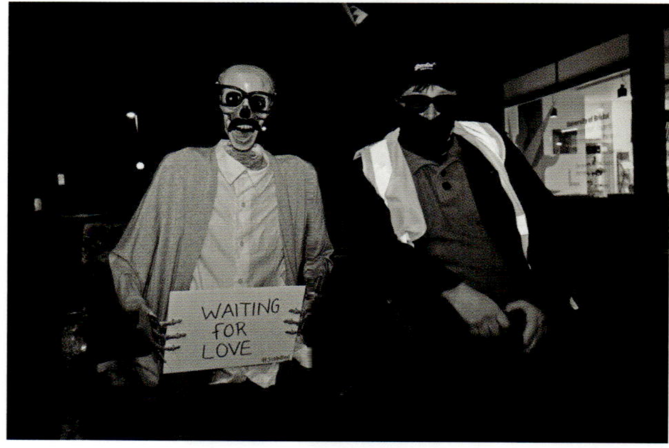

way for people without any wealth or social prestige to assert their seemingly irrelevant selfhood amongst the anonymity of the modern city. Instead of the face becoming the signature, the signature becomes the face.

The Broken Window theory

It is widely perceived that graffiti is an expensive burden on a local community that not only costs money to remove, but lowers property values and even encourages further costly acts of criminal damage. This negative view of street art has been popularised by the so-called Broken Window theory developed by George L. Kelling and James Q. Wilson. ('Broken Windows: The Police and Neighbourhood Safety', The Atlantic Monthly 249.3, March, 1982, pp. 29-38). They argue that permitting minor crimes, such as graffiti, littering or vagrancy, creates a visible invitation to commit further and more serious crime in a given area by suggesting that there is no security or sense of community.

In 2013 Mary Portas was tasked with regenerating a failing high street in Weston-super-Mare and I was privileged to be involved in this project. With the collaboration of artists and landlords the run-down premises that had fallen into a state of disrepair were gradually rejuvenated and beautified by the vivid colours and shapes of the street art and graffiti. This can be seen as a counter argument to the "broken window theory" and its stereotypical presentation of graffiti, demonstrating that street art, when done aesthetically, legally and in a communal fashion, can not only revive an area experiencing urban decay, but generate revenue and tourism. With the increase of online shopping and wage growth failing to keep up with inflation, physical stores are increasingly resorting to creating a "shopping experience" in order to draw customers in and remain profitable. Arguably, by offering something visually engaging and tangible, urban art can help improve our regional economy.

"But it's just a stencil?"

I have heard this comment so many times at festivals and on social media. In some ways this dismissive attitude parallels the public attitude toward contemporary and abstract art when critics say "my child could have painted that!" The "easiness" of some conceptual art prioritises the meaningful idea over any craftwork, whereas the "easiness" of stencil art is often a practical requirement of speeding up the physical creation when doing a legally ambiguous activity. In that over generalisation, the two artistic styles seem almost opposite. By giving you the ability to pre-make your art, this stencil minimises the installation time and makes it relatively quick and easy to paint your images or text, especially when painting in low-light levels and in places which are busy or under a lot of CCTV surveillance. Although I wouldn't class myself as a stencil artist I do dabble with this type of art quite a lot and have become well-known for it.

Stencils themselves can be seen as part of the urban landscape. Living in a cardboard box is stereotypically associated with urban homelessness and cardboard often makes up a lot of the street litter in our cities. By transforming this symbol of detritus and the downtrodden into a piece of art can be seen as a recycling and socially transformative act.

A stencil is essentially a cut-out template of an image or word, often made out of cardboard, whose hollowed-out sections can be filled with colour, leaving behind a duplicate image painted on the surface. In multi-layer stencils, several of these stencils are applied to the canvas or wall in a specific order, with each individual layer adding additional details and different colours to the overall composite picture. While multiple layers can add complexity and depth to your work, they require more time to execute, increasing the chances of being apprehended. So the number of layers that will be used is a question every stencil artist asks themselves beforehand. Layering colours can be slightly tricky or annoying at first, as each layer of pigment you add on top can mix with the layers already painted. For instance, a yellow layer on top of a red background will possibly become orange. The time-consuming effort involved in creating layer after layer of a stencil will be pointless if the detail is too far away to be seen or perhaps in high security areas where the risk is too high. When painting on a horizontal surface, the stencil can be weighted-down with, for example, bolts, washers or stones. This can also free-up your hands to paint more easily and quickly.

The size of the stencil is important in sometimes contradictory ways. On the one hand, it needs to be big enough to make a visual impact amongst all the advertisements and graffiti in its specific location with, for example, larger images needed for rooftop settings. On the other hand, sometimes the image has to be quite small in busy or well-populated areas such as high streets where installation time has to be vastly reduced.

Speed is of the essence. The main reason is, obviously, avoiding law enforcement. And by leaving the

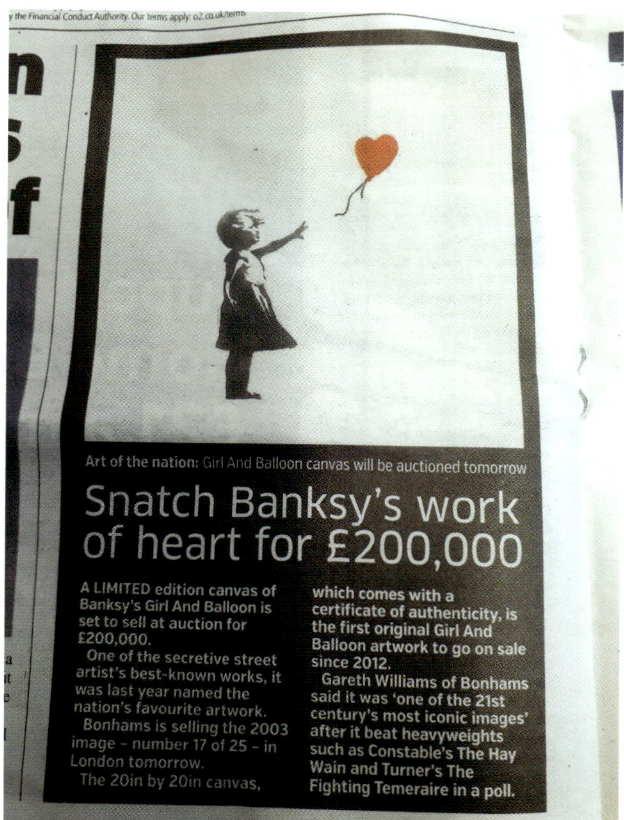

Art of the nation: Girl And Balloon canvas will be auctioned tomorrow

Snatch Banksy's work of heart for £200,000

A LIMITED edition canvas of Banksy's Girl And Balloon is set to sell at auction for £200,000.

One of the secretive street artist's best-known works, it was last year named the nation's favourite artwork.

Bonhams is selling the 2003 image – number 17 of 25 – in London tomorrow.

The 20in by 20in canvas, which comes with a certificate of authenticity, is the first original Girl And Balloon artwork to go on sale since 2012.

Gareth Williams of Bonhams said it was 'one of the 21st century's most iconic images' after it beat heavyweights such as Constable's The Hay Wain and Turner's The Fighting Temeraire in a poll.

scene of the crime quickly, there is less chance that a member of the public will see you and later reveal your identity if painting anonymously. Also, painting speedily complements the often high-paced style of living that takes place in large cities.

The location is, in a way, a part of the artwork itself. The image is often a response to a local issue and may playfully incorporate the physical paraphernalia of the city, such as drains, manhole covers or lampposts, into the actual work. This can be said to defamiliarise the public from the mindless commuting, consumerism or urban decay that takes place daily in their grey and monotonous landscapes. To a certain extent, street art is an urban form of *plein air* painting, where you react to the constantly shifting levels of public activity and the chances of suspicion. This means that, on rare occasions, a piece may have to be abandoned midway through

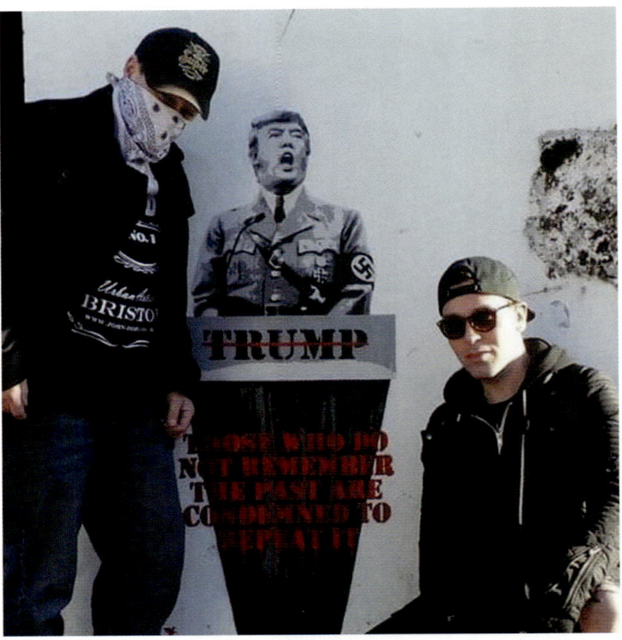

painting. Location can also be physically risky. When somewhere elevated, highly secure or visible it may paradoxically be better to pretend you have permission and to wear something like a high-visibility jacket in order to gain temporary access or look less suspicious. Designing your stencil forces you to think ahead and be environmentally and situationally aware because painting outside and vertically in the wind, rain or heat is quite different to painting flat in controlled conditions. And in some places your art may last a long time or gradually be tagged or painted over by other artists throughout the years in a kind of palimpsest. In other areas the life expectancy for an artwork can be just a couple of hours, where councils or competing crews may completely paint over your work. In the centre of Bristol, for instance, the artwork is rotated quite frequently, so one should perhaps not put a lot of time and resource into an image that may not last the day there.

The bigger the stencil and the higher the wind speed, the more risky it is to execute an artwork on your own. Painting with the aid of other others can mean there is assistance in holding the stencil tightly against the surface and preventing it from becoming detached, this can help to reduce overspray and increase the speed of production. Constructing your stencil of a good quality card or Mylar is also a good investment or else when you hold the stencil up to attach it to the wall for the first time it may catch a gust of wind and break apart.

When painting external or going large the most important thing in my opinion is increasing the size of bridges. A bridge is the uncut material which holds all of the parts of the stencil together thus keeping it from falling apart. Bridges often hold what is known as islands in place which are the parts of the stencil inside the external cuts or hole. Increasing the size of bridges adds strength and stability to a stencil, to resist damage from wind and rain. When doing multi-layer pieces it is possible to hide the bridges as you go under the next layer or when you get competent enough on large pieces just freehand that in. In the studio the bridging can be a lot smaller because it is usually laid flat in a wind-free environment.

Often, the labour-intensive process of creating a hand-cut stencil means that you have to reuse and adapt the same image in order to recoup your original investment. This also means choosing each image wisely and planning for future use. Each reuse of the stencil can risk damage from rips, tears and the build up of paint which can reduce the image quality and remove the details.

There are lots of tutorials on the internet which explain how to make your first stencil and it's probably worth starting with small, single-layer silhouettes and experimenting with the various graffiti paints and nozzles. The flatter or tighter you hold your stencil to the surface, the crisper and cleaner your image will look. Once you have your stencil the rest is down to practice or trial and error to find ways to paint that work for you. People's skills also develop over a period of time.

Up until a few years ago, most stencils were painstakingly cut by hand with a scalpel but these days technology has meant that this is not always the case. Artists can now get their images laser cut by a machine doing the cutting for them. This removes the individual time, care and labour from much of the creative process.

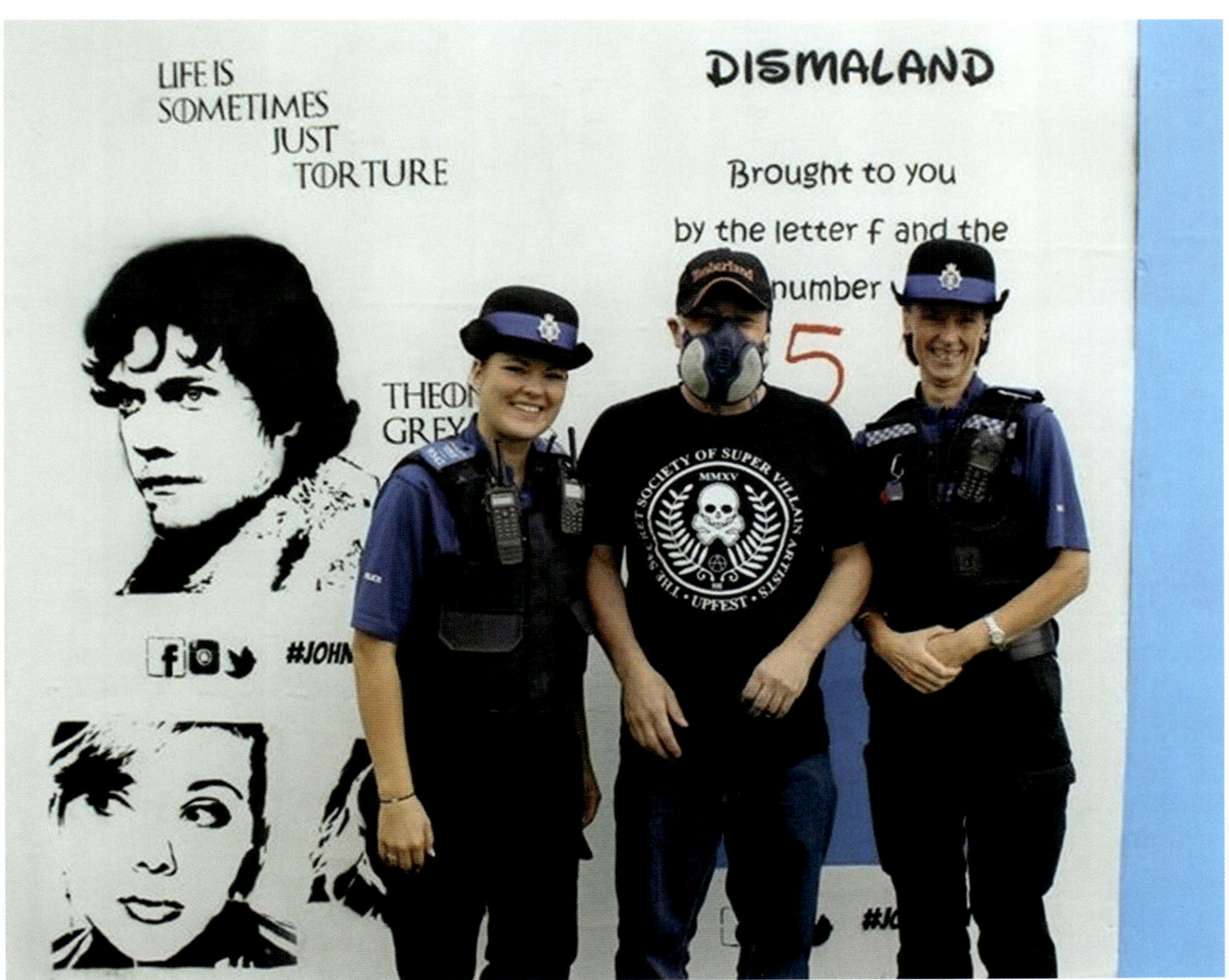

Not to mention some of the idiosyncratic mistakes. To me there is something impersonal about this and it is a technique that some artists go a long way to deny using. Over time, street art has become much more Warholian in its production methods. Some might say that if this technology is there and it works efficiently then why not use it? It may even be ideal for single-use stencils and the urgent need to respond to something topical quickly. I suppose I am just saying be honest as you are only stroking your own ego. Or, if stencilling onto a canvas, why not just Photoshop and print straight onto the canvas itself?

So what makes a good stencil? It's hard to say. Sometimes you don't need multi-layers and, from time to time, text on its own has been enough to catch people's attention. One of the most iconic images in street art is Banksy's *Balloon Girl* which is an extremely easy stencil to cut. I think it's important not to compare yourself to anyone else, just have fun with it. It's great for all ages and ANYONE can do it.

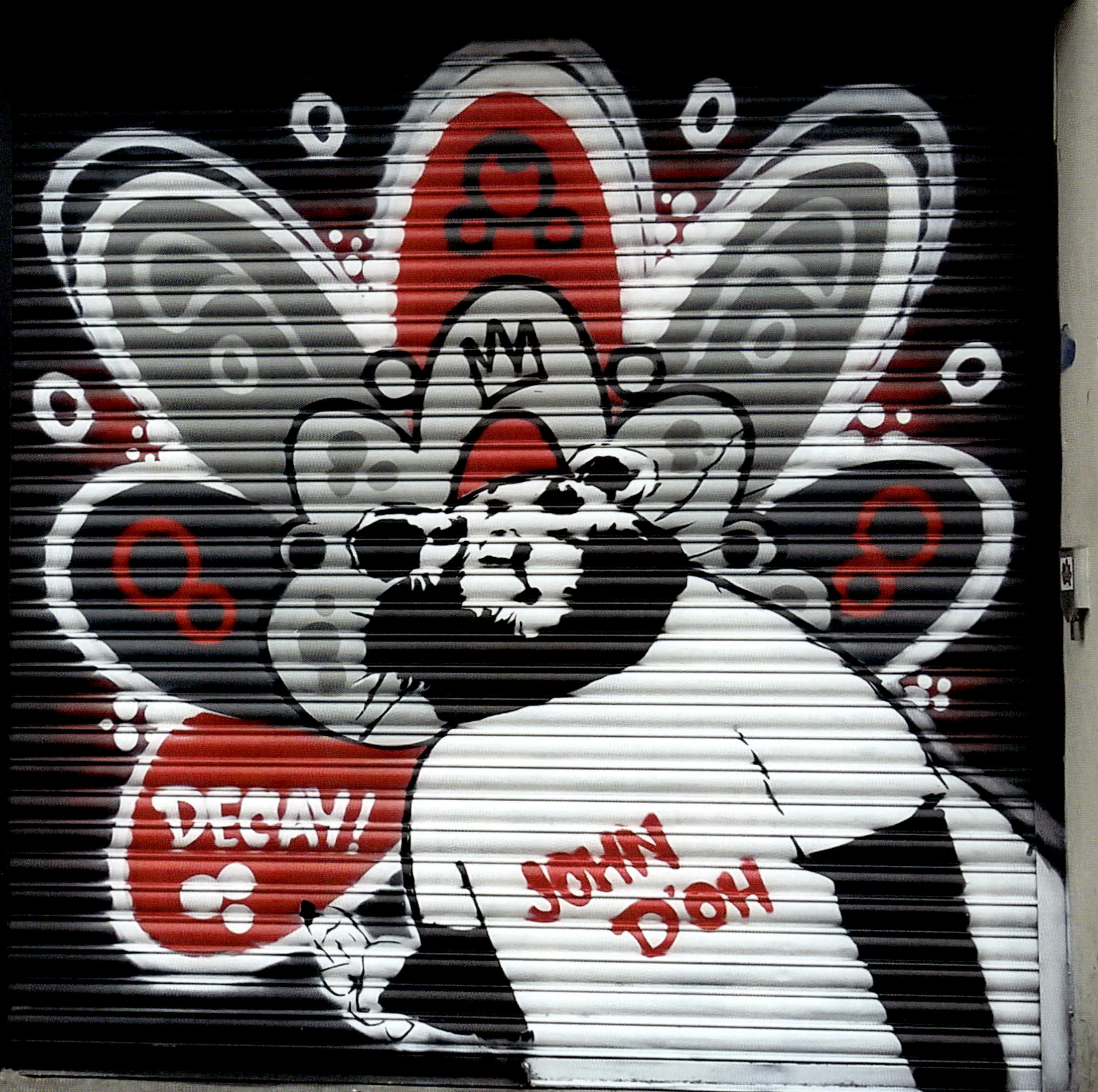

the rat lives !
DECAY!
JOHN D'OH

My Street Art

I have been exhibited all over the world but there is something special about painting on a wall. Street art has an illicit thrill of working against time and authority. Simultaneously, there is a sense of certainty in that you know somebody will definitely get the chance to see your art in the busy city as opposed to a small, elite and perhaps intimidating gallery. I suppose that, for me at least, street art is about getting a message across in the moment and hopefully raising a few smiles in the process. Urban art and graffiti is meant to be a temporary art, reflecting the diversity and fast-paced nature of city life, but it is surprising how many artists keep patching up their own work. This attempt to fix an image seems to have a conservative and individualistic function, attempting to preserve the singular identity of an artwork against the changes of time, society and environment.

In 2017 I went to Lonely Planet's street art book signing. The event also screened the *Stealing Banksy* film and followed on from this with a talk and public debate on contemporary street art. The discussion was really interesting as there was a good mix of options and experiences in the audience. While listening, however, I realised that there are a lot of people who are just into

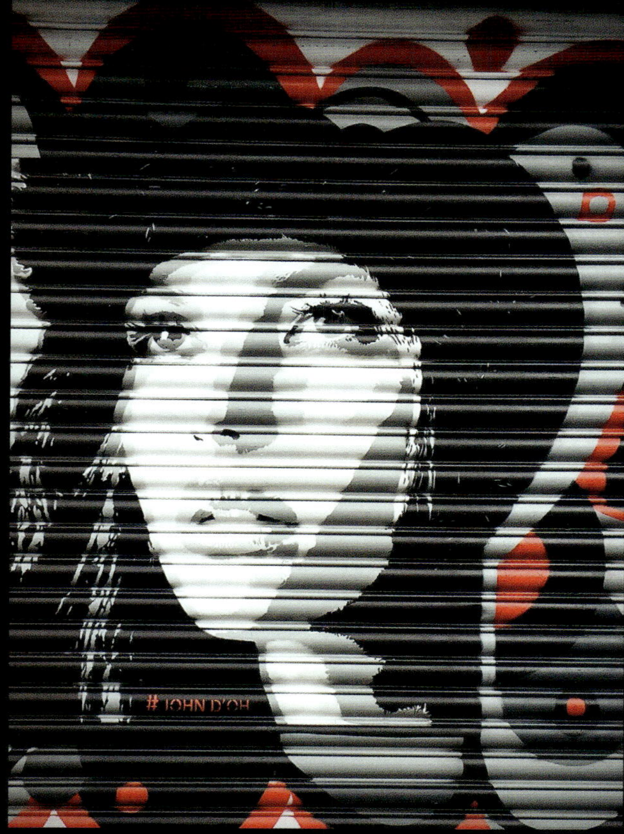

Shutter painted with fellow artist and friend Decay on North Street in Bedminster on 09/07/2016

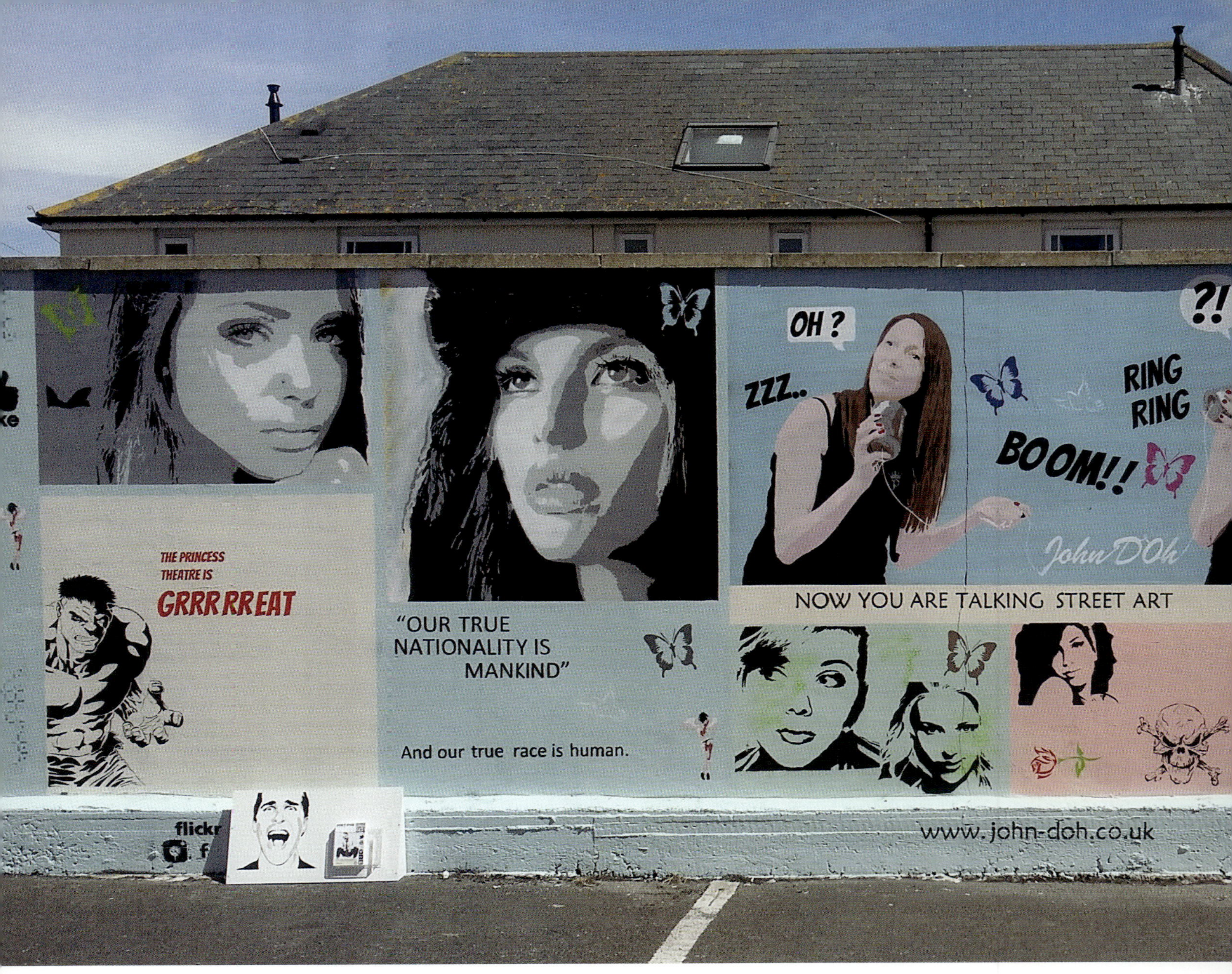

Burnham-on-Sea Paint Festival, Princess Theatre car park

street art and graffiti for fame and fortune.

The idea of having to churn out artwork just to pay the bills, regardless of the message or content, is something that doesn't appeal to me and changes an image from being art into being a commodity. After painting a piece on the street, I am almost instantly contacted by people asking when I will be reproducing the image as a print. Mass production is presumed to be a foregone conclusion and is now the established norm. In fact, most small galleries won't let you exhibit without producing a run of prints to sell. I myself was contacted by a Bristol gallery who wanted me to host a solo show but only on the condition of creating a line of prints. I agreed and invested a lot of time and effort in producing the required set of prints. However, after all that, the event was cancelled because the landlord wanted the

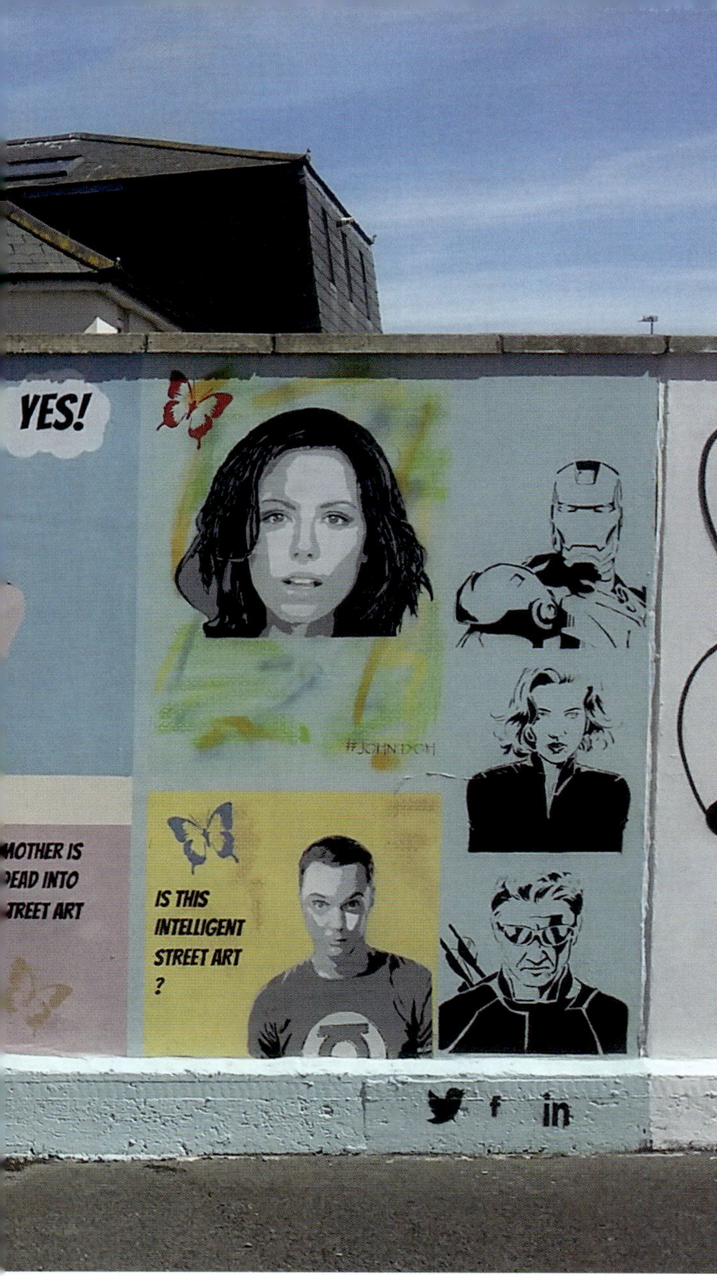

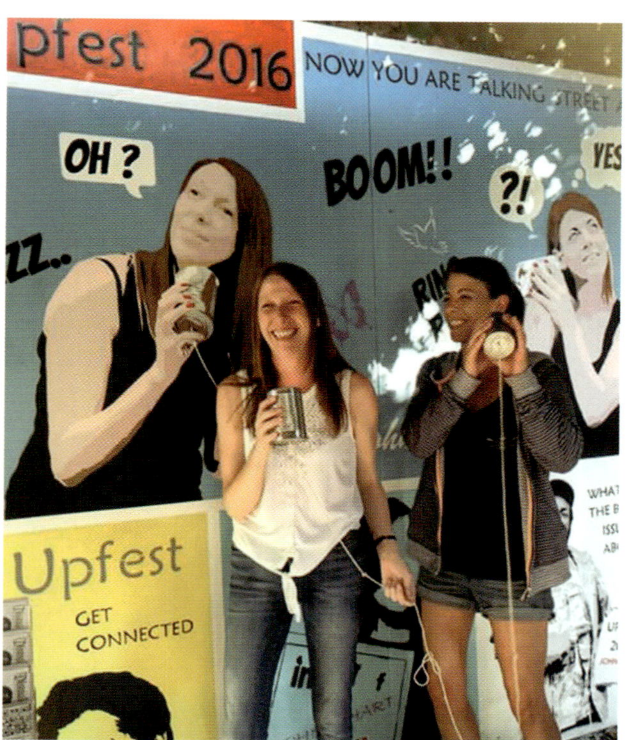

Upfest paint festival in Bristol 2016. Incorporated a couple of friends into my art. Pitched the concept of my name between two string cans and they loved the idea

property back from the pop-up gallery.

Street art can take many forms and I try to experience and combine as many different styles as I can. I do not claim to be a master of any of these particular methods, but I have learned and developed from each piece I have made. Street art also encourages an interdisciplinary approach to art, requiring broad practical skills, painting and even photography. The main thing is that you give it a go, not every piece you produce will or should be a masterpiece and we all learn from our mistakes. It's amazing how often you look back and see that some artists have improved, others have faded away and many are simply producing the same stuff that they have been making for years.

With the increasing popularity of social media it is getting easier than ever to get your images seen, meaning that even an image painted in an empty car park or in your own house can become quite popular. However, I personally don't think counting the number of likes or followers you have online is a measure of success or quality as even a quickly taken selfie of a good looking person in their underwear will gain an instant, fickle and frankly meaningless popularity. In fact, some people attempt to buy popularity instead of earning it through creating meaningful art, spending their wages or benefits on purchasing followers or bots in order to look more popular, successful or influential than they really are. Although if you are paying out all

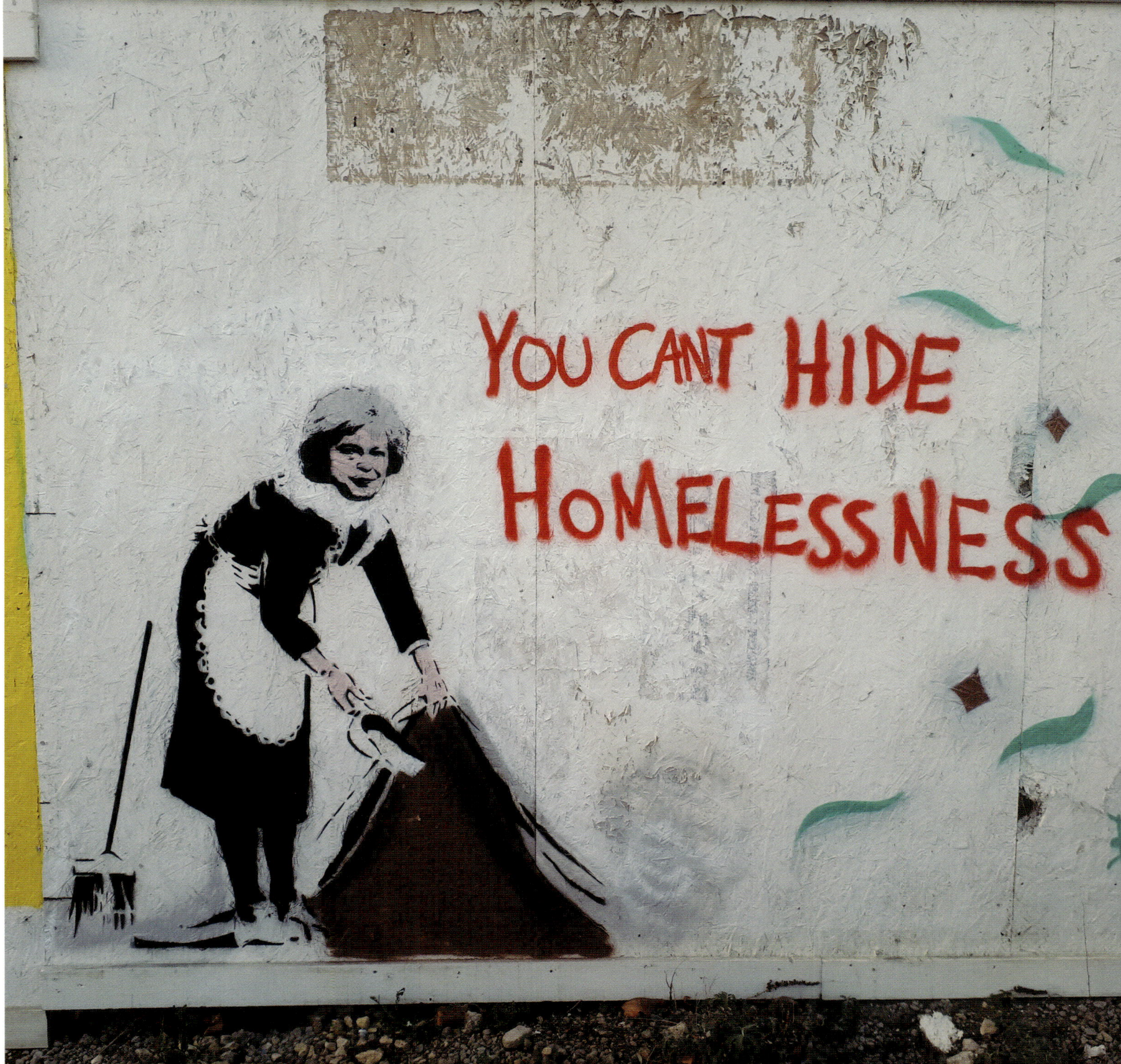

YOU CANT HIDE
HOMELESSNESS

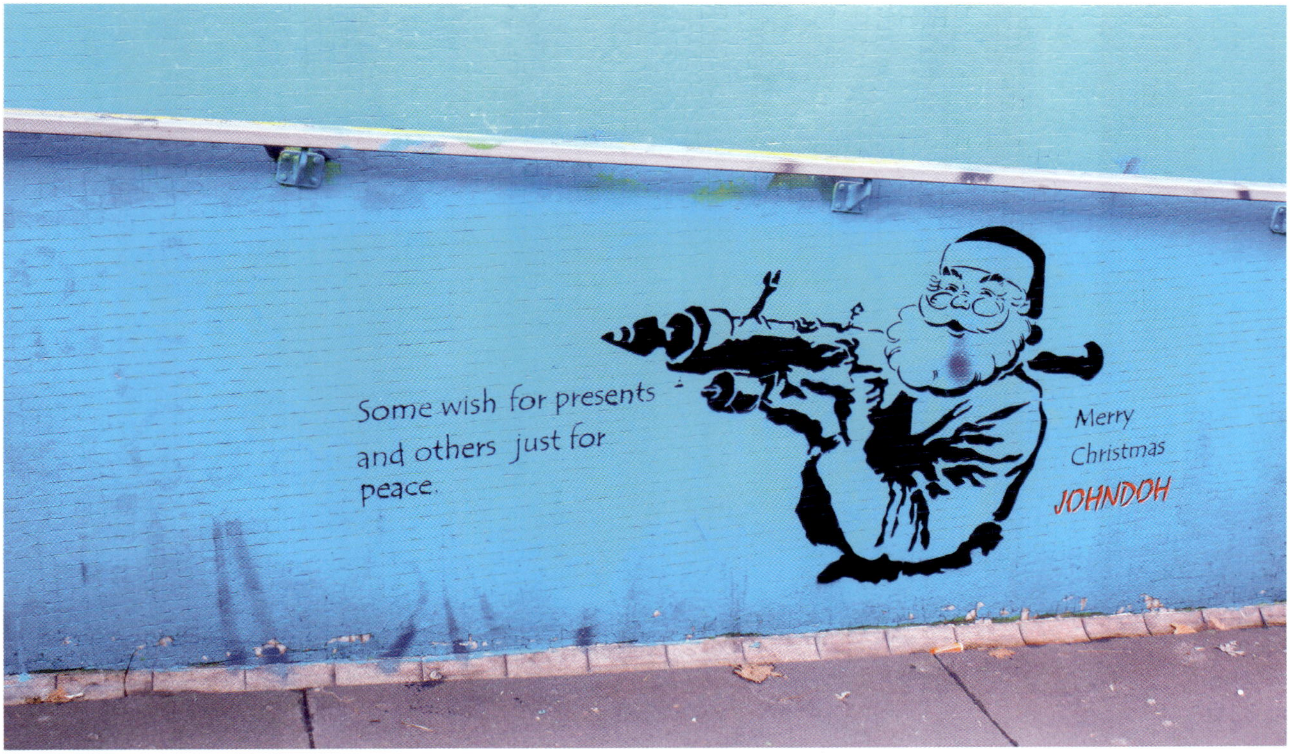

Left hand page:
Painted in a car park in Cheltenham on 14/12/2017. Shared widely on social media and was featured online by the newspaper the Canary

This page:
Top:
A Christmas message, Bristol Bear Pit on 16/12/2016

Bottom:
D'ohvader mosaic tiles installed off of Brick Lane in London

this money and getting only a few likes, then I'd argue that you aren't making a good investment and are simply giving your ego a narcissistic boost. It is possible to build a following with hard work and dedication but this really does require time, effort and interaction with many different artists, organisations and companies. Putting this in context, the important thing is getting people to associate the image you have posted with you and your message or else it may become just a random and superficially pretty image that people share online. This is perhaps why Banksy has put some of his artwork online, such as *Mobile Lovers*, originally without any accompanying text explaining where the location was. This lack of direction forces people who wish to fully view the artwork from searching the screen back into searching the tangible, urban environment. Arguably, street art is becoming overly virtual and is therefore decontextualised from the very city streets that it emerged from and gave it meaning.

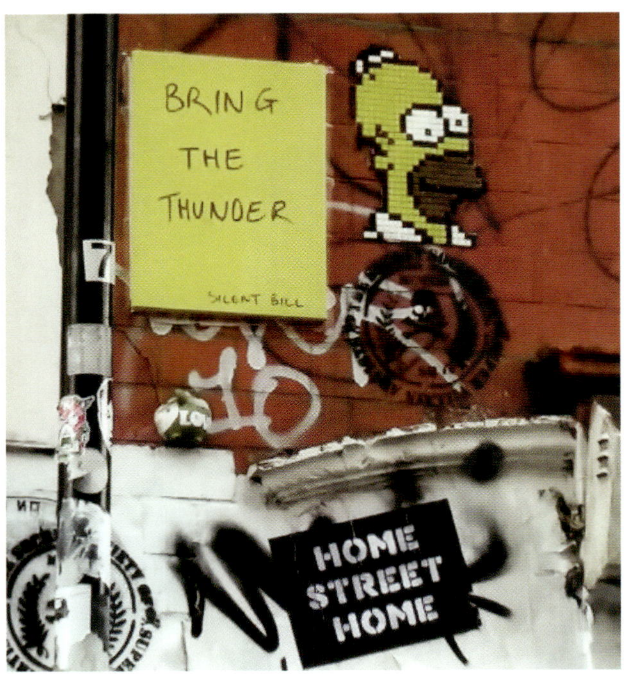

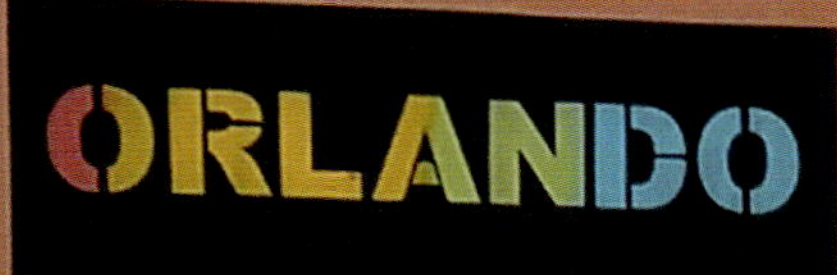

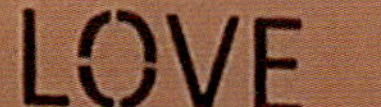

LOVE ....

KNOWS NO COLOUR OR GENDER

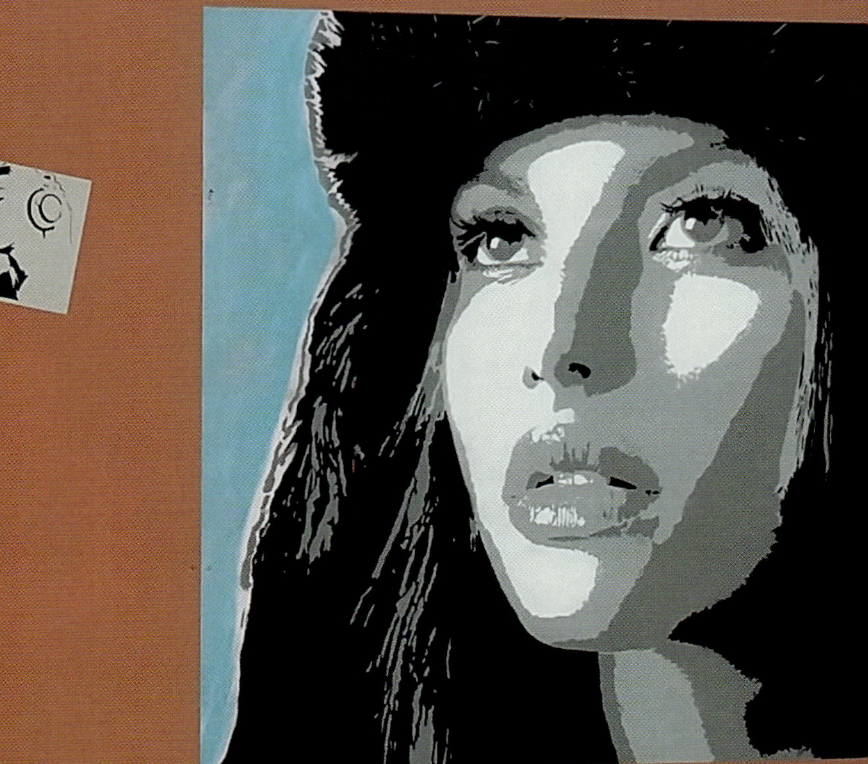

"OUR TRUE
NATIONALITY IS
MANKIND"

And our true race is human.

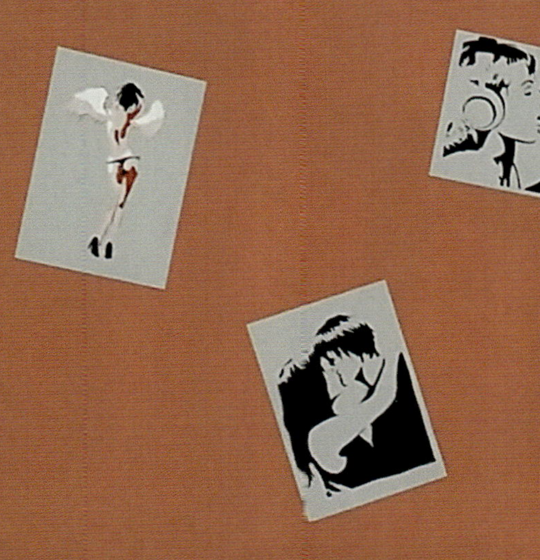

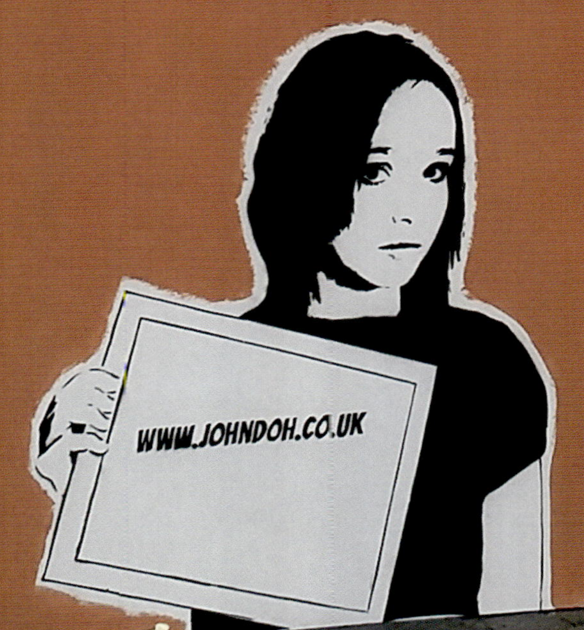

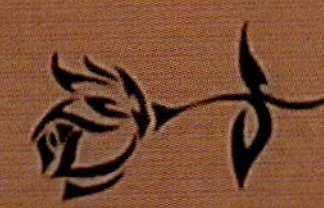

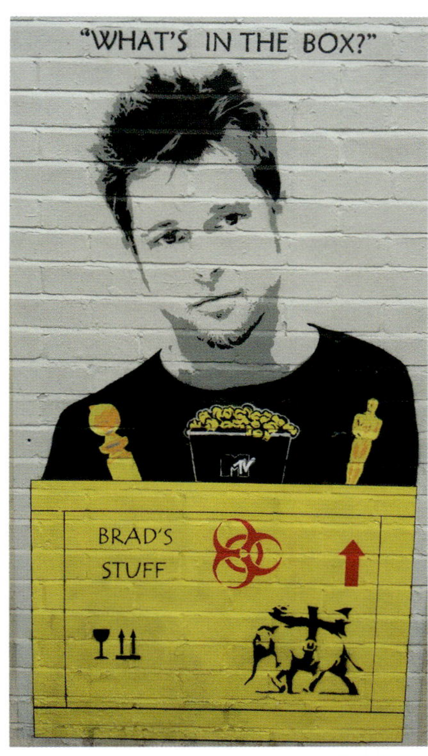

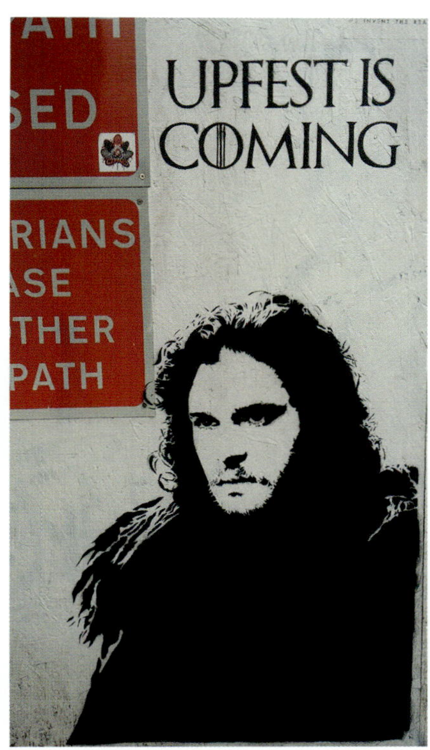

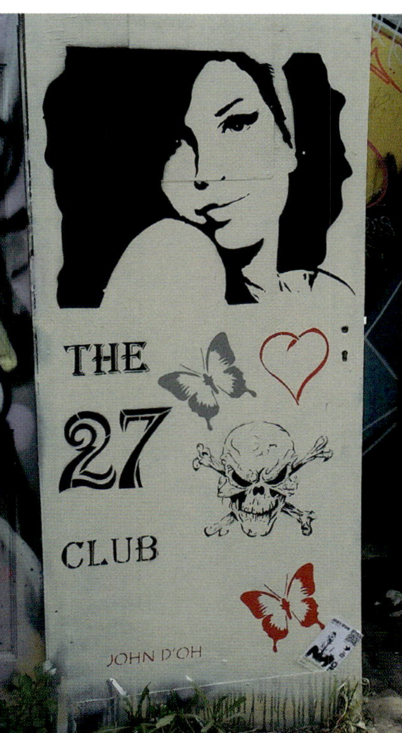

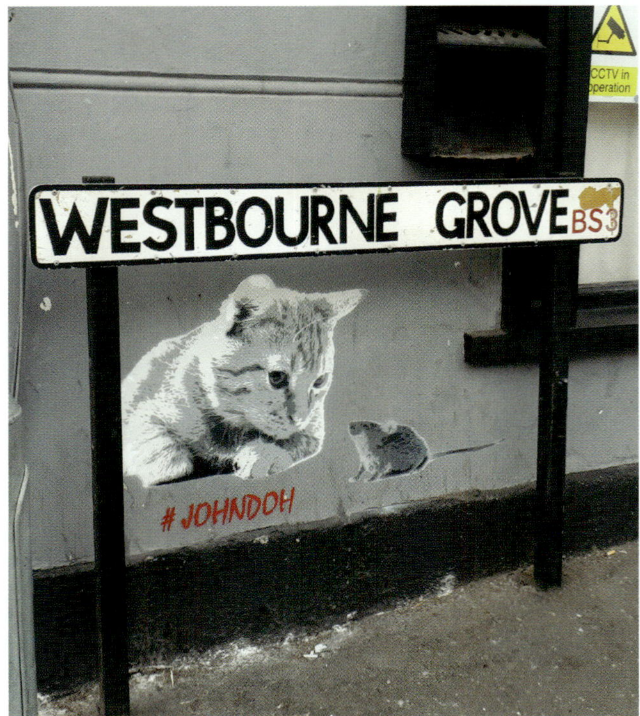

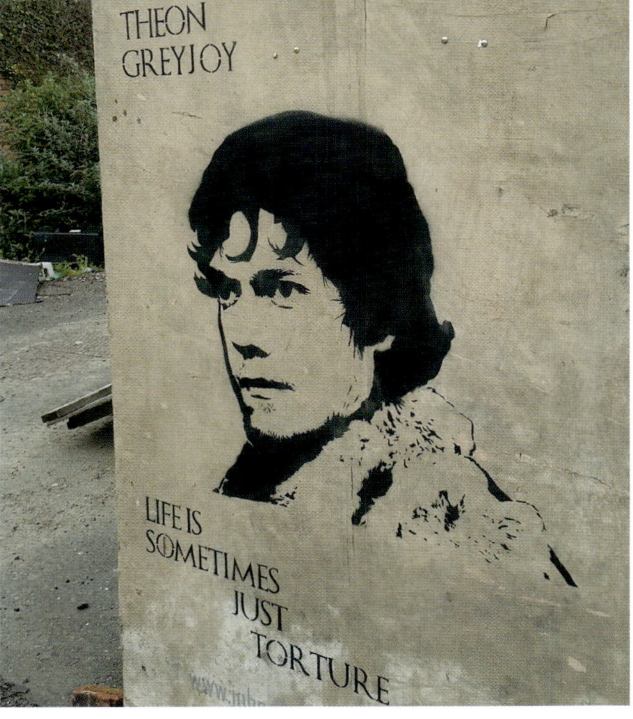

Left hand page: Painted at City Of Colours paint festival in Birmingham 2016 for the Orlando terrorist attack that killed 49 people and wounded 53

This page: "What's in the box?" painted in Burnham-on-Sea depicting the separation of Brad Pitt and Angelina Jolie. The quote taken from the movie seven staring Mr Pitt. 25/09/2016

Upfest is Coming was painted for Upfest 2017 and lasted under an hour before being painted over by another artist. Image used and slight change of wording from a popular television series Game of Thrones

27 Club. Amy Winehouse painted in Nomadic Gardens, Brick Lane London

Cat and Mouse painted on the Black Cat pub in Bedminster 28/07/2018

Theon Greyjoy. Another character from Game of Thrones with my own quote relating to the storyline. 15/05/2016

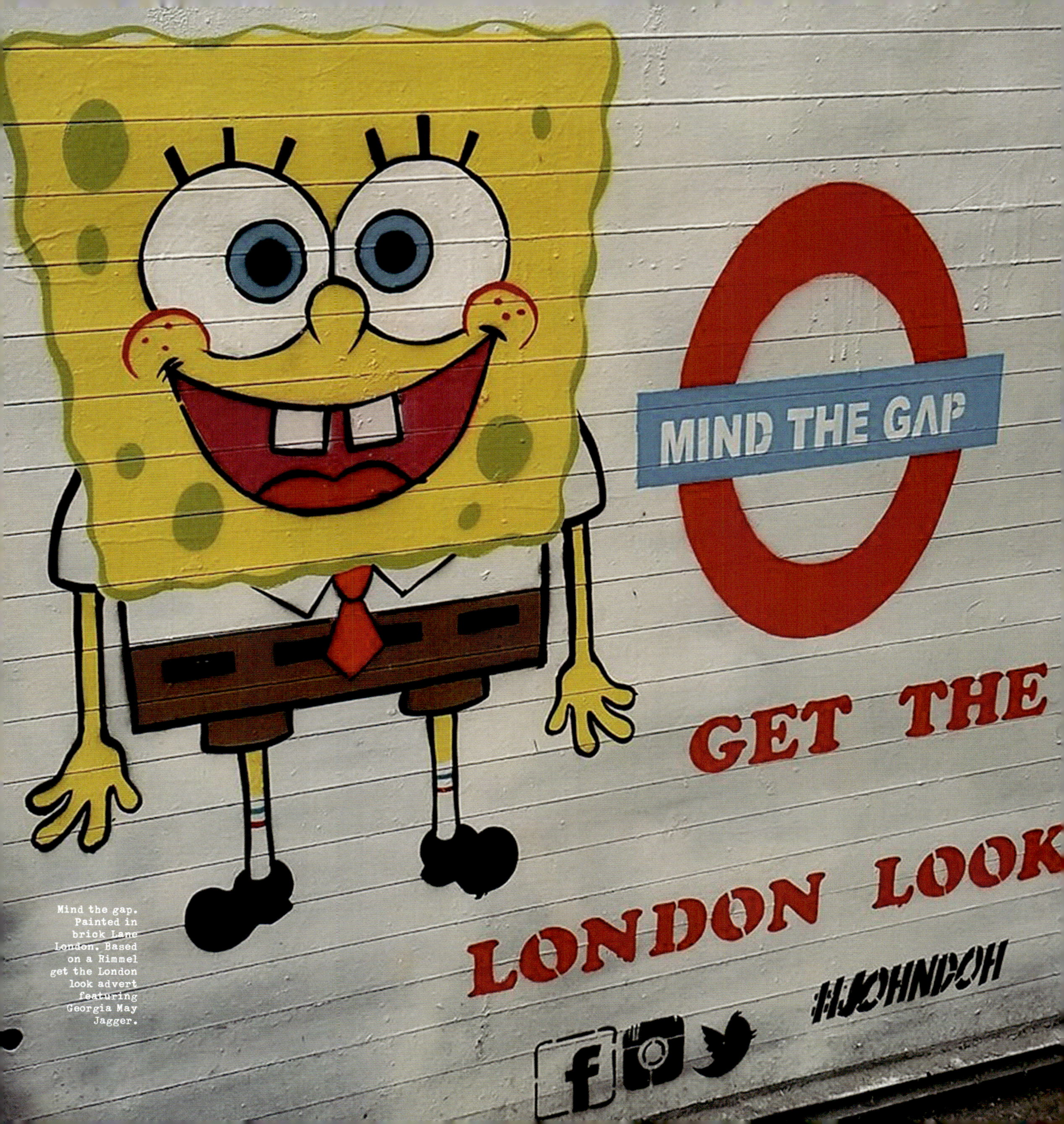

Mind the gap. Painted in brick Lane London. Based on a Rimmel get the London look advert featuring Georgia May Jagger.

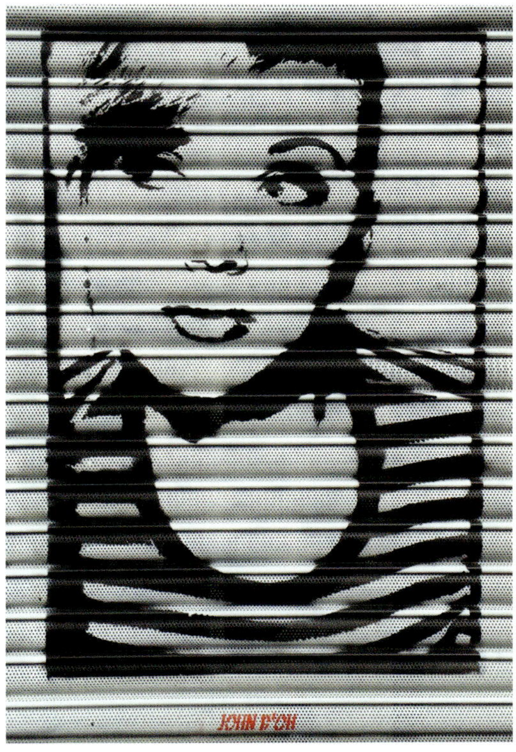

JOHN D'OH

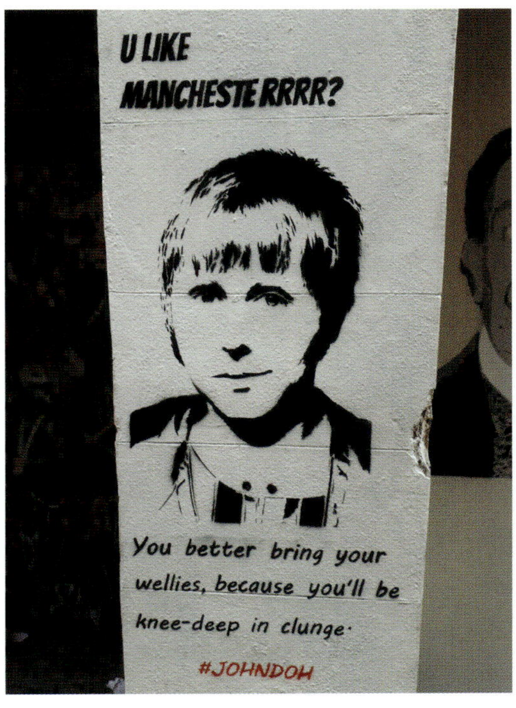

U LIKE
MANCHESTE RRRR?
You better bring your
wellies, because you'll be
knee-deep in clunge.
#JOHNDOH

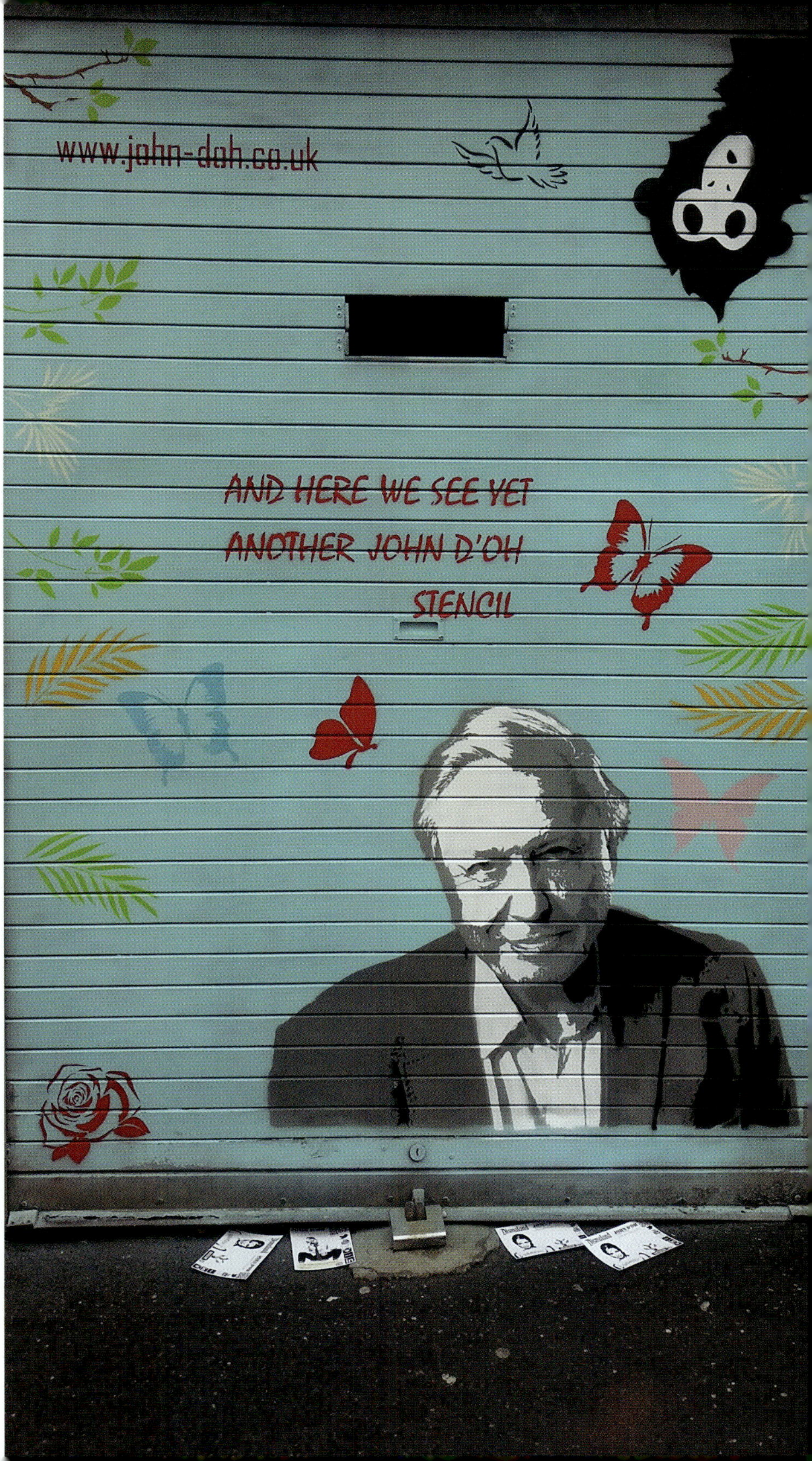

www.john-doh.co.uk
AND HERE WE SEE YET
ANOTHER JOHN D'OH
STENCIL

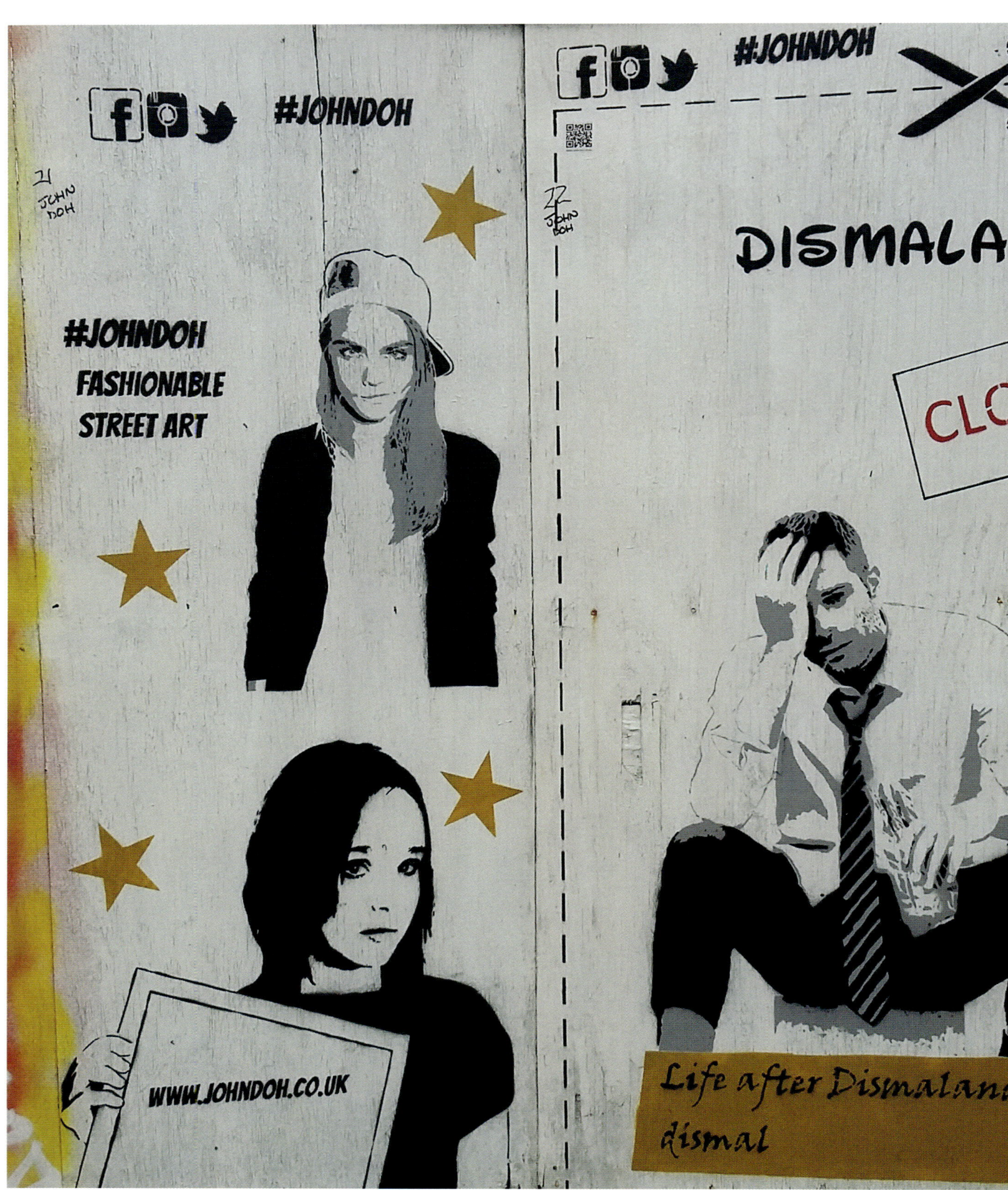
#JOHNDOH
#JOHNDOH
FASHIONABLE
STREET ART
WWW.JOHNDOH.CO.UK
#JOHNDOH
DISMALAND
CLOSED
Life after Dismaland is dismal

The piece on the left was painted on the closing night of Dismaland which I was lucky enough to attend. It was arguably one of the most well-known pieces of street art painted in Weston-super-Mare. It made the attention of many local, national and international papers and was even stolen because people thought it was an original Banksy but later returned after some police involvement.

It was painted for the Birnbeck Regeneration Trust after a campaigner who had seen and enjoyed the *Paris Hilton and Tinkerbell* piece that had been painted on opening night of Dismaland contacted me and asked if I would be interested in generating a bit of interest for the Trust through one of my paintings or stunts.

The piece was later auctioned off in order to raise money for the worthy cause and to help prevent the local landmark from crumbling into the sea. In addition to this, I helped the Trust put together and arrange Weston-super-Mare's first ever street art and graffiti festival. The event was a big success and it was the first time that Weston had seen such a mixture of artists and styles, encouraging local artists and providing money for the Trust and the whole community. I think it is particularly heartening that those wishing to revive a piece of grand and old-fashioned Victorian architecture were willing to embrace the chaotic and unapologetically contemporary art of graffiti as an equally important part of the town's culture. However,

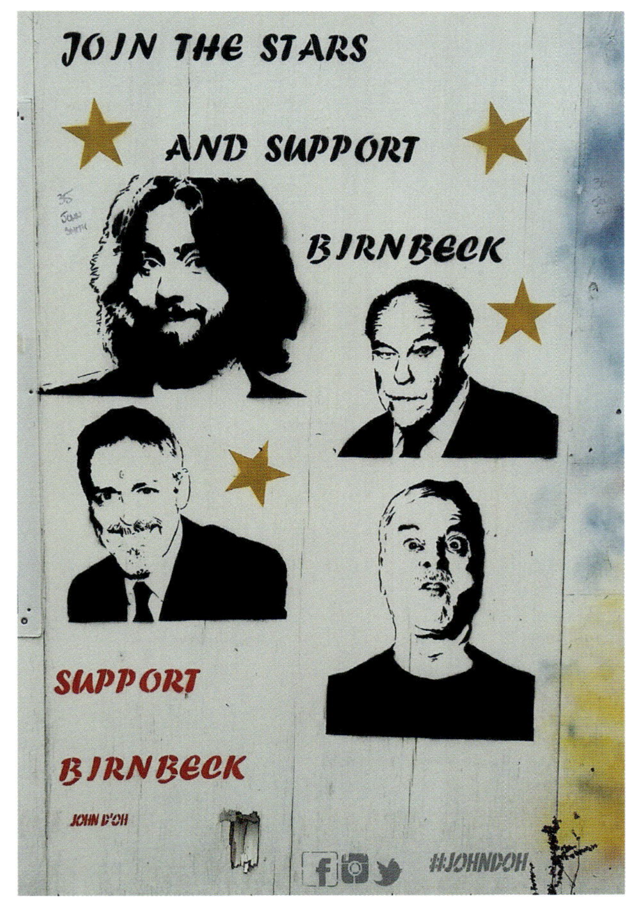

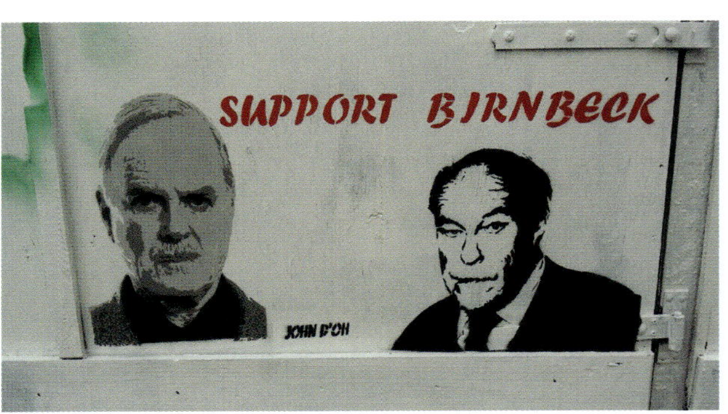

some of the artwork painted as part of the rejuvenation effort was covered in scribbles and messages in what was described by local newspapers as "mindless vandalism", which has caused the rejection of additional festivals, fundraising and art.

I painted a canvas which was presented to the stage and film actor Timothy West who visited the pier to show his support. Timothy West, along with comedians John Cleese, Griff Rhys-Jones and Justin Lee Collins, has been backing the ongoing campaign to save the derelict pier which continues to this day.

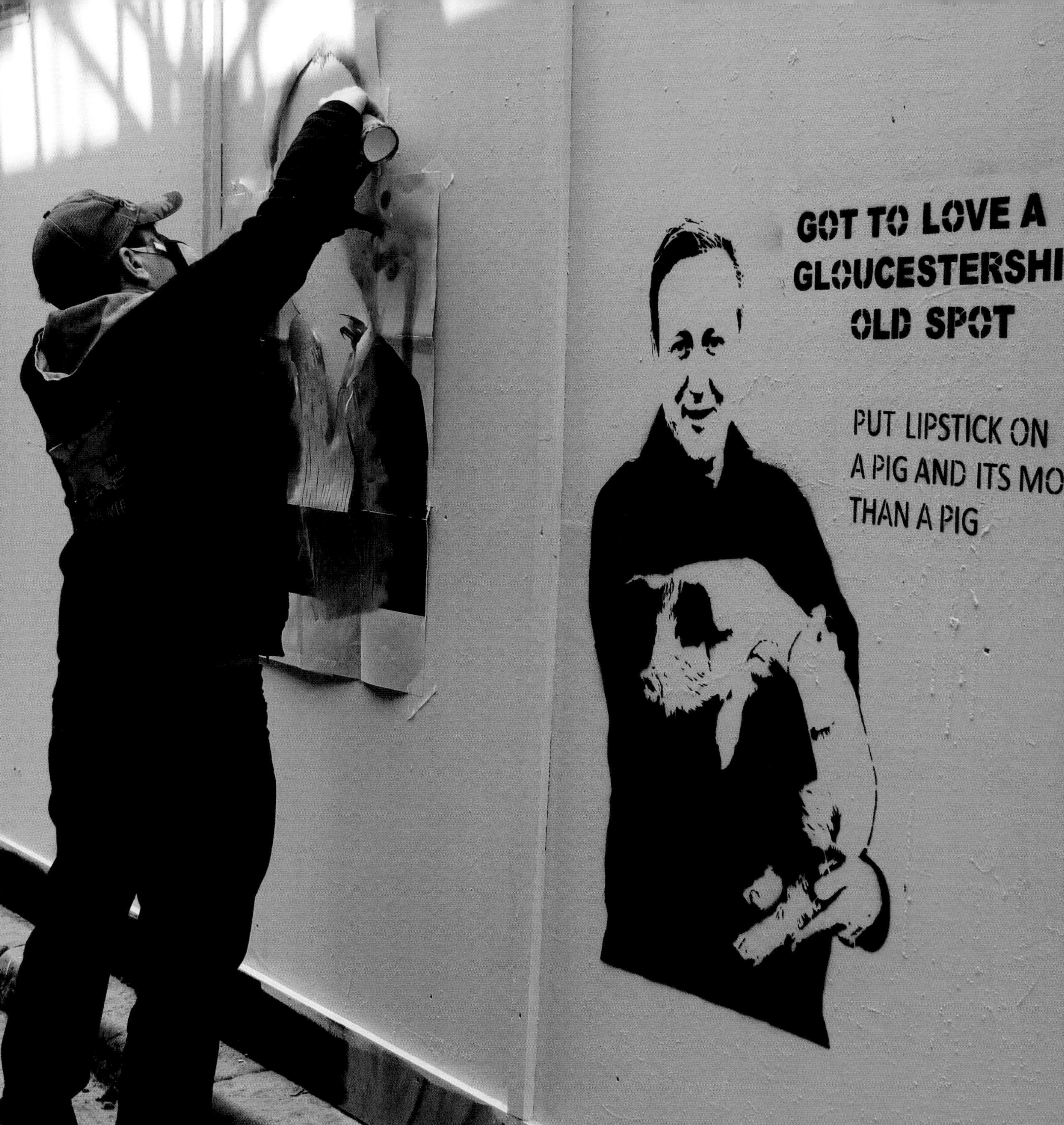

GOT TO LOVE A
GLOUCESTERSHI
OLD SPOT
PUT LIPSTICK ON
A PIG AND ITS MO
THAN A PIG

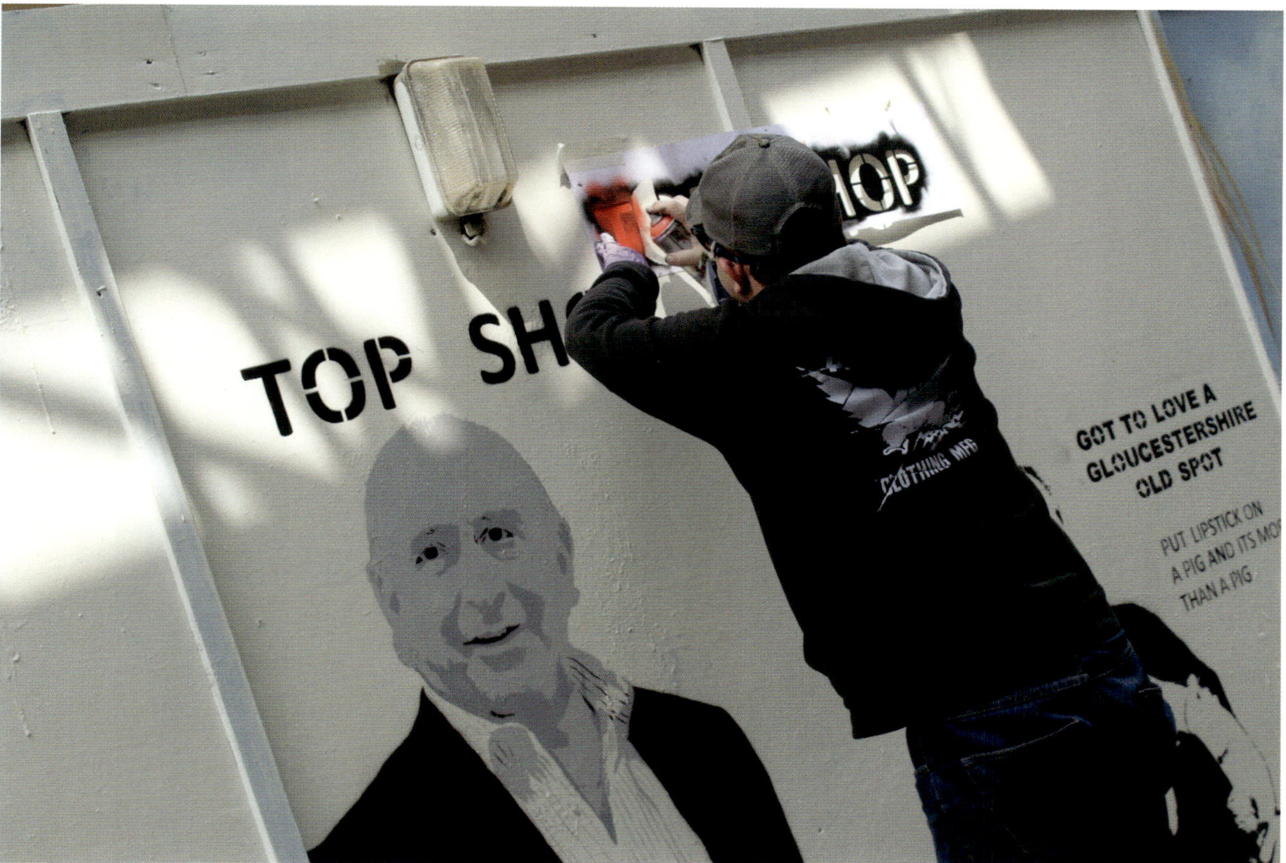

Painting an image of Top Shop owner Philip Green waving to pensioners from his £100 million super yacht after asset stripping BHS and raiding its pension fund. Completed on 28/05/2016

BLACKHALL STREET AND I WANT TO BREAK FREE

I don't often visit London but when I do I try to be as productive as possible. For me, London is a very large open air gallery with the potential for many people to see, share or criticise your work.

London can be considered both the birthplace and heart of British street art as a contemporary mode of artistic expression. Emerging in the 1970s out of the rise of punk, the political graffiti espoused a nihilism, individualism and aggressiveness that loudly voiced dissatisfaction with the declining manufacturing, decreased economic growth and prolific stagflation of the time. In such a context, buying a spraycan for almost nothing and painting something illegal, non-mainstream and opinionated for all to see was both a cheap thrill and a way of organising and creating an identifiably outcast, underdog and contrarian punk scene.

On the other hand, London's attitude to street art in more recent years has become more authoritative and bureaucratic, reflecting its transition into the world's financial centre and a 'global city' with an international image of Great Britain to maintain and project. For example, in the run up to the 2012 Olympic Games, local authorities and organisers wanted to control what 'illegal art' would be shown to the world and its tourists. Worried that too much graffiti would make the UK appear dilapidated, unprofessional or vulnerable to crime, councils, the police and the government actively targeted street art more aggressively, buffing over

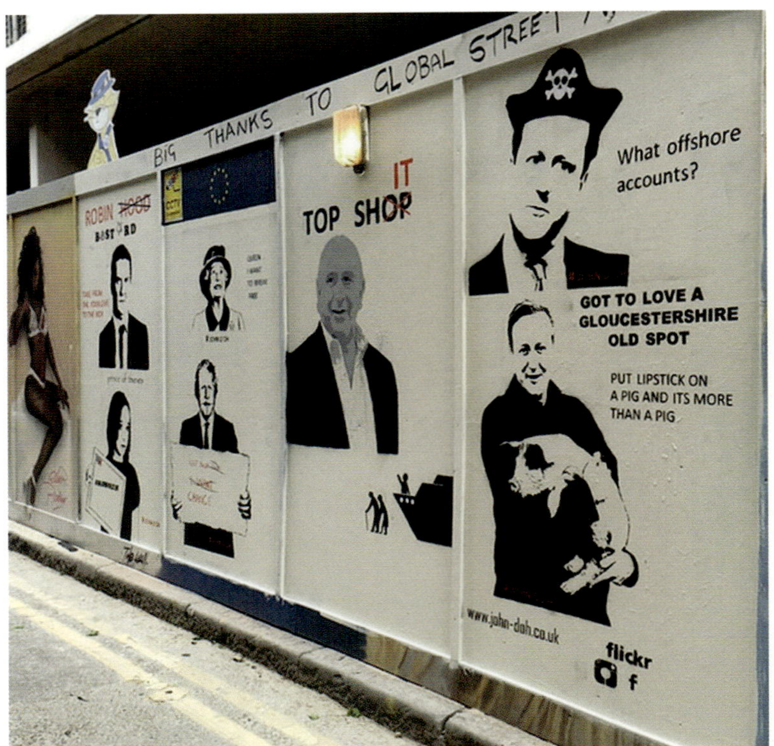

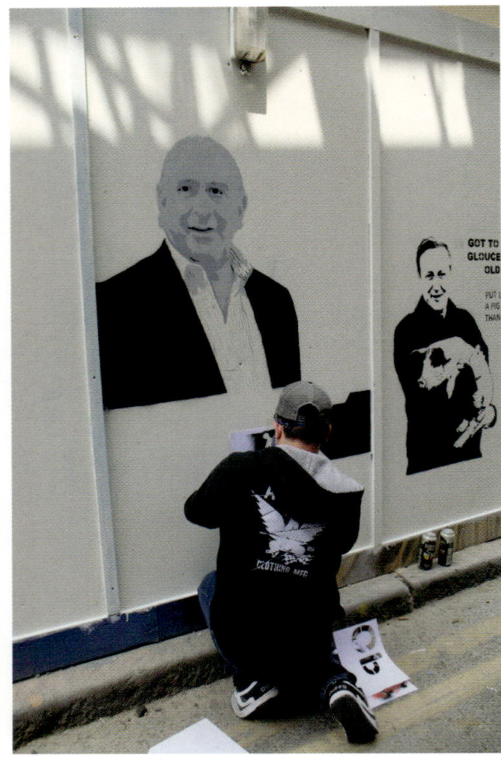

images, increasing arrests and securing more prison sentences. The only permitted urban art in London would be paid for by sponsors, celebrate Britain or sport and would be sold to art dealers afterwards.

In my last big visit, Blackhall Street in Shoreditch was my first stop where I had pre-booked a selection of hoardings through Global Street Art. I was up early because I wanted to get up as much art as possible before attending 'The Meeting Of Styles Festival' in the Nomadic Gardens just off of Brick Lane. I set about painting nearly five metres of hoarding with a range of politically themed art. My artwork didn't last long. It was removed by builders who presumed it was a Banksy and were hoping to make easy money. This was despite my name and website being prominently displayed.

In addition to this I had pre-painted quite a few pieces of art on boards which I was hoping to quickly and easily attach to walls or hoardings around Brick Lane in Shoreditch, with even a piece or two dropped into the Nomadic Gardens. I painted a few more pieces around Brick Lane mostly on shop shutters which lasted a few days but Brick Lane is an ever-changing canvas.

The pieces of art entitled I Want to Break Free depicted an image of the Queen looking up at a blue European Union flag with the well-known title of the song by the British rock band Queen punningly written next to her. The art was in response to a front page story claiming that the Queen, who is constitutionally not meant to express a political opinion because of her unelected and inherited position, had expressed her views desiring to leave the European Union. This was one of the biggest rows, among many, of the referendum campaign. The art was not done to motivate voting one way or another, but was intended to highlight the increasingly bitter and scandalised tone of the debate. It must have got a bit of attention because most of them were quickly removed, leaving just one in the Nomadic Gardens that remained there for more than a year.

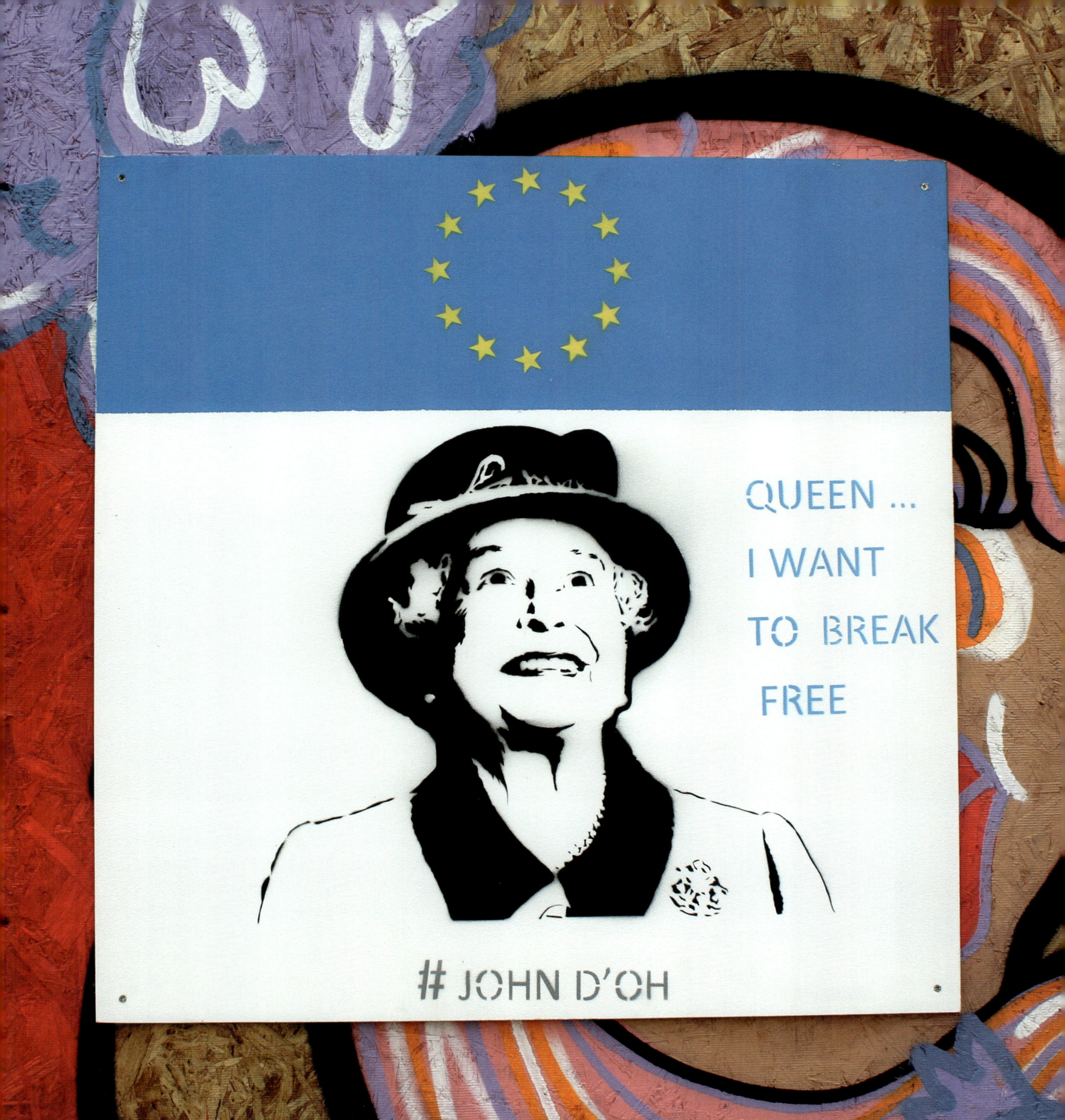

QUEEN ...
I WANT
TO BREAK
FREE
JOHN D'OH

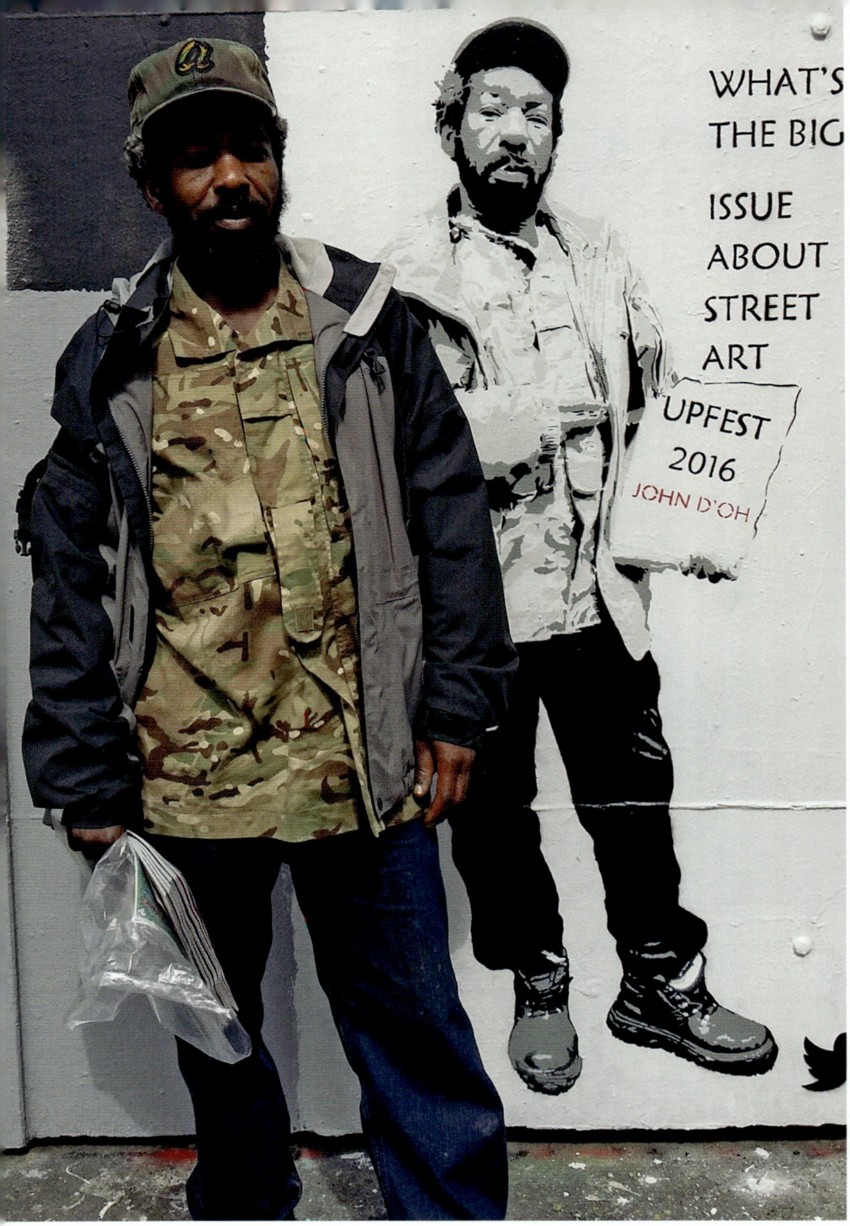

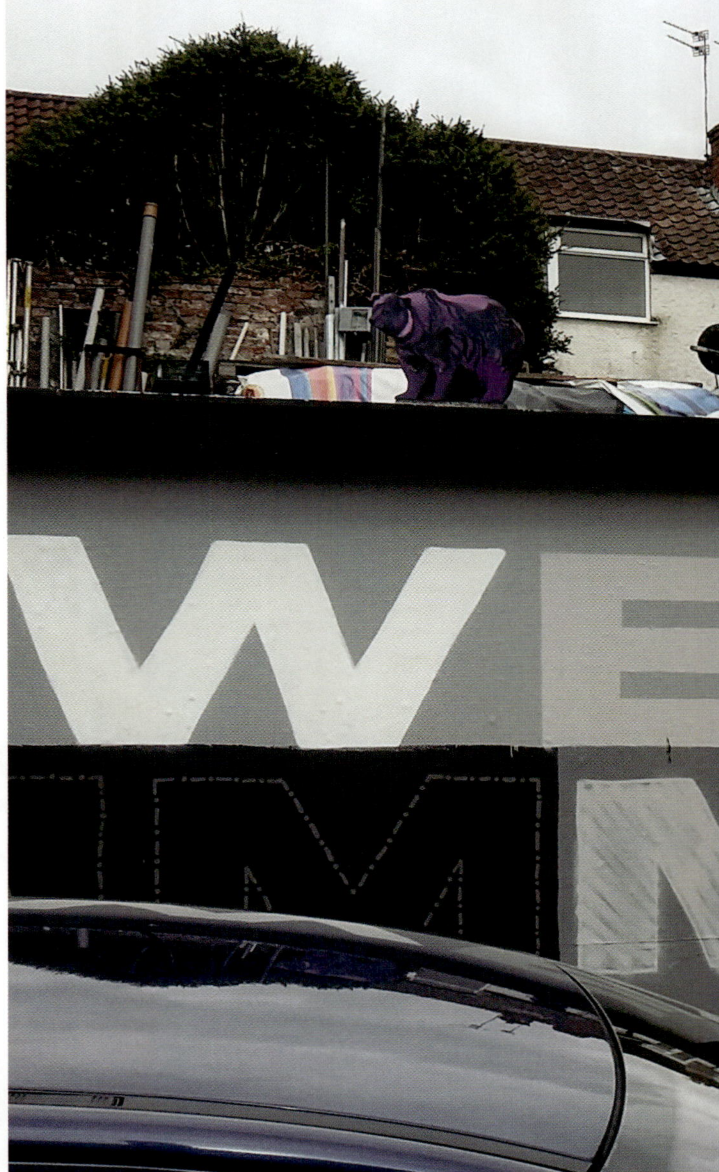

JEFF

What's the *Big Issue* about street art?

I have known Jeff Knight for quite a few years and I don't think I have ever seen the guy in a bad mood. He always seems upbeat and cheerful. He is perhaps one of the best known *Big Issue* sellers in the country, having been positively featured in local papers and on international websites for the combination of his strong work ethic and his eternally affectionate, jocular manner. There was even a petition set up by Bristolians to have Jeff carry the torch during the 2012 Olympic Games.

He came to Britain two decades ago from Jamaica without family, friends or a place to live. He has always been a fan of street art and, as immigration had been featured heavily in the news in an increasingly negative way, I wanted to paint someone who was both an immigrant and a part of the Bristol community in a

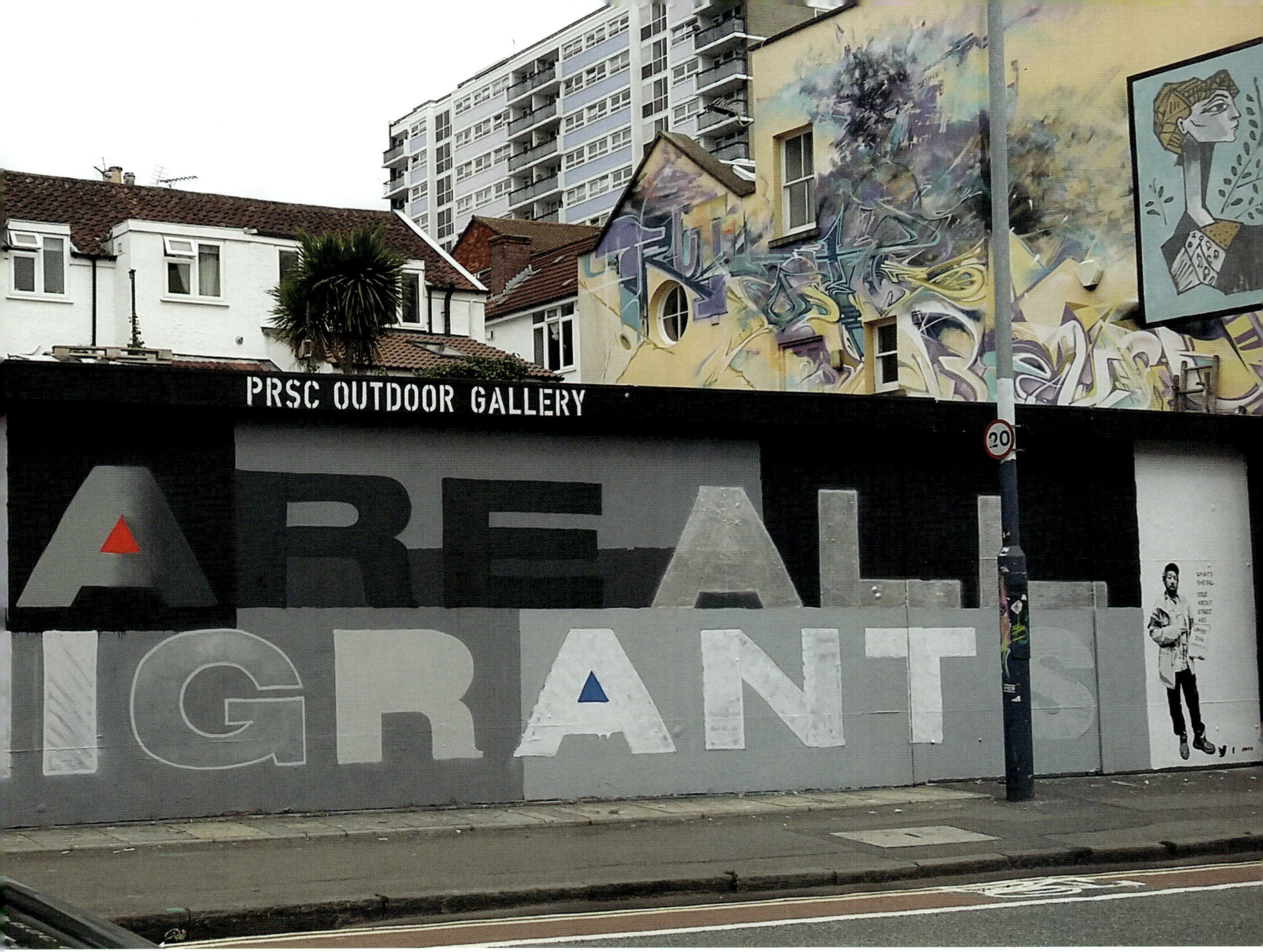

positive manner. The first time I painted the artwork was in the Stokes Croft area of Bristol. I had been driving around looking for a surface to paint on and had come across a wall with "We are all immigrants" freshly painted on it. Luckily, there was a blank space just beside it and I couldn't resist painting Jeff in, giving an example of such productive immigration. Not only was this close to the spot where Jeff often sells the *Big Issue*, but this location was on Jamaica Street which, representing the country he was originally from, fitted in perfectly.

Unfortunately, it was mistaken as an advertisement for Upfest, Europe's largest street art festival, and was whited out because the owner did not permit or agree with advertising in general. I painted two more images in Bedminster which stayed up for over a year and they have been featured in the *Bristol Post*, the *Big Issue* magazine and even featured in "the UK's most striking street art" on *MSN.com*.

Bristol Big Issue seller Jeff Knight in Stokes Croft, Jamaica Street, Bristol

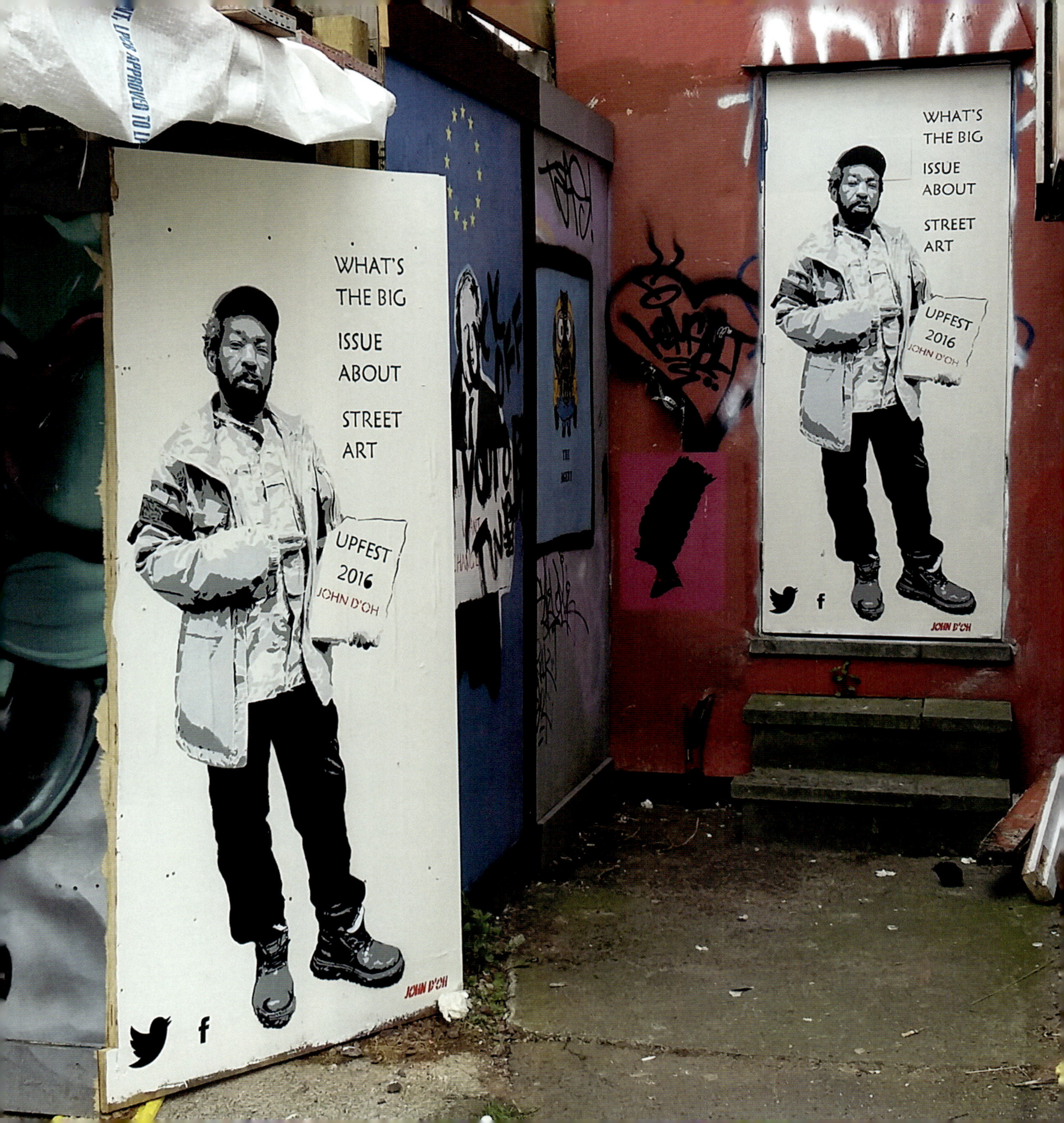

WHAT'S
THE BIG
ISSUE
ABOUT
STREET
ART
UPFEST
2016
JOHN D'OH
WHAT'S
THE BIG
ISSUE
ABOUT
STREET
ART
UPFEST
2016
JOHN D'OH

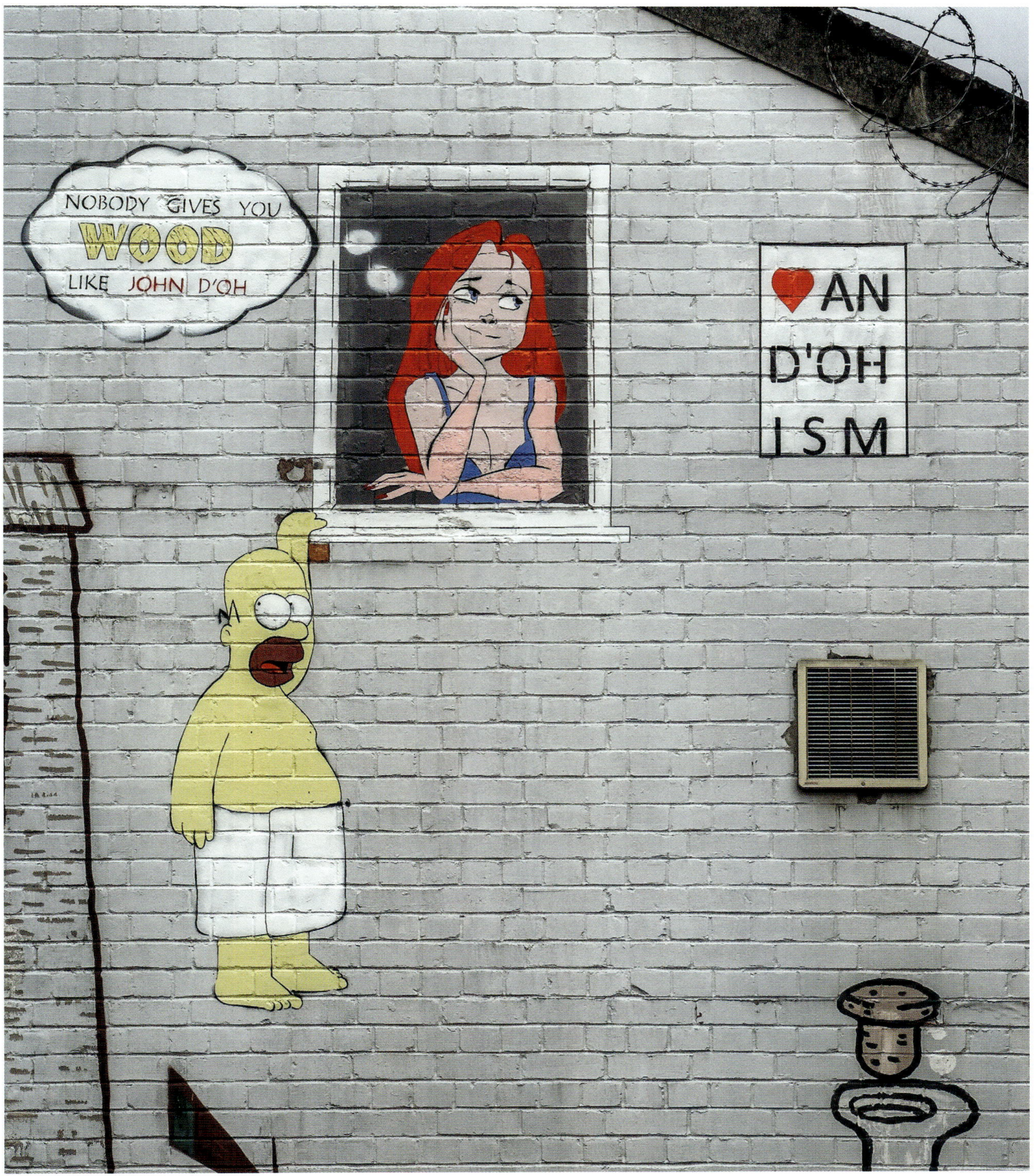

Hanging out with Banksy and Nick Walker. Painted behind printing shop in Stokes Croft, Bristol

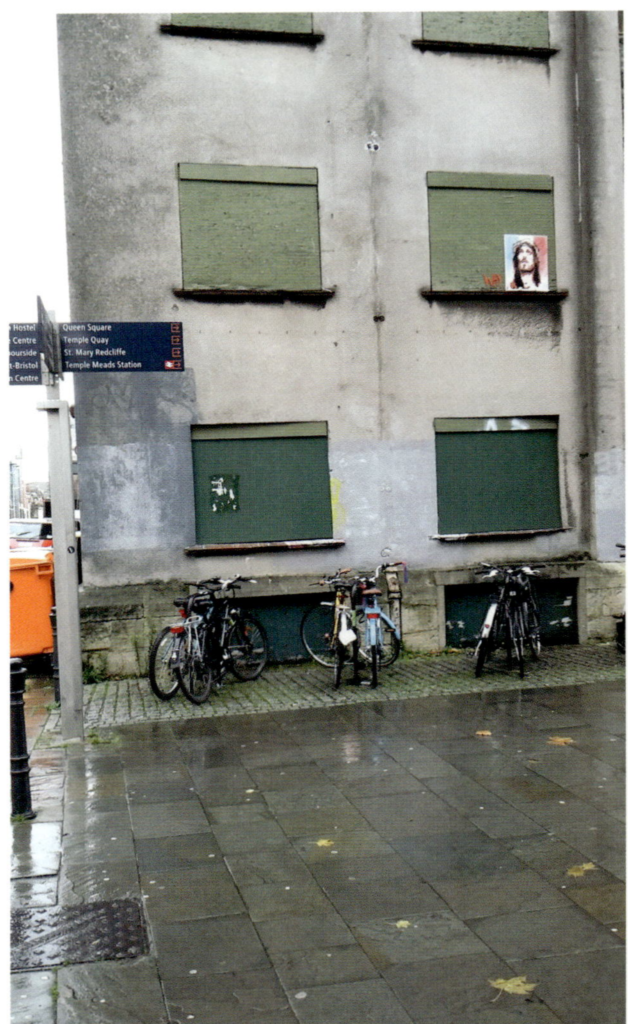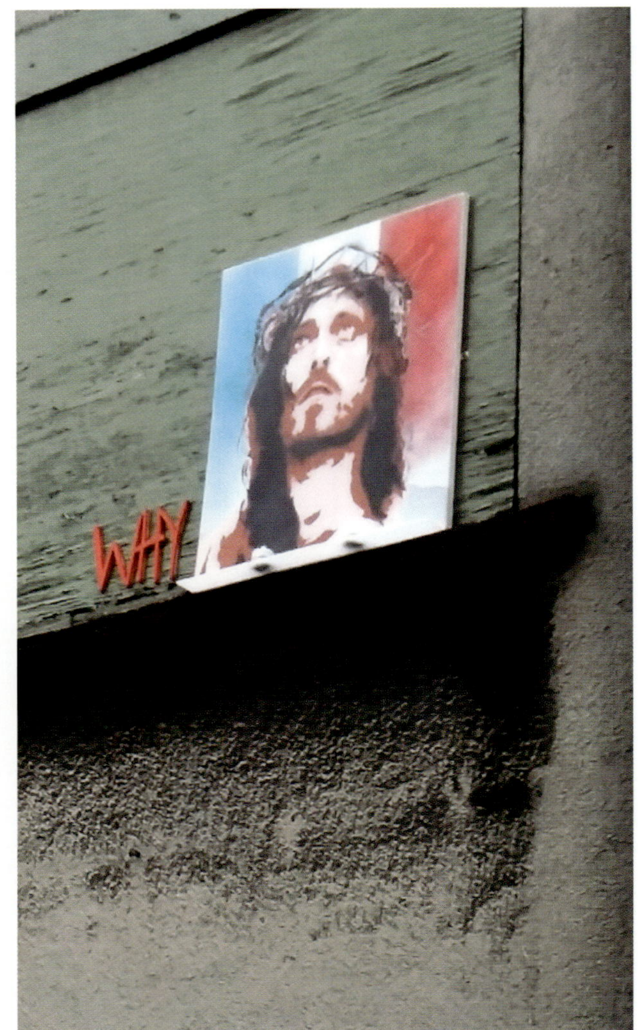

JESUS

(Installed on 16/11/2015)

This was my tribute to the lives lost in the Paris terror attacks on November 13, 2015. This has to be one of my longest running and surviving pieces in Bristol and that is probably because it is a difficult location to climb up to. It was installed close to the Arnolfini and Queen Square in Bristol by using a telescopic ladder at full stretch above a bike parking area in heavy rain. Health and safety was given a back seat. The artwork had a projecting shelf with battery-operated tea lights which flickered and lit up the image like the votive candles offered at a religious altar or shrine. They worked for a few days continuously before the batteries ran out. Artwork with a religious theme in this incredibly politicised and tragic context hopefully shows that freedom of religion and freedom of expression are certainly not mutually exclusive acts that need to be violently in conflict.

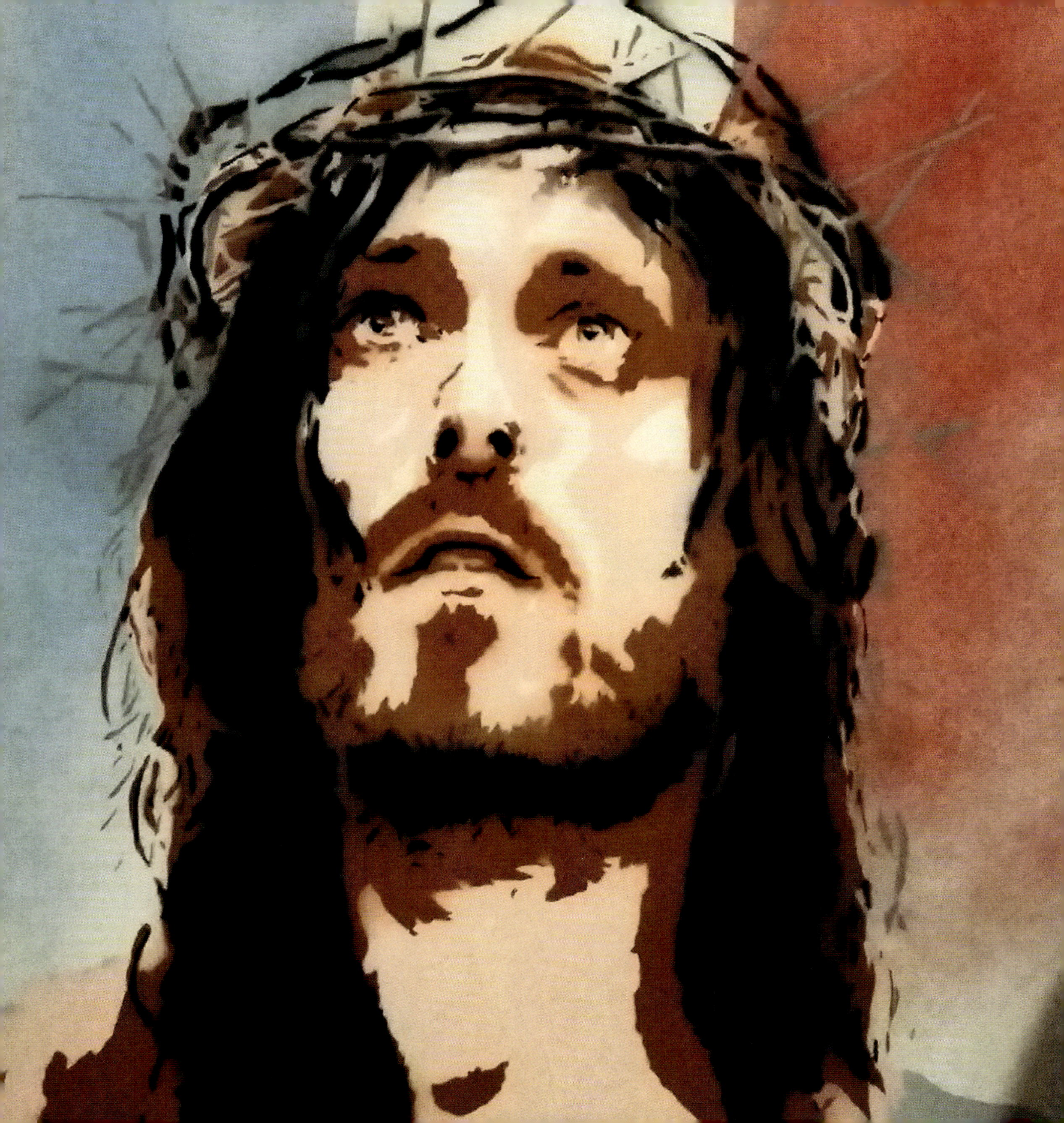

DAVID CAMERON AND THE PANAMA PAPERS:
"WHAT OFFSHORE ACCOUNTS?"

In 2016, journalists analysed and published documents from the Panamanian law firm and corporate service provider Mossack Fonseca. The 11.5 million documents contained personal financial information about wealthy individuals and public officials. Some of these people were using shell corporations for illegal purposes such as fraud, tax evasion and evading international sanctions. The names of Conservative Party lords and donors were found prominently amongst the papers, including JCB chairman Baron Anthony Bamford, oil industry executive Tony Buckingham and Baroness Pamela Sharples. Most famously, David Cameron and his wife Samantha were found to have sold shares in his father's offshore company for £31,500 four months before Cameron became Prime Minister.

The Prime Minister claimed that it was "a private matter" and then declared that "there are no shares", but eventually admitted that he "had previously" had shares and that it was no longer relevant for a austerity-focused government that depends upon taxation to be run by a man whose family, friends and party had benefited from money that had "avoided" taxation. According to the *Guardian*, David Cameron's father Ian Cameron was a director of Blairmore Holdings Inc, an investment fund run from the Bahamas which managed tens of millions of pounds on behalf of wealthy families. Since Blairmore was founded in the early 1980s, it allegedly avoided ever having to pay tax in Britain by hiring a small army of Bahamas residents to sign its paperwork and fill roles such as treasurer, secretary and vice-president despite the documents proving that all big investment decisions were taken in the UK.

Following the death of his father, Cameron was left £300,000 tax free as an inheritance. Cameron claimed not to know whether the money had benefited from a tax haven status due to part of the estate being based in Jersey. It also emerged that his mother transferred two separate payments of £100,000 to his accounts in 2011 as "gifts", seemingly allowing the family estate to avoid a potential £80,000 worth of inheritance tax. Protesters and MPs from both Labour and the Liberal Democrats were demanding that the Prime Minister resign.

My piece was originally done in London. It depicted Cameron in a cartoonish pirate hat saying "what offshore accounts?" It was repainted in Bristol and featured in the *Bristol Post*. Depicting Cameron as a pirate wasn't simply a comment on how his family had apparently used foreign countries to steal and store taxpayers' money like a common pirate. Countries and domains such as Ireland, the Bahamas and Luxembourg have been accused by journalists and politicians of "piracy" by attracting multinationals and foreign investment from the other countries they are based in or actually manufacturing in by lowering its tax rate or changing its taxation law, thus "stealing" other government revenues. In that way, it is perfectly appropriate to describe Cameron as a pirate. Amusingly, "John Doe" was the pseudonym used by the person who leaked the private documents, and I felt a similar sense of holding power to account and fighting corruption as no doubt the whistleblower did..

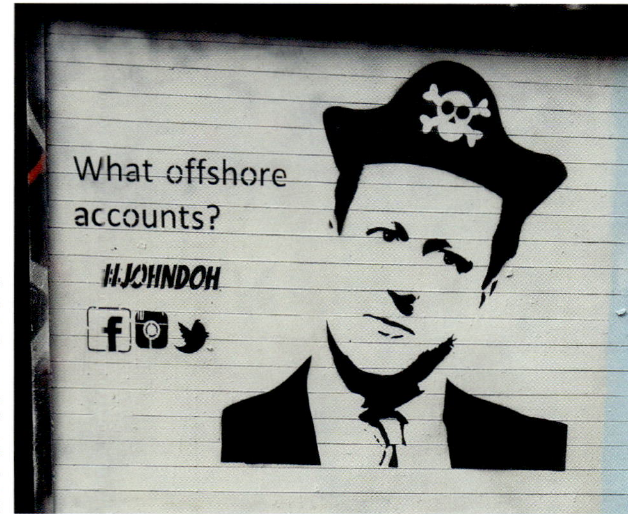

What Offshore Accounts painted at locations in Bristol, Gloucester, Swindon and Brick Lane in London. Opposite painted in Bristol Bearpit on 10/04/2016

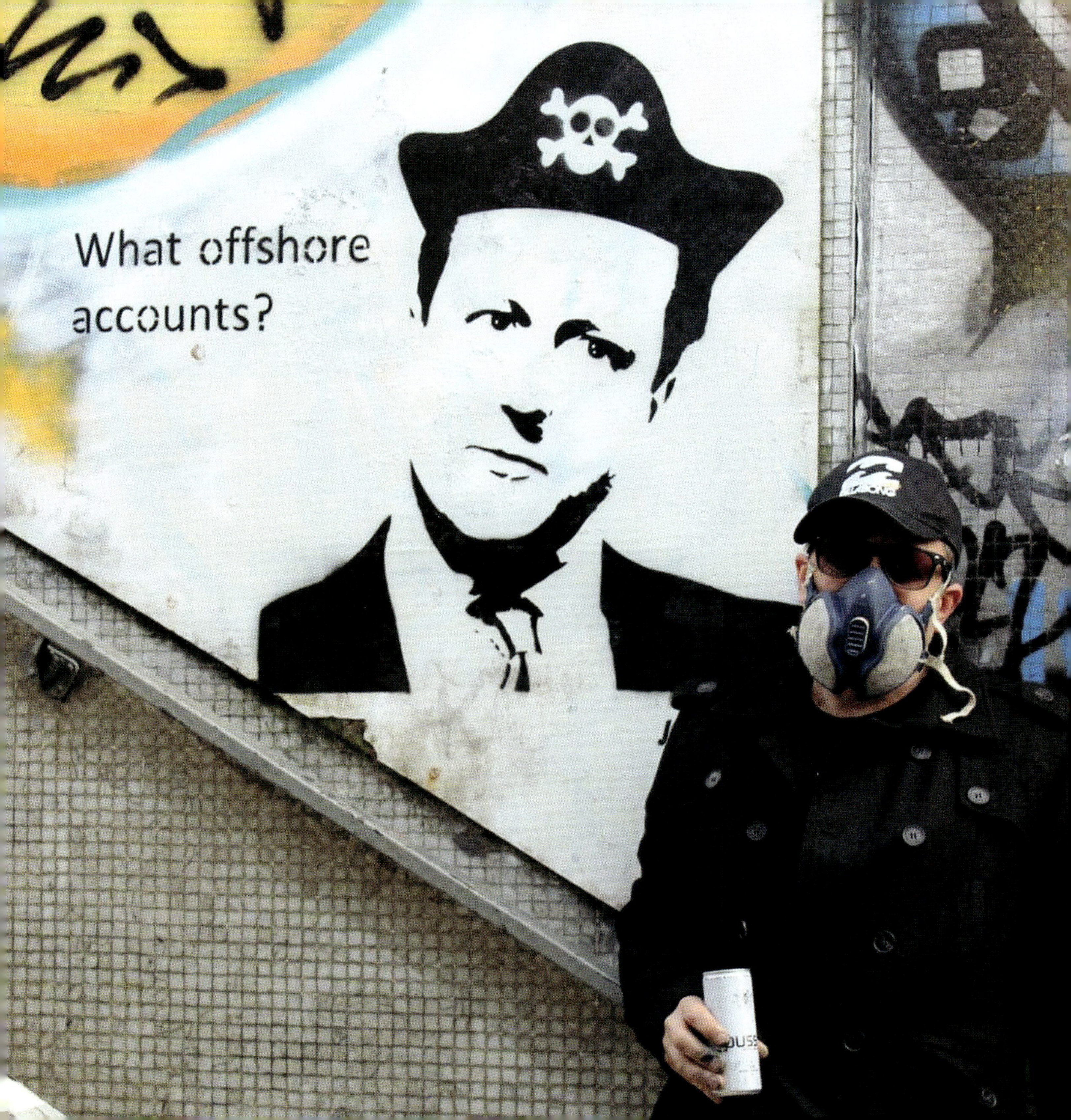
What offshore
accounts?

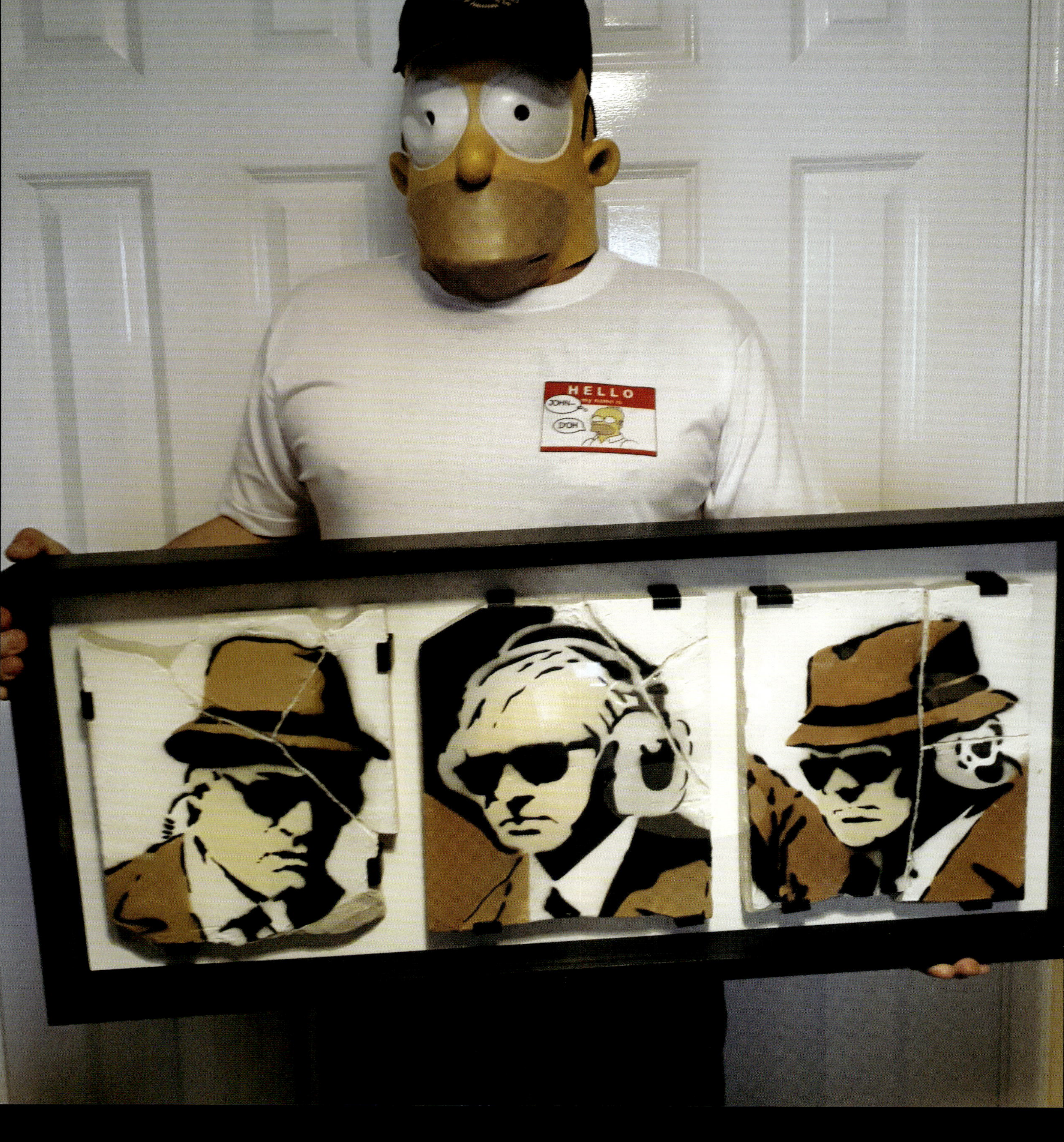
HELLO
my name is
JOHN
D'OH

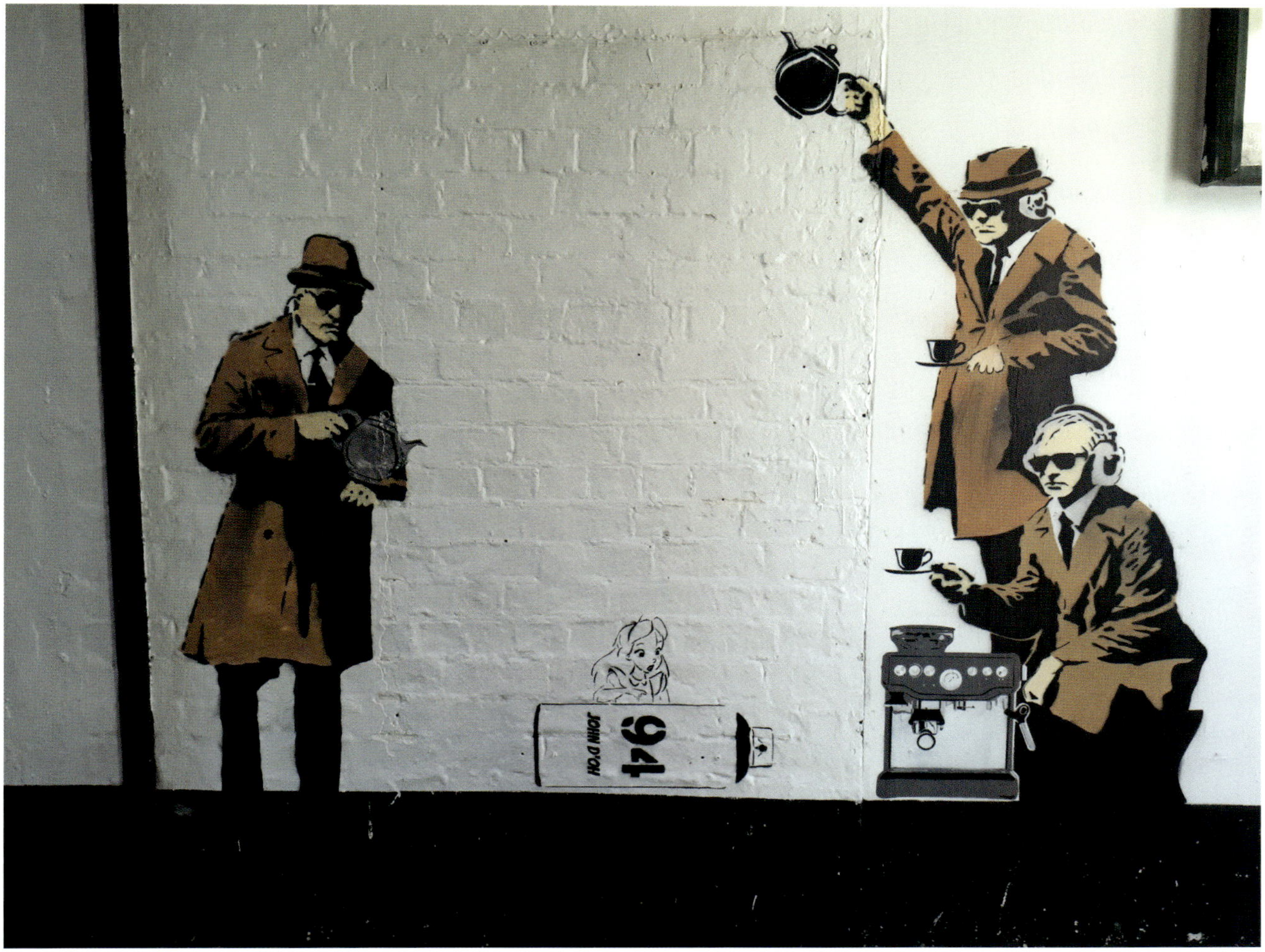

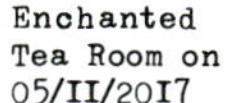

JOHN D'OH SPYBOOTH

"Are you Banksy?"

Arguably, I have been compared to or, perhaps more accurately, mistaken for Banksy more times in the media than any other artist. It often surprises me that I get so much press attention because my street art is mostly just an enjoyable hobby. My art tends to be topically relevant, humorous and fairly light-hearted so I suppose it can be useful in filling half a page on a slow news day. A day without major headlines generally allows a renewed focus on ignored topics or overlooked local issues, including the often sidelined area of arts and culture. On the other hand, in order to generate sales or views, the media may manufacture a minor scandal about controversial graffiti, street art and vandalism on a day without "important" news. And an apparently new Banksy piece normally ticks both of these boxes.

If something I have painted is suspected to be a Banksy it usually has a short lifespan. Initially, comments describing the work as "fantastic" or "wonderful" appear online. However, once the artwork is denied by Pest Control, is discovered not to be a Banksy by some art critic or you simply come forward and claim responsibility for the image, it becomes just another piece of street art and the interest and praise vanishes almost instantly. In this way, street art mirrors the official art market and culture industry, where the attribution of a major artist's name to a work can massively increase its value and media attention.

I sometimes feel a bit guilty on occasions where my art has been covered in Perspex, boarded over or stolen and put online for sale because there must be a lot of disappointment when the real authorship is revealed. But that is normally short lived as I personally feel that art painted on the streets should stay on the streets. Instead, we often witness artwork being cut out of walls and sold to the highest bidder by profit-orientated organisations such as the Sincura Group and Bankrobber. Whether they succeed in removing the art from the environment or not, they can often cause physical damage to the piece, something that is made explicit by what happened to Banksy's *Spy Booth*.

Enchanted tea shop and *Spy Booth*

I really liked the *Spy Booth* piece that Banksy did in Cheltenham; it was witty, well-executed and topically insightful. The people of Cheltenham were generally upset by what happened to the image: It was vandalised, painted over and, in the end, turned into a pile of rubble when builders attempted to remove it.

Whilst painting at a street art festival in Cheltenham, I was lucky enough to find a nice white wall just off of the high street on the side of the Enchanted Tea Shop. I thought it would be nice to return the destroyed mural to its hometown but with my own twist, swapping the microphones for teapots and the tape machine for a

coffee machine. It was a cold, early morning start and I had to sit and wait for it to get light enough for me to see and paint properly. I did get caught in the act by a couple of members of the public on that particular occasion but that is to be expected sometimes. Despite it really being just a Banksy imitation, in a technical sense it is one of the more complex images I have created. Even when reproducing another street art image, a lot of effort and time is involved. If you look at the many images of the original you will notice not one photo has captured all the artwork in its entirety because the telephone box obscures elements of the individual stencils. Not only was it necessary to replicate the image from a number of different photos from conflicting perspectives, but I also had to resize the figures in order to fit it on the specific wall and in order to make it proportional to the scale of the teapots and coffee machine. In addition to this, when painting a reproduction, you have to try to replicate the original shading while also trying not to be seen by painting speedily. It wasn't quite as good as I would have liked it to be – another 10 minutes undisturbed and I think I could have got it even more accurate and polished. The piece did really well and was reported by the BBC, local newspapers and did the rounds on social media. In fact, news crews appeared there by midday. It's a homage to the original and a bit of fun.

I love Banksy's art and we seem to have a similar sense of humour and a generally similar political outlook. He has immense cultural influence, helped change the way members of the public treat street art and has been an inspiration for many artists. He has achieved more in his own lifetime than many other artists do and, no matter what he does in the future, there will never be anyone like him.

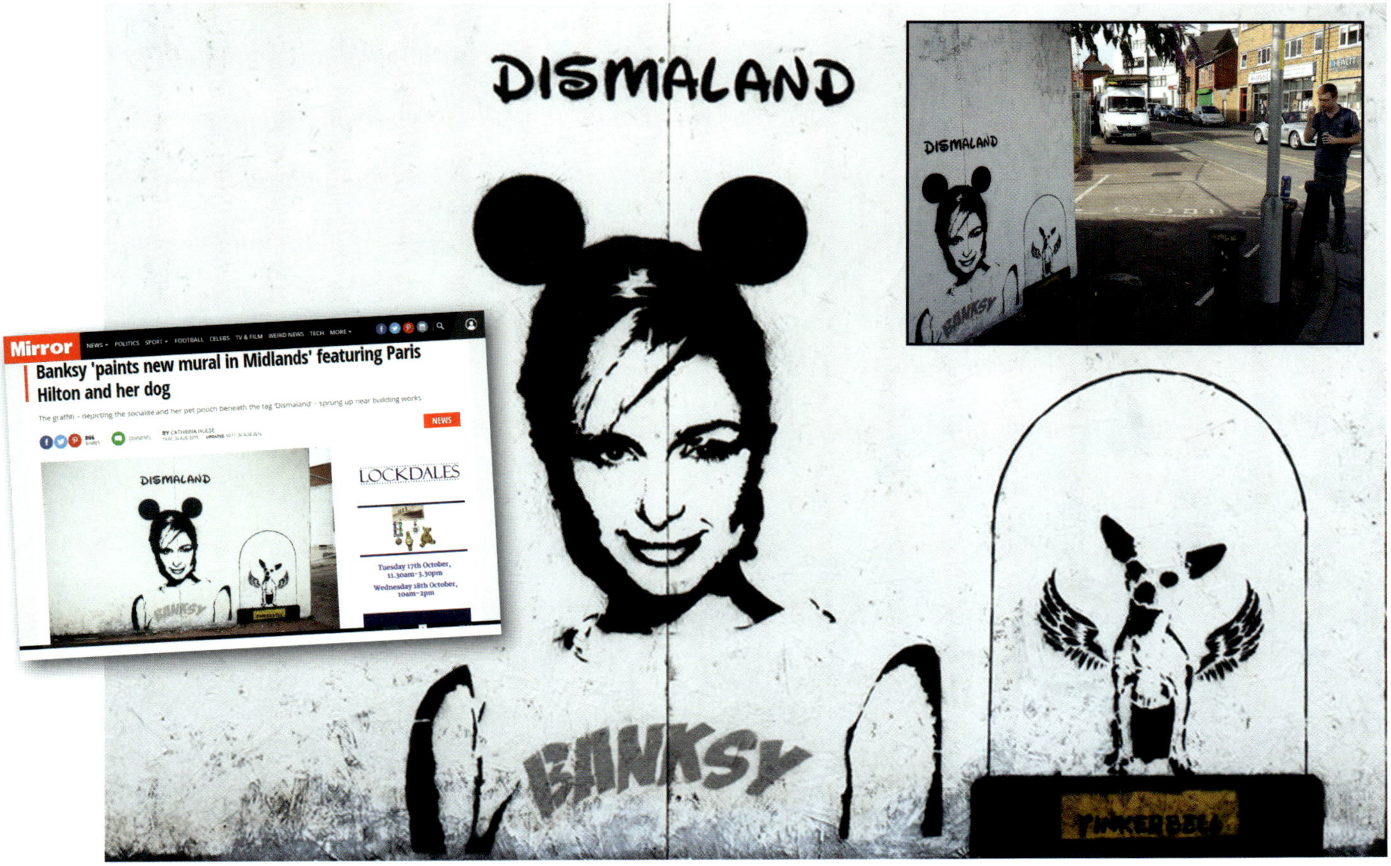

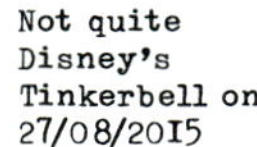

PARIS HILTON

Paris Hilton and Tinkerbell

The famous-for-being-famous Paris Hilton had recently "dedicated" her Instagram page to her well-known Chihuahua Tinkerbell after its death. By replacing her pet with its namesake cartoon character, I wanted to show how sentimentality can be exploited and commoditised. In the same way that Disney's fairy only exists because the other characters believe in her, much of our celebrity culture succeeds only because the public believes in and invests in these individuals regardless of their talent or contribution.

This was painted in two separate locations. Firstly, I attended the VIP opening event of Dismaland and felt that my image paralleled Banksy's criticism of our Disneyfied and celebrity-based popular culture. Consequently, painting it just a hundred meters away from the ironic theme park seemed contextually appropriate. The artwork was painted on hoardings at Weston beach and was painted just as the sun was going down in nearly complete darkness. Secondly, I was painting in Kidderminster at a street art festival the next day and decided to paint it there as well. The piece was a big success and was boarded over for protection. It was even valued at a very high price and was about to be put on an official auction site. The artwork, which had been mistaken for a Banksy, was featured in local, national and international newspapers.

Burnham-
on-Sea, at
Parkfest on
03/10/2015

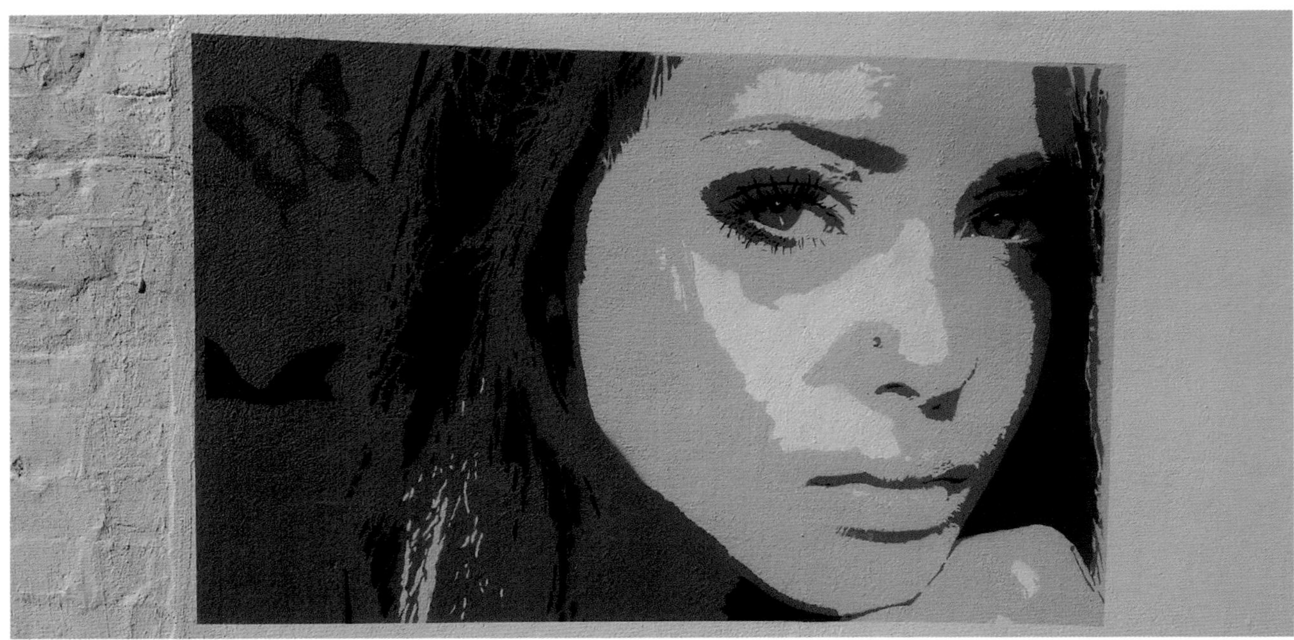
JOHNDOH

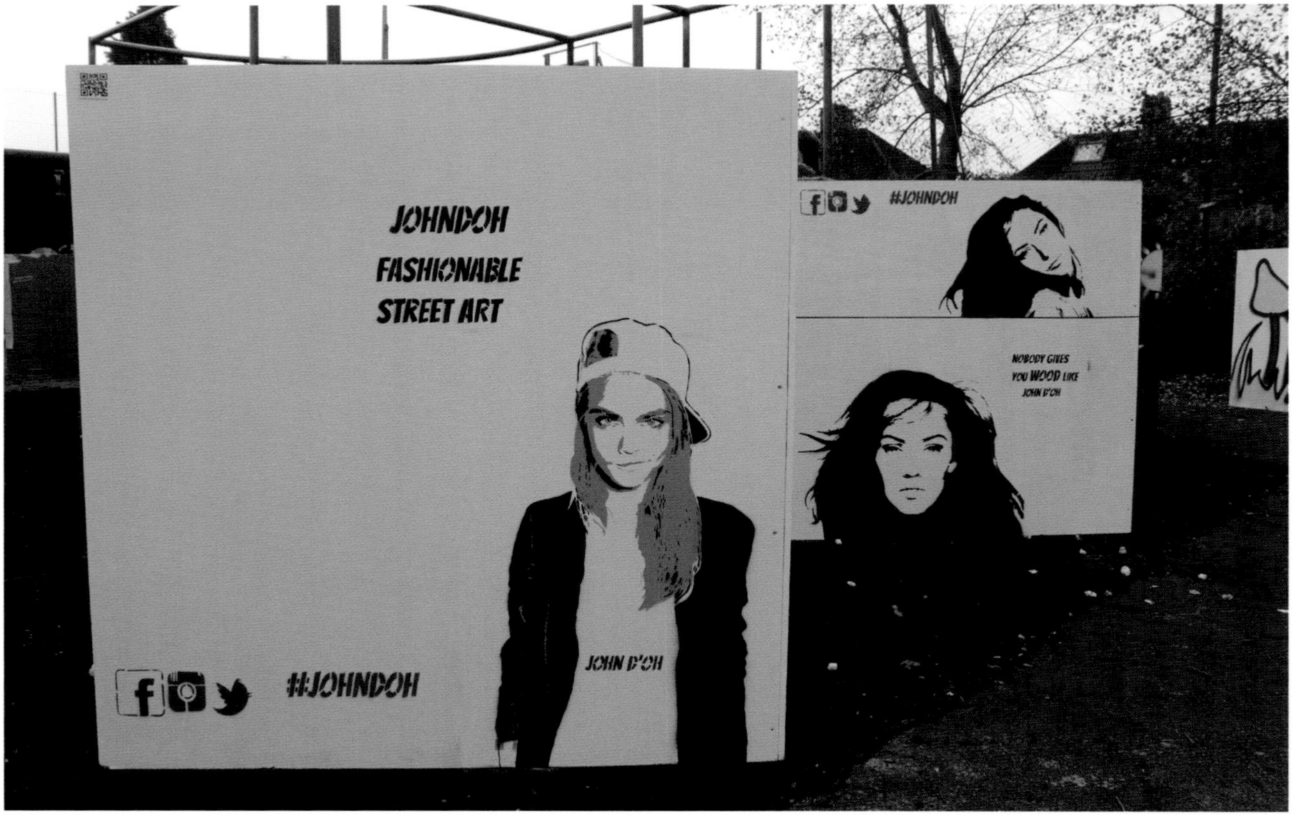

FASHIONABLE
STREET ART

#JOHNDOH

#JOHNDOH

NOBODY GIVES
YOU WOOD LIKE
JOHN D'OH

JOHN D'OH

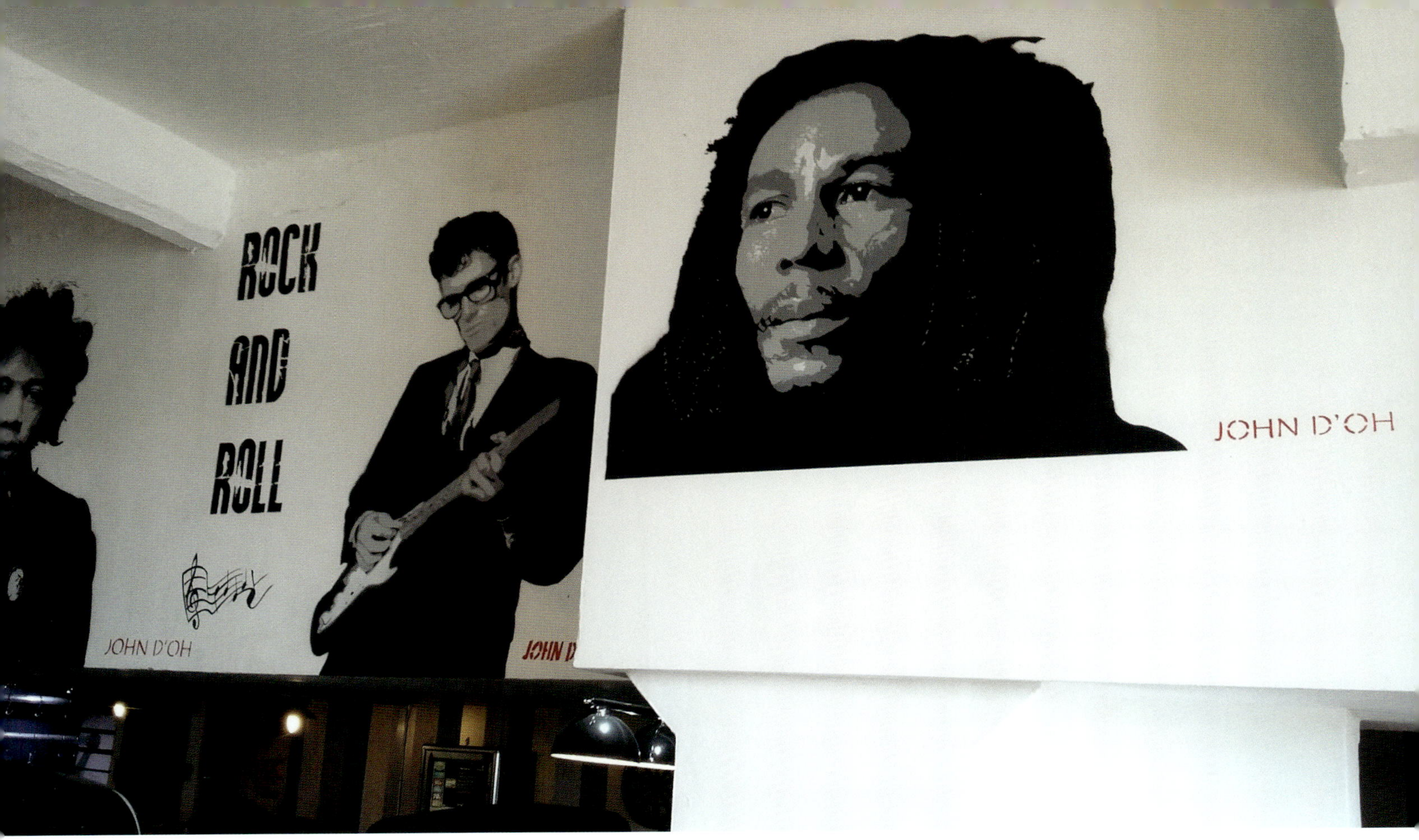

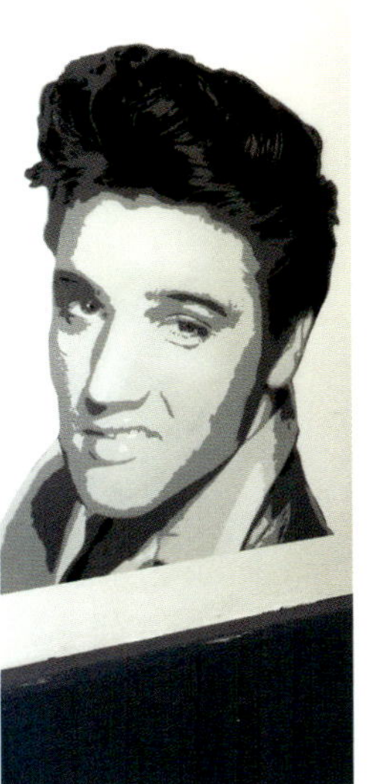
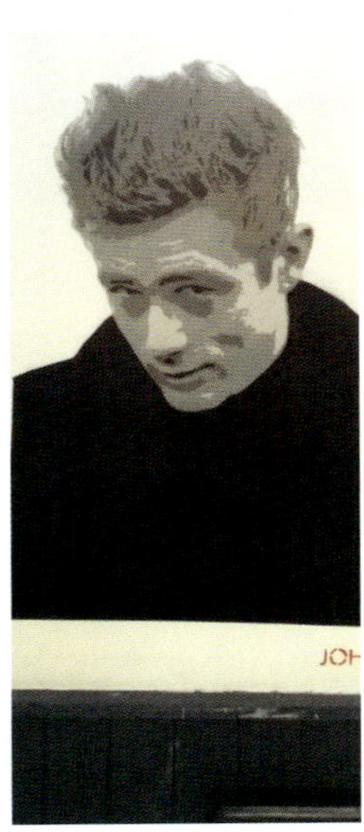
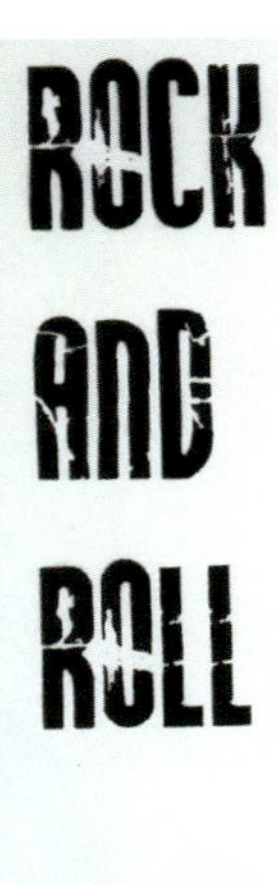
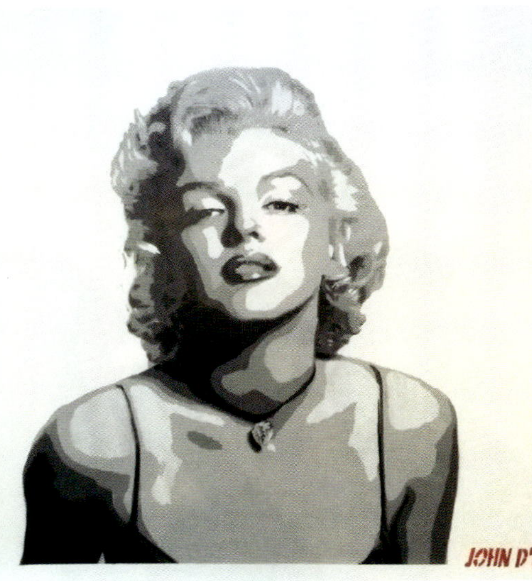

Inside the Old Pier Tavern, Burnham-on-Sea on 03/2017

Bull Inn
Worcester
28/04/2018

Vape shop in
an industrial
estate in
Cheltenham
19/11/2017

Old Butchers
shop Upton-
upon-Severn
11/02/2018

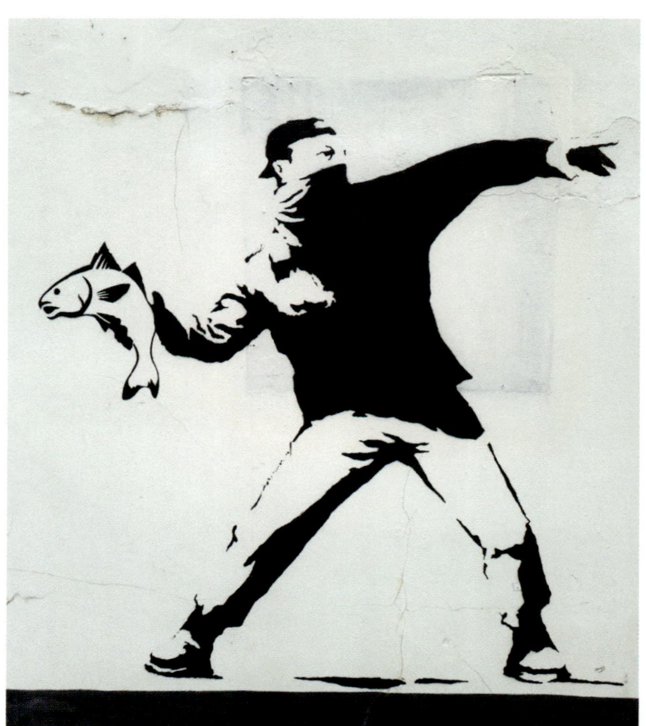

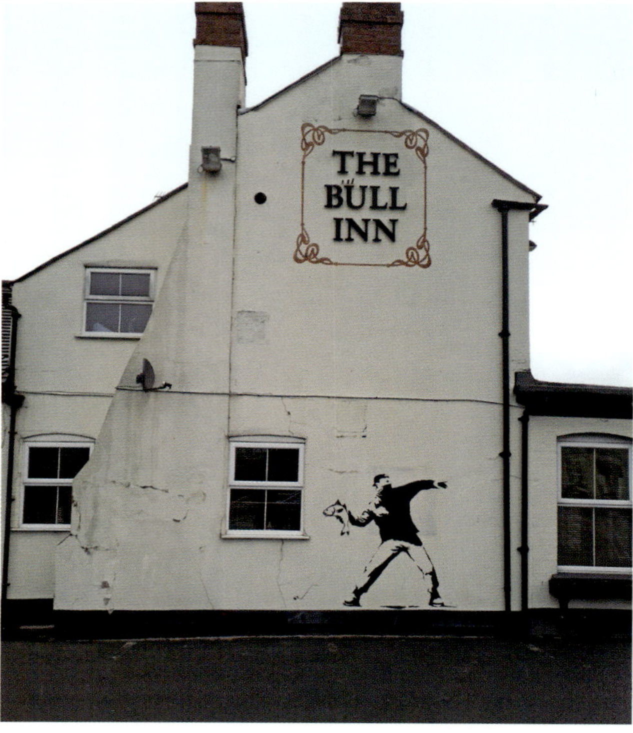

THE
BULL
INN

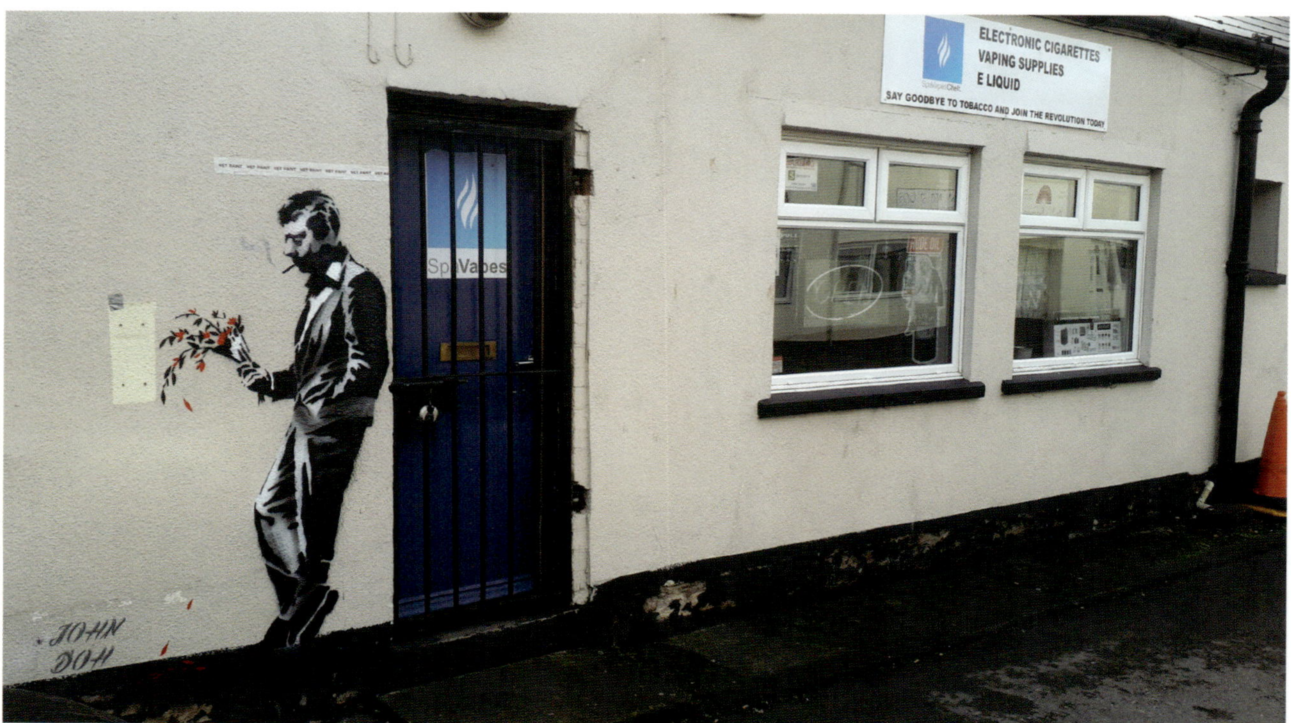

ELECTRONIC CIGARETTES
VAPING SUPPLIES
E LIQUID
SAY GOODBYE TO TOBACCO AND JOIN THE REVOLUTION TODAY
SpaVapes
JOHN
D'OH

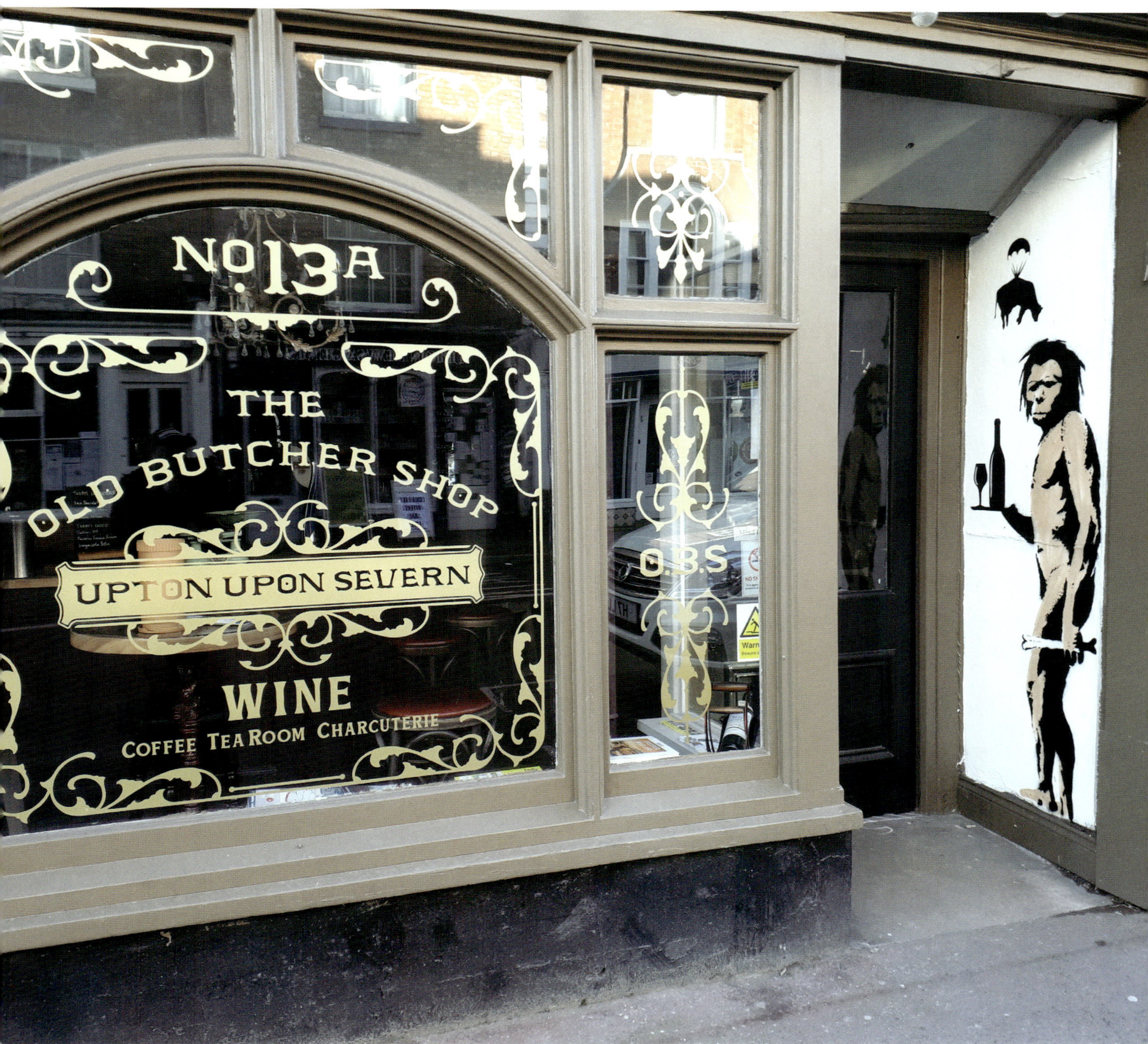

NO.13A
THE OLD BUTCHER SHOP
UPTON UPON SEVERN
WINE
COFFEE TEA ROOM CHARCUTERIE
O.B.S

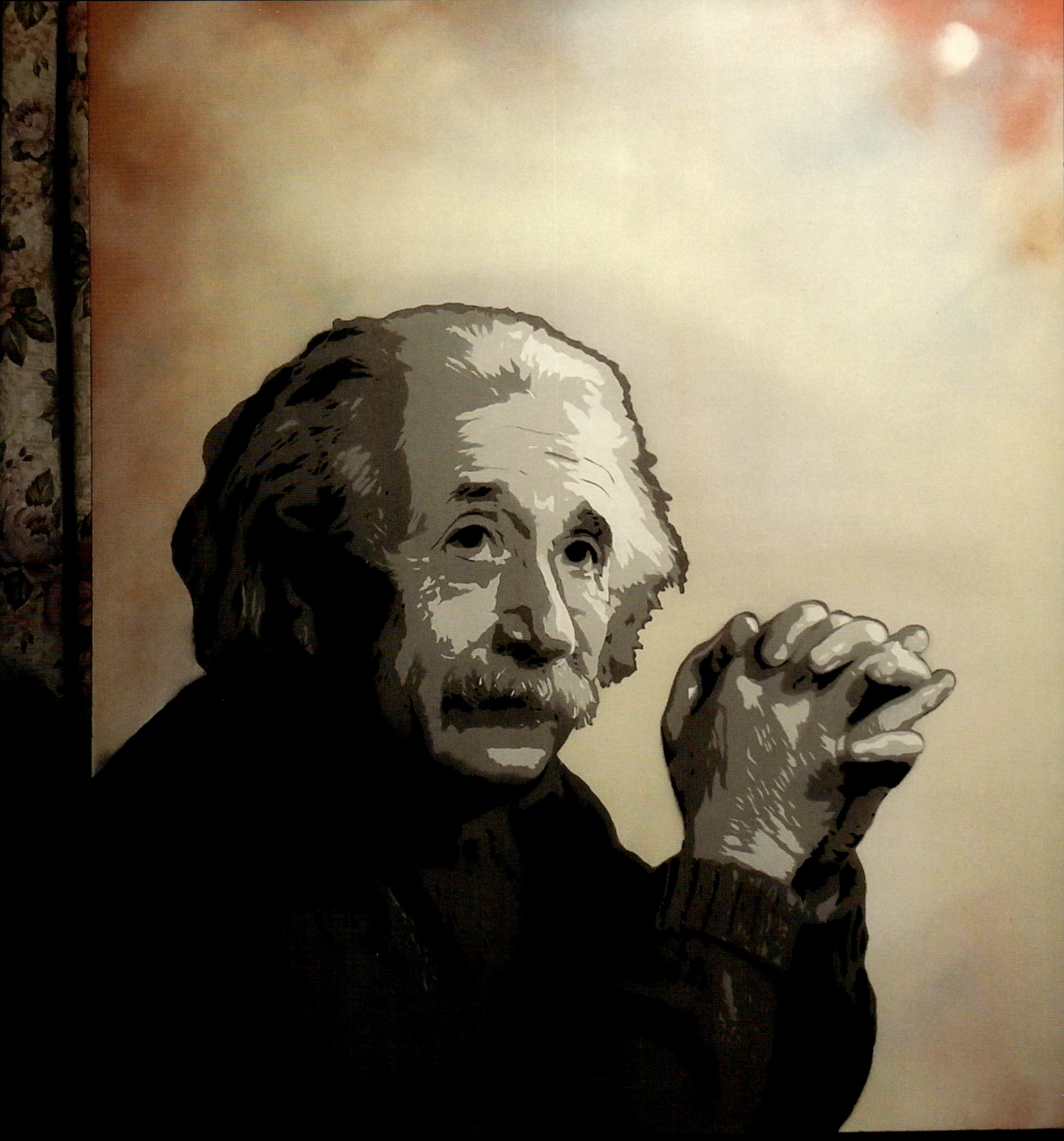

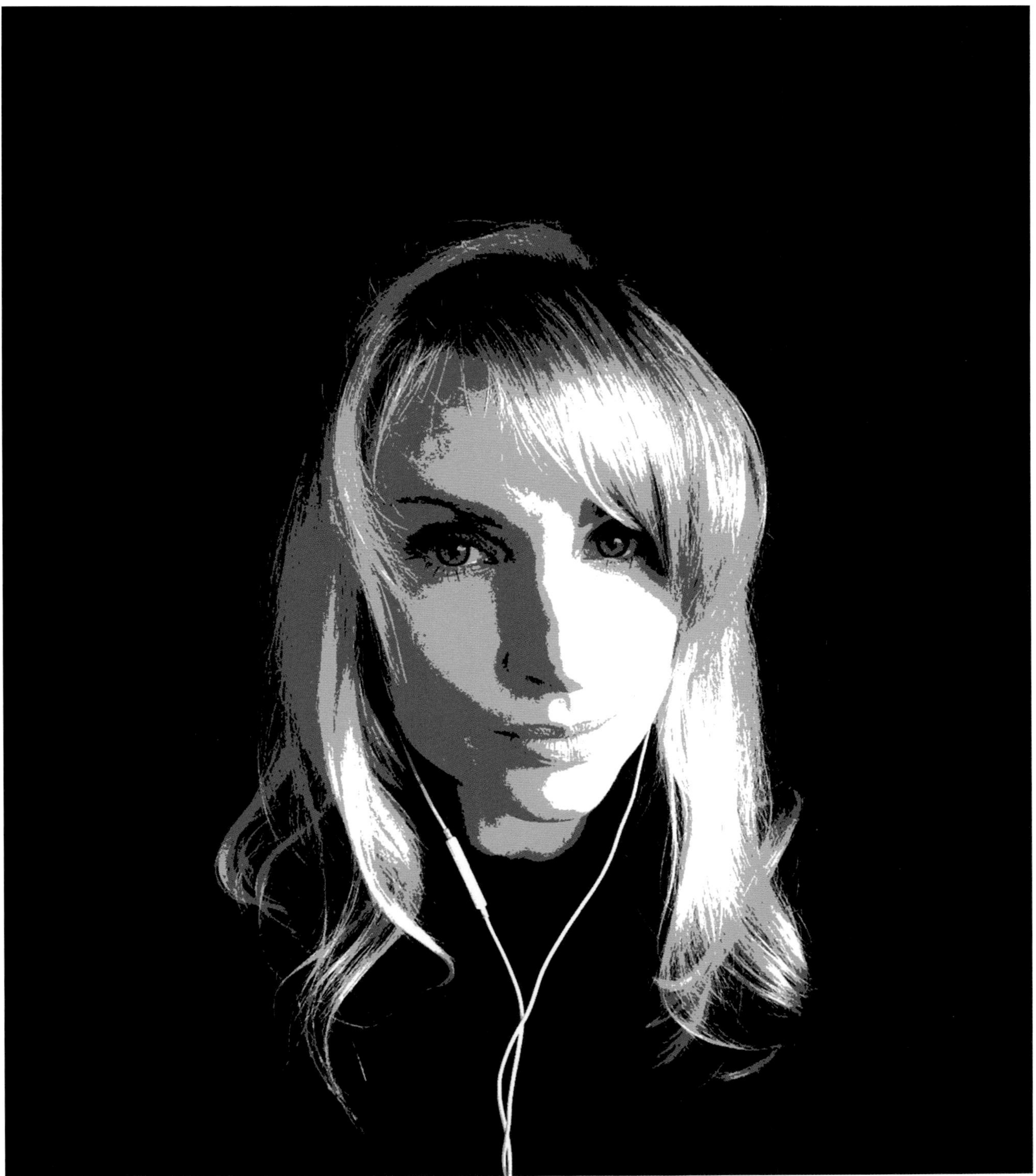

Einstein
canvas

Rebecca Holms.
It's nice to
occasionally
add your
friends into
artwork.
17/02/2018

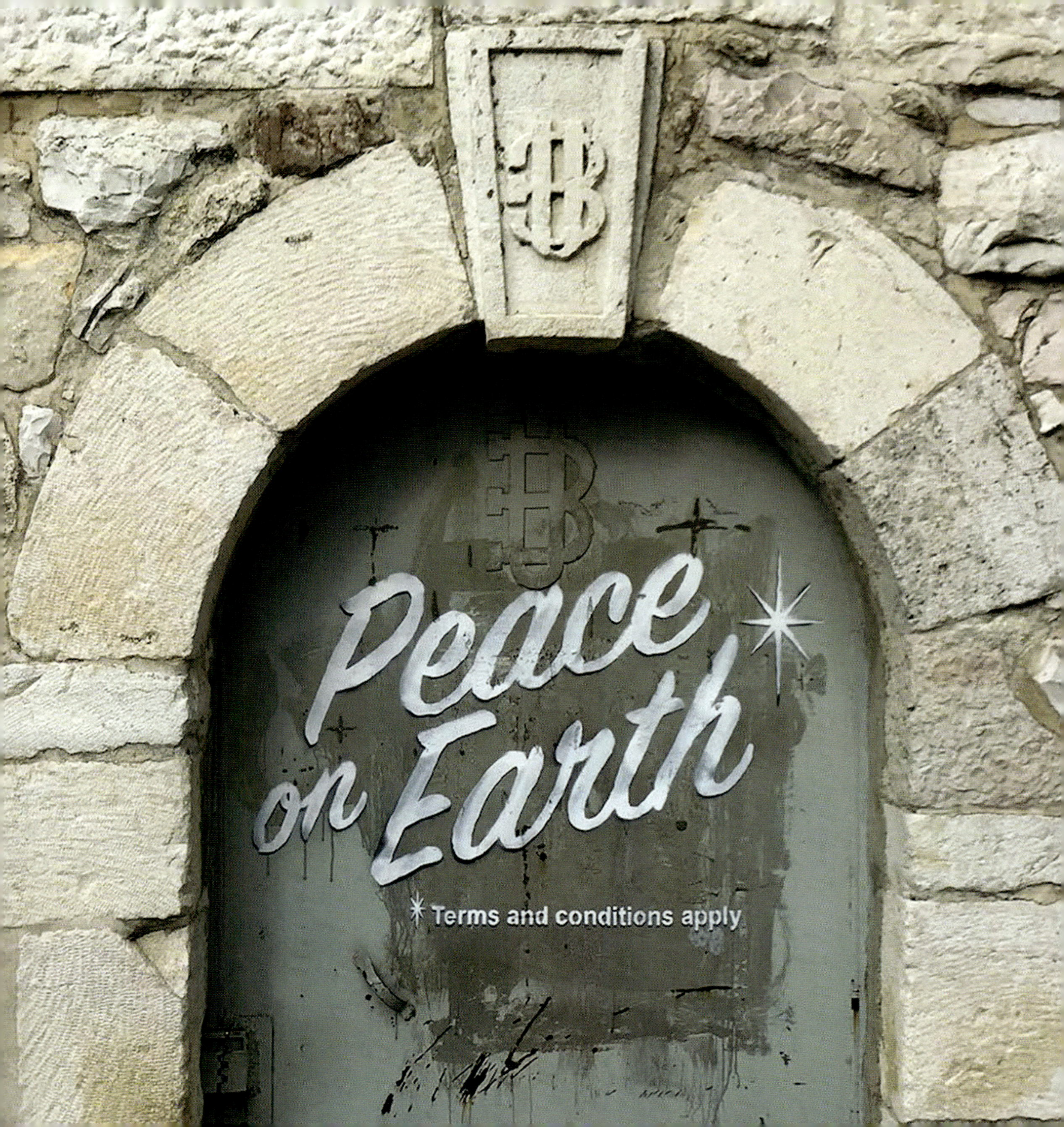
Peace
on Earth
* Terms and conditions apply

Where is Street Art Going?

Museums, galleries and the public acceptance of urban art

Has there been a change in attitude towards the acceptance of urban art?

Museums still seem reluctant to accept street art as an art form. Even though it is extremely popular in Bristol, especially after the Banksy vs Bristol Museum exhibition, street art is hardly featured in the major galleries and local museums. In fact, exhibitions that could be a massive draw to the city are constantly turned down, including a chance to showcase work by the upper echelons of street art such as Shepard Fairey.

But if you put street art in a museum or gallery does it loose its integrity?

In 2014 the Sincura Group put on an exhibition called Stealing Banksy which featured artwork that had been literally cut out of walls and taken from the street. Banksy himself condemned the exhibition and posted on his website *Banksy.co.uk* saying:

The Stealing Banksy exhibition taking place in London this weekend has been organised without the involvement or consent of the artist. Banksy would like to make it clear – this show has nothing to do with me and I think it's disgusting people are allowed to go displaying art on walls without getting permission.

I feel that the removal of an artwork changes everything. The local context and specific urban landscape that the art is situated in and corresponding with cannot be recreated in any institution or exhibition. In some cases, as with Banksy's *Love Plane*, only a portion of the artwork is removed. This disfigurement removes integral parts of the image that are necessary for understanding the original themes or context of the piece.

In these situations, the removal is normally well documented by newspapers, effectively transforming articles of journalism into examples of provenance. When these art objects are put on display it is not for the public interest or for cultural purposes. Instead, museums and galleries are compelled to exhibit the expensive art and property of the super wealthy as the publicly-funded institutions can no longer afford to purchase cultural artefacts in the contemporary art market. Furthermore, for the wealthy elite who own the art, this effectively works as a publicly-funded advertising campaign, because the value of artwork increases as more members of the public see it.

Looking at street art is like studying the aftermath of a crime scene. As in a heist film, you marvel at how the artist has scaled a large height, avoided CCTV or security and painted in the dark of night. This sense of threat, danger and achievement is all gone the minute it is removed.

Banksy vs Bristol Museum 2009
Unbeknownst to even those within the street art community, I was the only other artist to have pieces dotted around this well-known exhibition. I gave the donation boxes a makeover and was heavily involved in the set up of the event. I even did a bit of conservation work on 'Ballerina With Action Man Parts' which had sustained some damage in transport – if you look very carefully you can still see the hairline cracks on the legs.

I won't divulge too much about the set up but I can confirm that there were no secret underground tunnels as some Bristolians believed, as recounted by Marc Leverton in *Banksy Myths & Legends*. There certainly was no free run of the building as protocol had to be followed and most of the art removed was irreplaceable, expensive and culturally important. It was all done extremely professionally.

Where Is street art and graffiti going?
The popularity of street art seems to be growing and growing. When you talk to people at festivals, it's the people who you would think would detest it that like it most. The elderly absolutely love it and really like the splash of art and colour. There are some really talented artists out there that any city should be proud to display on its buildings and walls.

However, what is perhaps less widely known by the general public is that there is a lot of censorship within the graffiti scene. A lot of walls are controlled by street art companies and the art work you are allowed to see is often by select artists which they are paid to promote.

It is big business now and these companies even make money by charging artists to put their art up on their social media platforms. If our public space continues to be censored by local authorities and manipulated by global street art companies, the future of street art could end up no different from the advertising boards we are forced to endure every day.

Street art can also occasionally be territorial. If you see the work of predominately one artist work or crew in an area it is usually because of local favouritism, personal rivalry and financial competition.

Tagging is a subject that normally starts a lot of debate and is mostly disliked by the majority of the general public. They see it less as anything artistic and more like narcissistic self-aggrandising. However, if they wish to have meaningful and representational street art, then the public need to respect the culture that inspires it and perhaps accept more tagging. Yet increased tagging can cause a lot of problems as councils are forced to respond to increased levels of complaints from their constituents. This can sometimes cause a reactionary crackdown by councils, issuing more hard-line threats of arrest and making it difficult to paint. Perhaps the most evident example of this can be seen in Brazil. According to the *Guardian*, the populist right-wing mayor of São Paulo, João Doria, launched a "Beautiful City" policy in 2017 that will organise "cleaning events" where the colourful, ever-changing and sometimes offensive images are replaced with grey monochromatic paint. Removing street art and penalising those who create it is seen by the politician and his supporters as a way to combat urban decay and crime. The project utilises the aforementioned distinction between tagging and street art, claiming that once a mural has been "partially mutilated" by taggers, the state is justified in painting over a work.

The truth is that nobody knows which direction the art form will take in the future.

Anecdotally, some even say street art has peaked and is on a downward slope. As council funding gets capped, there could be less funding for the arts that would affect graffiti negatively. For instance, street art festivals which can be relatively inexpensive and can increase tourism dramatically for local councils might be scrapped. In Bristol, for example, there are even street art companies like *Where The Wall* that regularly take tourists around the city to show them some of the work and explain the ever-changing artwork.

Constant developments in technology will also have an effect on the scene. Artists are already starting to use computer (or computerised) numerical control (CNC) machines and 3D printers, but it won't be long before printers will be able to print holograms and other visual gimmicks affordably which could change paste ups and fly posting. Handheld printers are already capable of printing directly onto walls, mirroring and potentially replacing the traditional use of spray paint. Maybe graffiti paint manufacturers will produce a more environmentally-friendly paint that is easily removable and less of a problem for councils.

It's a good debate and if you ask one hundred people you will get one hundred different answers. I am even contributing to research for several university dissertations, so it must be getting increasingly popular as an area of academic study.

Has street art sold out?

I partially agree with a quote from Ben Eine in the *Independent* back in 2010: "Street art belongs on the street. But I'm a working street artist and I earn my money selling art in the style of street art via galleries. I don't get paid for what I do in public places. So I invest the money I earn in galleries back into doing the stuff I passionately want to do on the street." Ben thinks his approach negates accusations of selling out. He says: "If that's how artists are going to work, then I think it's cool. But if they're just a bunch of so-called street artists that make stuff in their studios and sell it in galleries, then they're making a bad choice."

However, that is where the similarities end as it appears that Ben's view have taken a rather dramatic change. The *Evening Standard* claims that, since 2013, Eine has customised scarves for Louis Vuitton and collaborated with Sir Richard Branson's airline *Virgin Atlantic*, whose first-class passengers could purchase Eine's work from an airborne gallery.

Personally, it's hard to say that you are *never* going to sell out and prioritise making a living over creating independent art, but there are certain people who couldn't tempt me with all the money in the world and Richard Branson is one of them. I'm not sure if Ben has sold out, but he is a very funny, inspirational guy and well worth watching in videos.

You see too many artists now selling prints in every colour of the rainbow trying to cash in, which are aptly named colourways. Companies contact you the minute they see something they think they can capitalise on, change and make 50% for the privilege. Even when you see artists theatrically painting on a wall it is just an arbitrary choice of location and image used as a marketing gimmick, because within hours a new print is available to purchase nearby or at the scene. Almost every potential artist wants to be the next Banksy and almost every art-purchaser wants to buy something as an investment that will constantly increase in value.

Street art can be seen as a personal expression of one's unique identity in anonymity of the crowded cityscape. The street can also be seen as an egalitarian gallery accessible to everybody, especially because the contemporary art market is extremely hard to enter, is dominated by specific artistic styles and is populated with graduates from certain elite schools. Graffiti is often seen as an act of rebellion (or vandalism by some) which communicates political and social change, but many companies are now buying into street art as a profitable business opportunity, sometimes even without the artists consent. Here, egalitarian ideals and individualistic expression are replaced by conformist and profit-orientated corporate messages that are antithetical to the aims of street art originally.

For example, the fashion company Moschino allegedly took a 2012 Detroit mural known as *Vandal Eyes* by Brooklyn graffiti artist Rime (Joseph Tierney) and used it without his consent on their Autum/Winter collection for 2015. Most notably, the artwork was controversially featured on a dress worn by Katy Perry during a red-carpet publicity stunt. Not only was Rime's art exploited, but his credibility as a graffiti artist was left in tatters. It was labelled as a publicity stunt by many, undermining his reputation as an independent artist of the streets. It's like putting Che Guevara on a T-shirt; it is the opposite of what he would of wanted, being an ideological opponent of capitalism.

H&M have also tried to use Machino's argument that vandalism should not have copyright protection when they tried to use a piece by LA Artist Revok (aka Jason Williams) in the background of their new men's sportswear campaign.

One has to admit that there is a certain amount of hypocrisy and self-centredness in a street artist who paints on other people's property without their permission suddenly complaining that a company is using his artwork without any prior consent. Governments, on the other hand, do not want criminals to profit from their crimes, including graffiti and street art.

This does have far-reaching implications for street art and graffiti. And, while the likelihood is that they will again settle before the trial takes place, these challenges are now becoming more frequent. I have had also had my own art used in an advert for Under Armour (an American company that manufacturers sports clothing and footwear) and sometimes it's nice to just credit the artist.

Even photographers are cashing in on it, often offering jpeg images for use or even tying to produce direct prints of artist's artwork for sale. Don't get me wrong, it is always nice to get your work documented by photographers, especially when the piece may be painted over within a few days, and I don't mind if there is a bit of moody sky or a scantily clad model in the shot. However, photographing or reproducing a direct copy of the artwork onto T-shirts, mugs or prints is just plain not right.

But for most, these issues are irrelevant. We live in a consumerist society and global marketing can make you a household name overnight. In such a situation, the political, social or economic messages behind a work may be watered-down for a long-term increase in fame and wealth.

As a side note, I also really don't get how people buy into the Mr. Brainwash thing. He commissions other artists to produce artwork, throws a splash of paint on it and then whacks a massive price tag onto it. This is commercialism at its worst and resembles the production processes used by some contemporary artists more than any street artist. And while some suckers genuinely line up in great numbers to hand over their cash, others just put their purchases straight up on eBay for a quick buck. This is known as 'flipping'. What does that tell you about the quality of the art as anything other than a financial investment?

Even when corporations try to directly recruit street artists for promotional work, they don't always get it right. One particularly vivid example is in a 2015 advert for the Hyundai i20. Throughout the advert, the car drives past street art that has been "inspired by" or "based upon" works by real artists. These pieces, which have only superficial alterations from the authentic artworks, were not done by or permitted by the original painters. It is easier and cheaper for large companies to recreate the street art images with less well-known artists than it is to hire and transport all the original creators from around the globe. This caused some controversy within the street art community, especially online, where those artists who had been paid to recreate the pictures for Hyundai were criticised for "stealing ideas" from other artists. Evidently, the territorialism that can be seen in the streets can also be seen in cyberspace, where different forums and online communities argue over the moral and legal "right" to borrow, adapt or copy another artist's work.

Here we can see how the desire to be "authentic" still remains important in street art. This desire to be "real" and have "ownership" undermines the subversive potential of the art form. Originally, street art appropriated normal words and images and, by randomly, aggressively or repetitively painting them where they didn't belong, emptied them of their meaning and value. These ad-hoc and seemingly "empty signifiers", as Jean

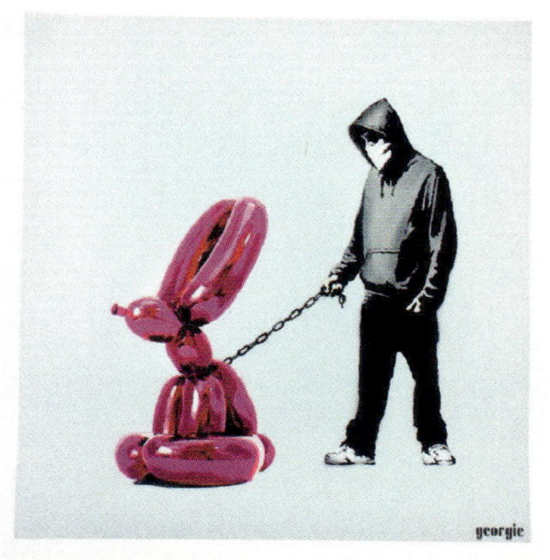
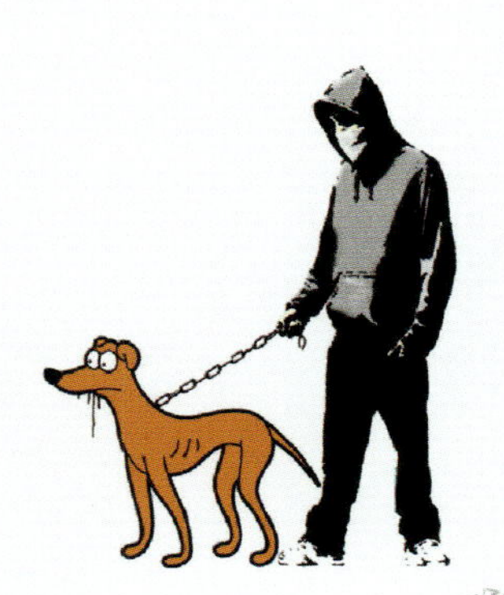
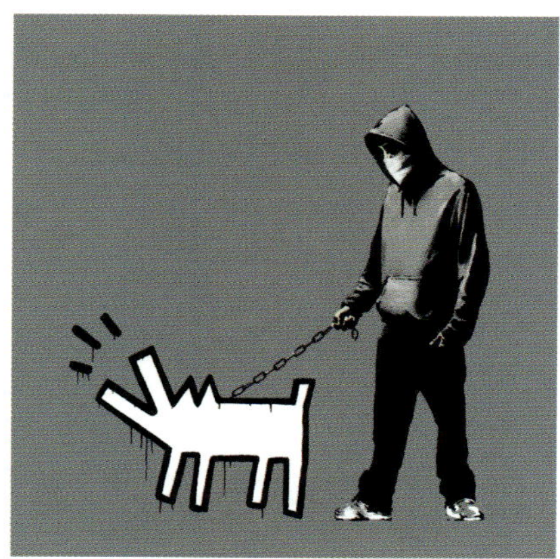

A selection of just a few of my favourite reworkings of Banksy's Choose Your Weapon, a tribute to Keith Haring's iconic barking dog. Top row artists Georgie, JBoy and Banksy. Bottom row, Angus and Lewis Bannister.

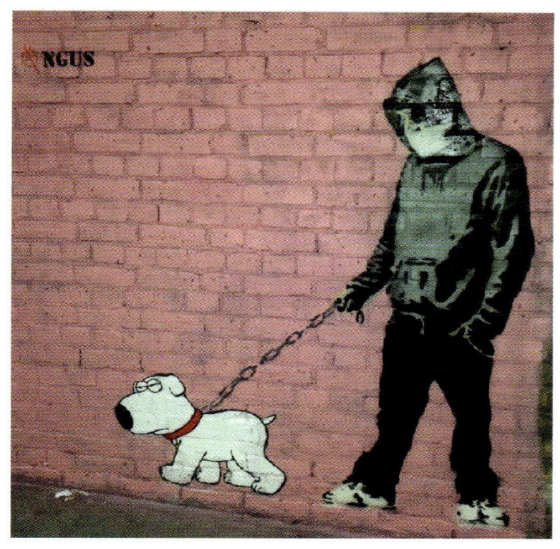

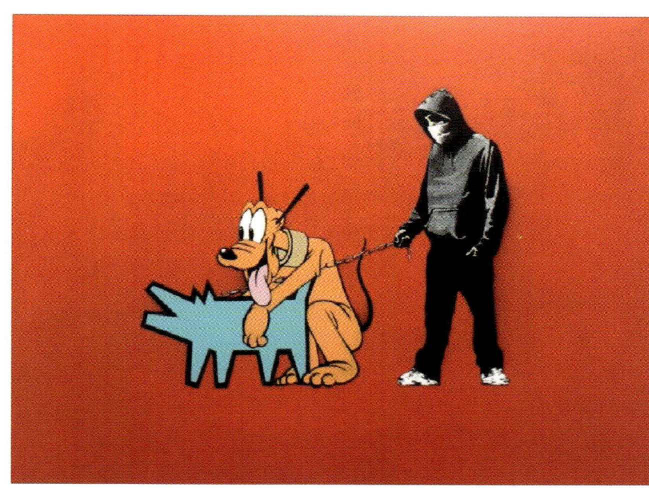

Baudrillard called them, couldn't be commoditised by companies and politicians. But now that graffiti has been defended as "authentic" self-expression of individuality, it can be purchased as a symbol of a "cool" and "real" identity outside the "mainstream" consumer culture in a hipster-like fashion.

So "sold out" is a debatable way to characterise street art, but it has definitely lost its integrity.

Copyright, plagiarism, satire, pastiche and parody
There have been recent developments in the United States which seem to suggest that street art and graffiti, whether guerrilla or commissioned, may hold some level of copyright. This has emerged only as a response to several artists suing companies and individuals for misusing their art without permission, such as a law suit against American Eagle and Terry Gilliam.

This could have a far reaching effect and some are even questioning if photographing street art is a breach of copyright as more and more photographers are now taking direct images of artwork and uploading them for sale on the internet. Personally, I like to have my work documented and circulated on social media, but have seen my art appear on T-shirts, plates and unlicensed limited-edition prints. I am a big fan of photography and nothing looks better than a well taken photo that can even make the artwork look better than it is. If you use artwork for a backdrop for a photo it is always courteous to let the artist know and maybe credit them. There really needs to be a respectful, reciprocal balance.

Plagiarism is massive in street art and graffiti often uses or satirises copyrighted characters from large franchises such as Marvel or Disney without any prior permission or care. Even other graffiti artists have their work borrowed, changed or mocked without consequence. It is generally considered as fair use.

I consider what I do a pastiche by taking an original piece of well-known art and modifying it to add my own humour. Some people may confuse satire, parody and pastiche. Generally, satire is where you ridicule the shortcomings and vices of society with social criticism, intending to cause improvement or inspire action. Parody is the very explicit duplication of another work in order to make fun of it exclusively, simply for comedic purposes. This compares with pastiche, where you're explicitly bringing up a scene or situation from another artwork in order to praise, celebrate or develop it. My work is definitely a homage in the latter category and is not sold and made just for amusement.

On one occasion I did leave a couple of fellow artists a little upset with my borrowings and they are perfectly entitled to voice their opinion. However, I did a bit of digging into their social media profiles and found out that they had not only replicated exact copies of Jamie Hewlett's *Tank Girl* on many occasions but had also plagiarised a number of record covers. What gave me the biggest smile though was he had even used my wood cut style in replicating some of his art and was trying to sell it too.

When is a Banksy not a Banksy?

A lot of unattributed work in a certain stencilled style is often attributed to Banksy by local commentators, newspapers and members of the public. In doing this, they often ignore the actual content of the work or the creativity of a completely different artist and prioritise a vapid culture of celebrity instead. In fact, sometimes a so-called artwork by Banksy might not always be a Banksy piece even when it appears on his website! For example, a tourist claimed he had taken a photo of the secretive artist at work in Bethlehem when painting the *Peace on Earth* graffiti. This later appeared on his official website. However, people in the scene instantly recognised the figure as British-Israeli artist Ame72, also known as James Ame, who is familiar for doing street art all around the world. He is a well-established artist in his own right whose art has been exhibited in renowned museums and galleries from Tel Aviv to Beijing.

By associating a well-known artist to an unidentified piece, a local community may gain attention and money from the interest generated. At the same time, the name "Banksy" carries certain socio-political associations for the general public which, by attributing to a perhaps random and ambiguous image, provides the piece of graffiti with easily understandable or politically acceptable meanings. It is perhaps similar to the "Shakespeare industry", where anonymous plays or indeed plays by other authors from the Elizabethan period are unproblematically ascribed to the mythologised playwright by competing editors and publishers who hope to increase sales by capitalising on the cult of the author and authenticity.

Sometimes, then, people may rework a Banksy in order to undermine and satirise his iconic public image and the sometimes overbearing influence it has over the street art scene. On the other hand, artists may remake a Banksy piece in order to borrow his recognisable and valued work for their own economic or social gain.

If you look at the variations of Banksy's *Choose Your Weapon* included here, you can see both of these ideas at play. By replacing the dog in the original piece with the *Balloon Bunny* by contemporary artist Jeff Koons, a man whose million dollar work has been described as kitsch, openly meaningless and self-merchandised, this artist may be claiming Banksy has become too closely associated with the art market. And perhaps replacing Banksy's dog with cartoon animals from *The Simpsons* and *Family Guy*, the other artists may be critiquing Banksy's incorporation into the popular culture he is so often criticising.

Banksy and copyright

Banksy hasn't used his well-known phrase that copyright law is "for losers" for a long time now. Instead, Banksy has increasingly copyrighted his own work and used his handling service Pest Control as his legal enforcers, coming down hard on anyone who steps out of line.

Bristol Museum felt the wrath when a badly marketed print of the artist's *Paint Pot Angel* was sold on its website for £5 and an American buyer sought authentication for his purchase from the artist directly. Bristol Museum and Art Gallery was forced to cease sale of prints and I believe the remaining stock was pulped. Originally the artwork was donated to the Museum after his 2009 exhibition entitled 'Banksy Vs Bristol Museum', but along with it came many stipulations. Bristol Museum currently owns the artwork in question and had been granted permission to produce the image in the museum's guide, so it assumed that this permission extended to produce other images and prints. It was a hard lesson and a public apology was issued. However, the debacle left a lot of members of the public split over whether the artist had become a hypocrite, undermining his "free-wheeling anti-capitalist routine" (*Bristol Post*). For some, it seemed to be a contradiction for an artist who likes to capitalise on his localist and Bristolian credentials to begrudge his home city's publically-funded institution from making money from £5 prints, especially after hosting his largest exhibition ever at the time.

If you're looking at copyright infringements, it is arguable that Banksy himself could have been sued by the Jean-Michel Basquiat estate when he painted Basquiat-inspired artworks on the walls of the Barbican in September 2017. Two pieces were painted, one featured a figure being frisked by two police officers and the second depicted a Ferris wheel which is a fairly common motif in Basquiat's work.

Should street art be protected?

In general, most cities consider street art to be an illegal act of vandalism and most artists risk arrest when painting illegally and not every city council wants public

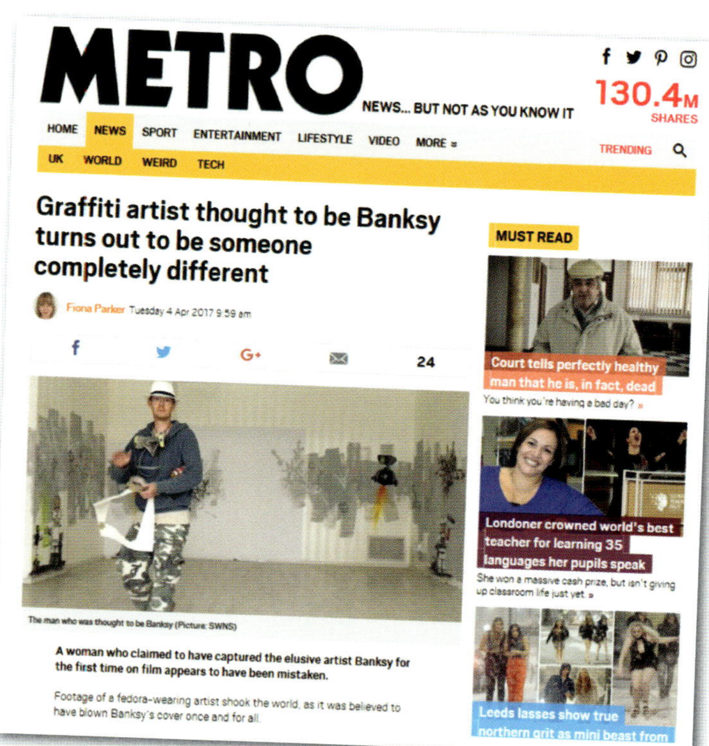

art put up, especially without permission or consultation of nearby residents. And if complaints come, it can be costly to taxpayers for art to be removed.

However, public perception appears to have changed. The art used to be instantly scrubbed away, but nowadays the first reaction seems to be "what's it worth?" and even councils now often think of tourism as certain artists can draw big crowds.

It is and will remain a grey area. As with the art in the Tate, one person's art is another person's pile of bricks. It depends on where it is painted and what the subject matter is, as anything deemed offensive or politically controversial is normally removed rather quickly.

There can also be issues with ownership because artwork painted illegally obviously has been done without the approval of the owner of the property, so it's up to the owner what happens to the artwork and not the local authority. Ironically, the public may even call for the so-called act of vandalism to be protected from other vandals, but this can obviously be complicated.

London Artist Stik standing in front of his artwork that was stolen

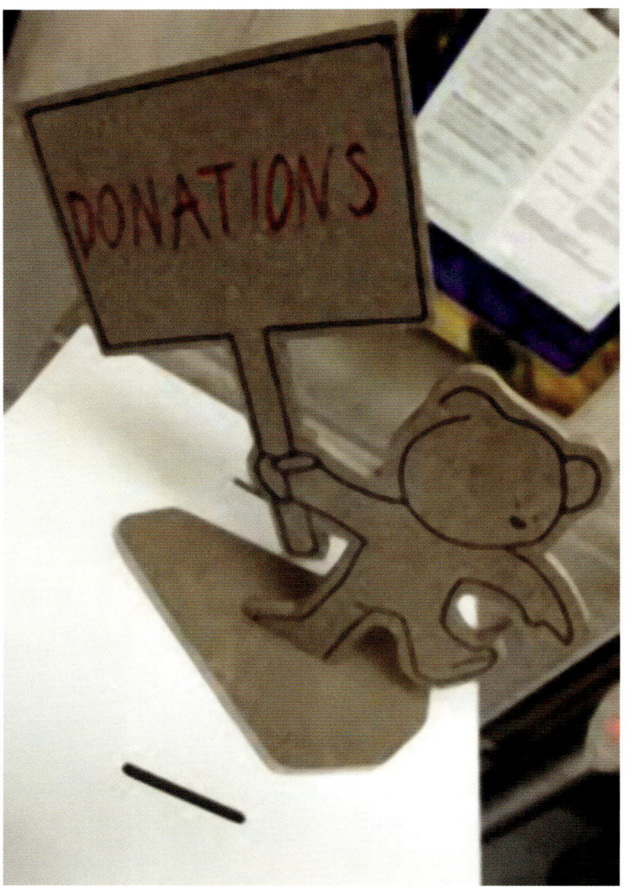

Painted by Banksy in 2014 in Folkestone, *Art Buff* was removed from an amusement arcade wall in order to be sold and provide money for a cancer charity. The charity was set up in memory of Jimmy Godden, a relative of the family who seemingly owned the wall Banksy had painted on. The artwork was taken to the U.S. to be sold but after a lengthy court case a British judge ruled that the mural was public property and had to be returned to Folkestone. *Art Buff* was removed by the London-based art dealer Robin Barton and his art dealership Bankrobber. Bankrobber, like the Sincura Group, you will see pop up time and again in many of the art disappearances. After investigation lawyers argued that the Godden family only owned the leasehold of the amusement arcade not the freehold, thus securing its return.

In 2013 Banksy's *Slave Labour*, which was painted on the side of Poundland in Wood Green in North London a year earlier, sold for in excess of £75,000 ($1.1 million dollars) at a private auction at the London Film Museum in Covent Garden by the Sincura Group, having previously been withdrawn from an auction in Miami after protests from Haringey Council. Sincura's Tony Baxter said in a statement:

The Sincura Group do not condone any acts of wanton vandalism or other illegal activity, however after carrying out extensive due diligence with regard the works provenance and ownership we are entirely satisfied that the mural was legally salvaged and that its current owners and its representative are acting in good faith by consigning the piece to us to act as the centrepiece of our forthcoming art show 'Banksy at the Flower Cellars'.

Removal and sale of such work is extremely controversial and not always successful. One memorable example was the removal of the *In the Spy Booth* artwork in Cheltenham – also involving Robin Barton from the Bankrobber Gallery in Mayfair. On this occasion the removal didn't go very well and the piece painted in 2014, which was granted listed status and retrospectively given planning permission by Cheltenham Borough Council in an effort to protect it, ended up as a pile of rubble.

When painted on walls owned by a local authority, some councils even decide what artwork can stay and what has to be removed. I have not been involved in this process personally but imagine it varies from council to council. To me, both street art and graffiti are temporary art forms to be enjoyed while it lasts and not something to be removed for profit and sold or placed in a museum where it loses it integrity.

The removal of artwork has been going on for many years and involving more and more artists. This process has had various outcomes. It has ended in a pile of rubble, it has resulted in the artwork being declared public property and returned to its original location and it has allowed pieces to be sold for hundreds of thousands of pounds.

The leader of Cheltenham Borough Council Steve Jordan said work had been taking place to repair render on the wall of the house after the council had issued an enforcement notice, but was unaware when contacted that the Banksy had vanished. "It is protected by a listing. I will have a look at what the situation is," he said.

Fragments of the *Spybooth* have since appeared for sale. Building owner David Possee took the bits to the council for safekeeping but was apparently given the opportunity to sell the broken pieces of the original artwork on the open market. The *Bristol Post* revealed that an unknown seller called 'G-City Graf Slaps' claimed the dusty pieces were "saved" and were now for sale to people making "serious offers".

The commercial exploitation of artists is on the rise, with more and more work disappearing from the streets. Back in 2011, East London artist Stik painted a children's community mural on a shipping container with a group of local children from Gdansk in Poland. This public art subsequently went missing in 2014 but then resurfaced at Lamberty Gallery Belgravia, albeit with the artwork having been cut into individual pieces and being sold for £10,000 each. Likewise, in 2014 street artist Bambi painted five shark murals for charity in Islington London in aid of the charity Art Against Knives, but overnight the art (with an estimated price tag of £20,000) was stolen.

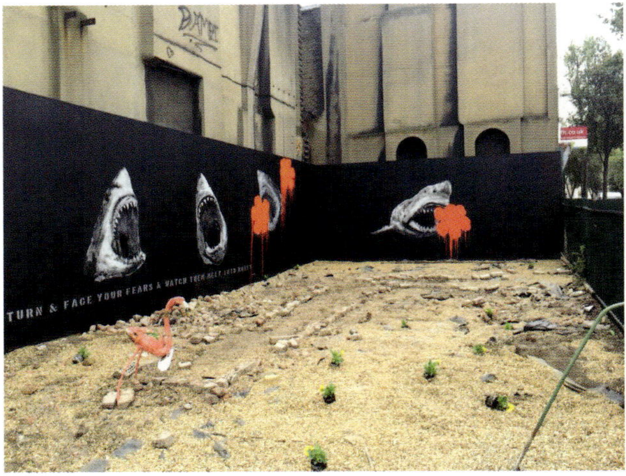

Authentication

In the future it is going to get increasingly difficult to authenticate art. Already technological advancements mean that 3D mapping is starting to become common place and used in Museums and Archeology, but I can see this spreading further as this technology becomes cheaper to use. Art can be replicated at a touch of a button and could be open for some unscrupulous art dealers to maybe copy or duplicate art, meaning it is possible that you may have authentication but not the original piece of art.

The second-hand art market is massive with art being sold in galleries and online in huge numbers, but you don't always get what you are paying for. Ideally, it is best to try and have a paper trail for your purchase: a receipt from a gallery where the art was originally on display, an original artist certificate of authenticity or a copy of an email or invoice if a purchase is directly from the artist.

In the case of art stolen or removed from the streets, there is usually no artist authentication and the seller often tries to prove provenance putting together newspaper articles, photographs from the artist's own website and any documentation from the removal company proving. Of course, if this is being sold for the second or third time, the names and paperwork from previous sales are often useful.

Appraisal from a recognised authority or expert on the artist can be sought but often they can get it wrong. Believe me I have seen my art valued at millions and then suddenly plunge and become worthless. But I always find the almost comically-exaggerated up-and-down amusing. Not so amusing for the buyers though, especially if you have spent millions and think you have work from one artist hanging on your wall and then it suddenly turns out to be by someone else.

Mobile Lovers and George Ferguson

Occasionally an artist may intervene or, in the case of Banksy's *Mobile Lovers* piece, may even come forward and help facilitate the sale. In 2014 Dennis Stinchcombe discovered the artwork painted next to the doorway on his Broad Plain and Riverside Youth Club and decided to remove the work in order to prevent it from being damaged. He then displayed it inside the youth club for the public to view. Bristol City Council argued that the artwork appeared on its property and the police removed the artwork from Mr. Stinchcombe on behalf of the local authority in order to secure an item of artistic value for the public interest. *Mobile Lovers* was then delivered to Bristol Museum and Art Gallery where it was put on display until ownership could be established. Banksy then wrote to Mr. Stinchcombe confirming his ownership, settling the dispute between him and the Bristol Mayor at the time George Ferguson. The artwork was later sold to a private collector for £403,000 with the proceeds going to Broad Plain Youth Club and a number of other voluntary sector youth clubs across the city.

When Banksy's *Mobile Lovers* was confiscated and in a highly controversial move I had to work quickly in order to respond to the scandal. I pictured George Ferguson, easily identified by his red trousers, as a balaclava-wearing thief. Here, *Mobile Lovers* is shown only from behind as a piece of wood, demonstrating how the political and social meaning of the painting had been replaced by a mere object or possession in the public eye. Besides, the work had been reproduced online and photographed by the public so much, which is ironic given that the work is critical of our current digital obsession, I didn't feel the need to reproduce the image

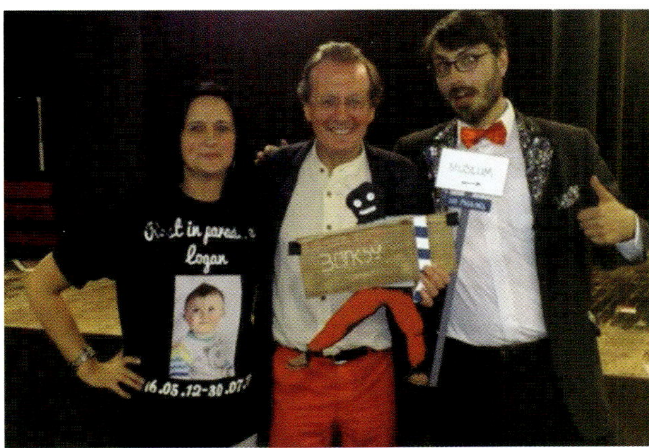

again. Moreover, the sign saying "no parking" tried to link the local authority's money-making fines and legal power with the taking of *Mobile Lovers*, highlighting how taking the artwork was tied-up with Bristol Museum's need for cultural and financial recognition. By showing Ferguson as a Banksy-esque figure and painting him in a similar stencil style, I tried to suggest that the Mayor's controversial "theft" of the artwork was not dissimilar to the kind of stunts Banksy himself uses to generate interest and discussion about his art. My work was put up for sale at a charity auction for Sudden Infant Death syndrome in memory of Logan Dyte, a 14-month-old child who had died the previous year. Ferguson purchased the work himself and posed for a photo with it for the *Bristol Post*. One could cynically argue that, in a similar way to how Ferguson posed in front of *Mobile Lovers* with the owner of the club after the scandal, such a move was done in order undermine and reduce any criticism of his actions. However, I have made George Ferguson the target of quite a few pieces and have met him on several occasions and he has a good sense of humour and takes these things all in his stride. As the *Bristol Post* itself said: "George Ferguson has proved he can chuckle over the very public Bristol saga surrounding Banksy's *Mobile Lovers*".

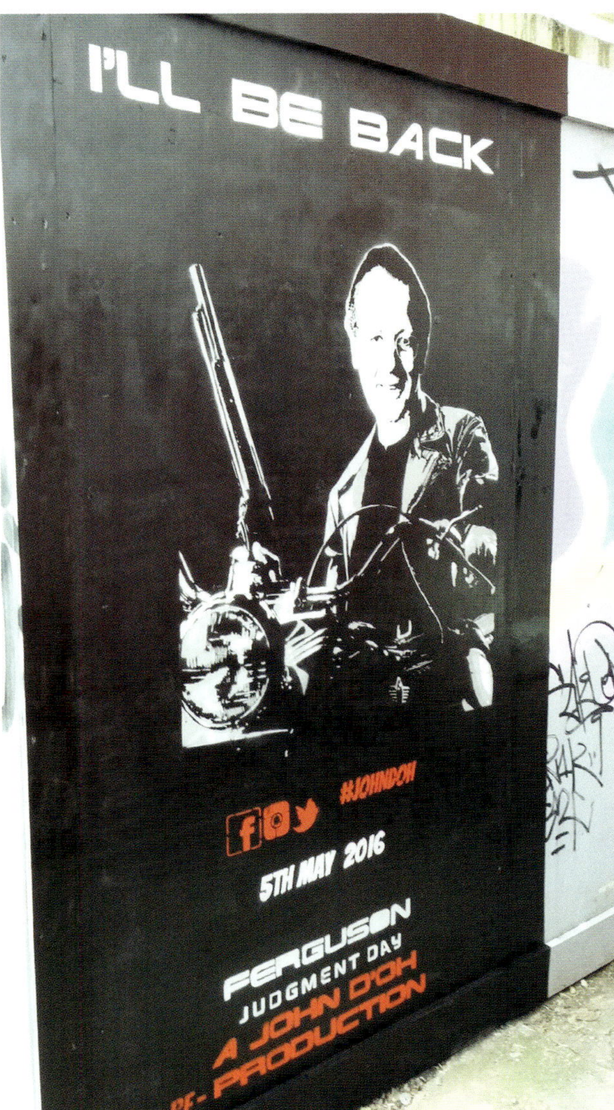

Painted for former Bristol Mayor George Ferguson's re-election campaign. The image and quote are taken from the film Terminator. Unfortunately for George he was 'terminated' and replaced by Marvin Rees when he was unsuccessful at securing a second term. 28/02/2016

Charity auction art purchased by George Ferguson. The humorous art depicted George removing Banksy's Mobile Lovers and taking it to Bristol Museum

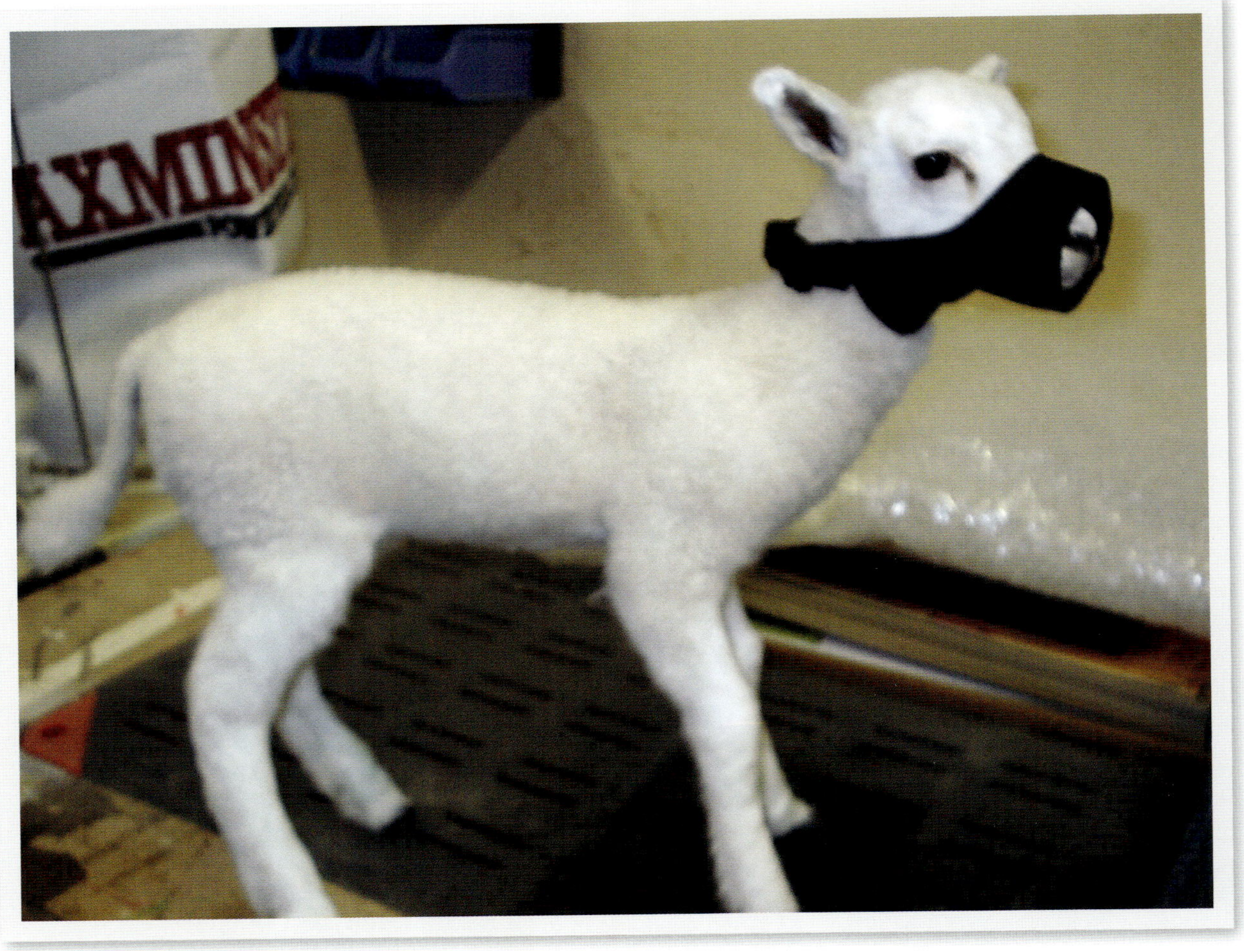

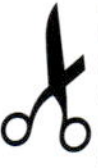

BANKSY VS BRISTOL MUSEUM: NEVER SEEN BEFORE IMAGES

I hope I won't get into trouble for providing these images, but it is many years after the event and most of the pictures are simply of a documentary or behind-the-scenes nature, not giving anything important away like the techniques or identities of those involved.

At the time of the installation, I remember several of us signing the same piece of paper promising not to release any information regarding the exhibition.

The paper, however, appeared not to be attached to any specific contract and, even when specifically asked, neither Pest Control nor the Bristol Museum provided a copy of what I had signed. So I doubt that it is legally binding or prohibitive. But just in case I have made the page easily removable by adding a "cut here" dotted line, allowing you to cease and desist with ease. Remember, "It's always easier to get forgiveness than permission".

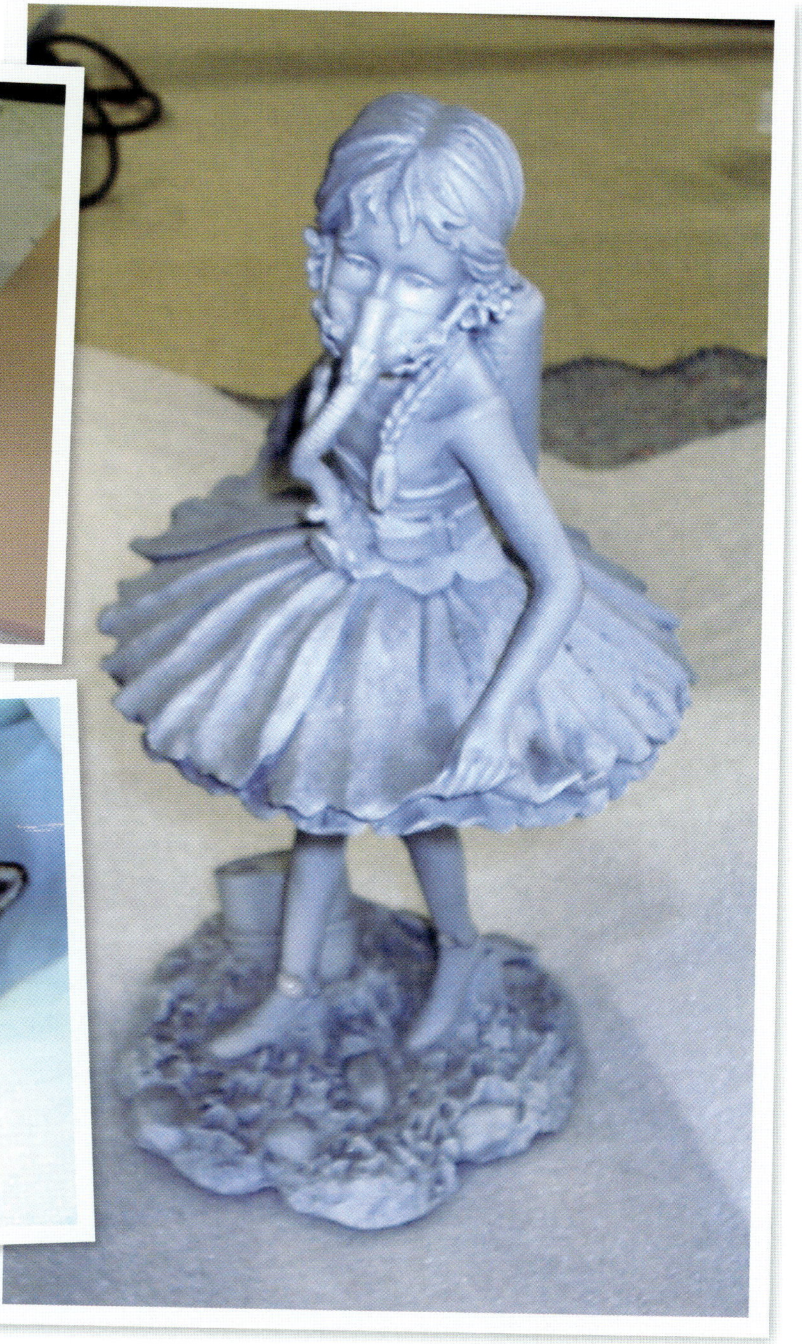

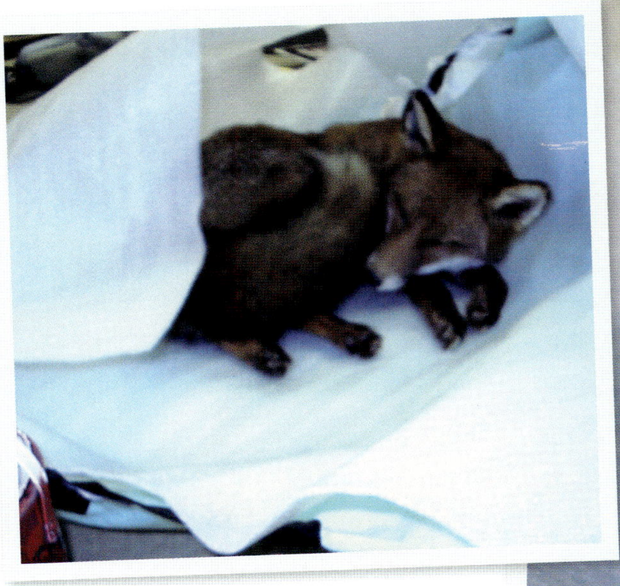

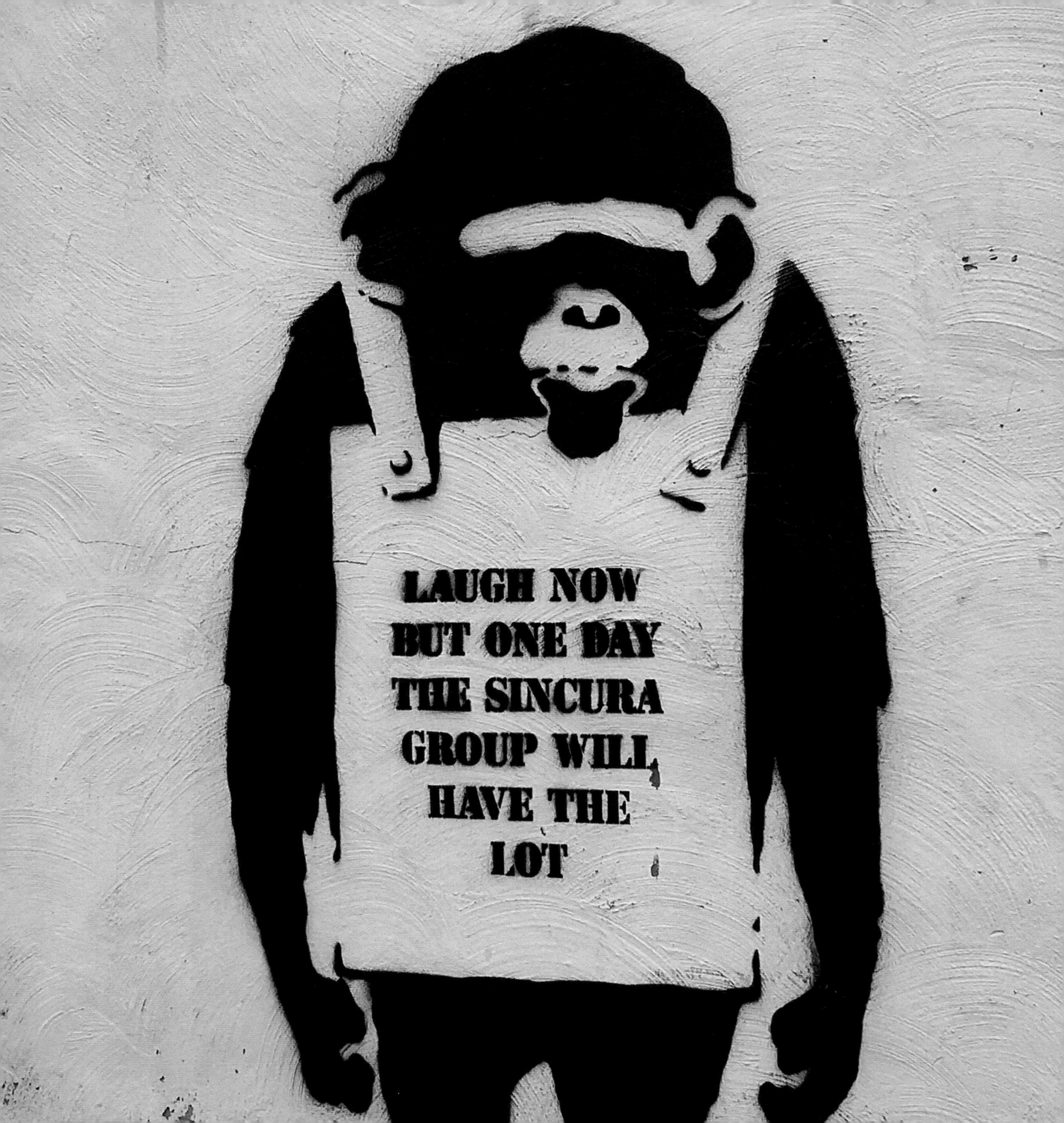
LAUGH NOW
BUT ONE DAY
THE SINCURA
GROUP WILL
HAVE THE
LOT

The Appropriation of Street Art and the Sincura Group

The Sincura Group describes itself as a provider of a "unique lifestyle management and bespoke concierge" service. More explicitly, they remove, curate and sell a range of street art and claim to have been involved with around 70% of all Banksy pieces that have appeared on the streets. The company itself describes its sales as "often controversial", perhaps hoping that the ethical and moral scandals surrounding the removal of artwork may generate a certain amount of interest, excitement and publicity around the organisation.

Now you have had an introduction to the Sincura Group, I will move on to a little protest that we staged over the removal of some Banksy work from Liverpool. A number of pieces had been removed to be conserved and housed in a purpose-built museum in Liverpool but the museum was shelved. The artwork was then sold to the highest bidder which was £4 million to a Qatari collector according to the *Sun* newspaper.

I went about painting Banksy-style street art around Liverpool, Wirral, Manchester and Cheltenham, with the collaboration of friend and fellow artist Silent Bill on a few pieces, in order to highlight the continuing removal of the disappearing artwork. Some art expert in Manchester was claiming that my replicated, edited and transformed Banksy images were too close stylistically to the original to be a copy. Unfortunately, the sale of the artwork still went ahead. It is always a struggle to stop individuals and organisations with deep pockets. Hopefully, the appearance of my art online and in several papers raised the public's and journalists' awareness of how these companies physically appropriate what can often be considered public art for their own private gain. This may at least make people more cautious to trust the official promises when other art is being "conserved" and possibly even stop the further removal of artwork. But I am doubtful.

The Sincura Group have also produced a book in which they claim to expose images of Banksy. It even features a photo of my own artwork critiquing the removal of the Folkstone *Art Buff* which I painted in

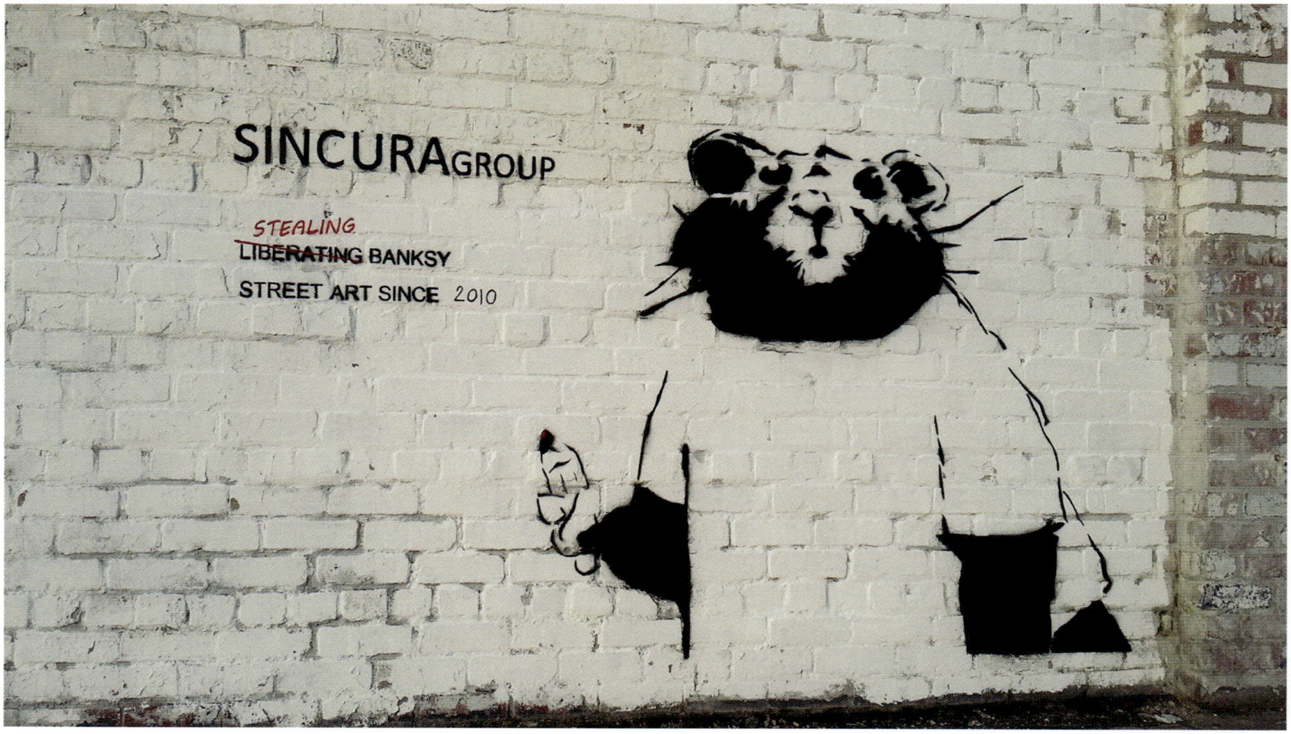

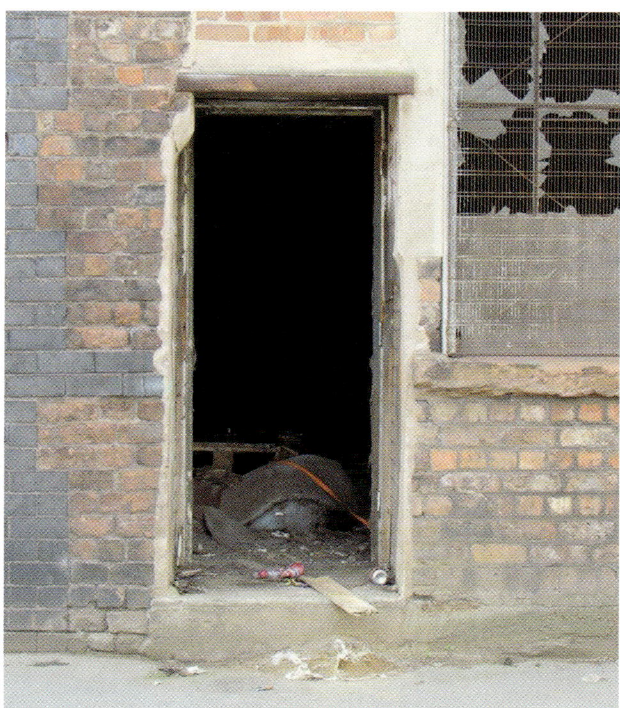

Manchester. The book does try to justify and explain the removal of art, providing the views of their clients and the owners of the contested walls. They claim that their removal of the image from its surrounding context is no different from how the work of Banksy and other famous artists is often placed on T-shirts, mugs and posters. In many of these cases, there is an overriding profit motive and often no formal permission given for the reproductions, whereas the Sincura Group does at least try to get permission from the owners of the wall and claim that they are protecting the artwork from degradation for future generations.

But if they do finally build a Street Art Museum in Liverpool in 2019 then at least something good would have come from this. The artistic response and the public disgust it aroused may have caused the Sincura Group to see street art as a cultural artefact that has more than financial value. Or perhaps a Street Art Museum, catering purely for the fashionable whims of public taste rather than for historical heritage or intellectual opinion in

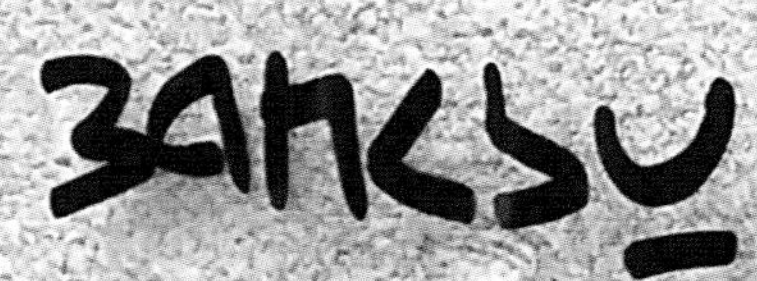
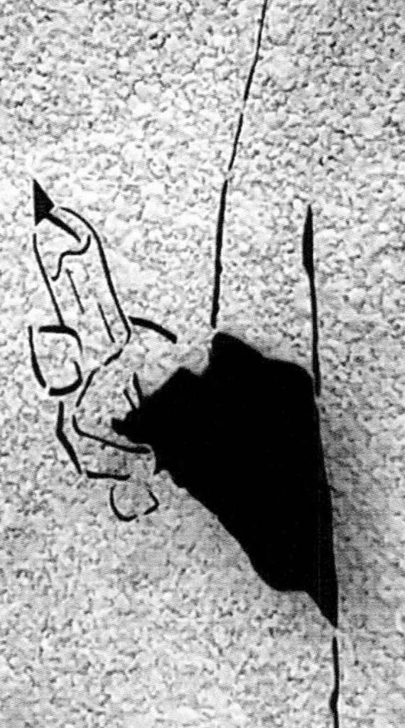
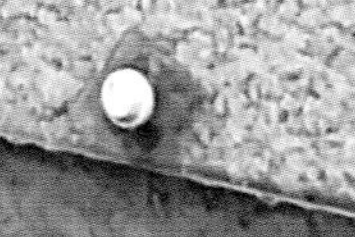

ART THIEVES
STOLE MY ART
WTF!
BANKSY

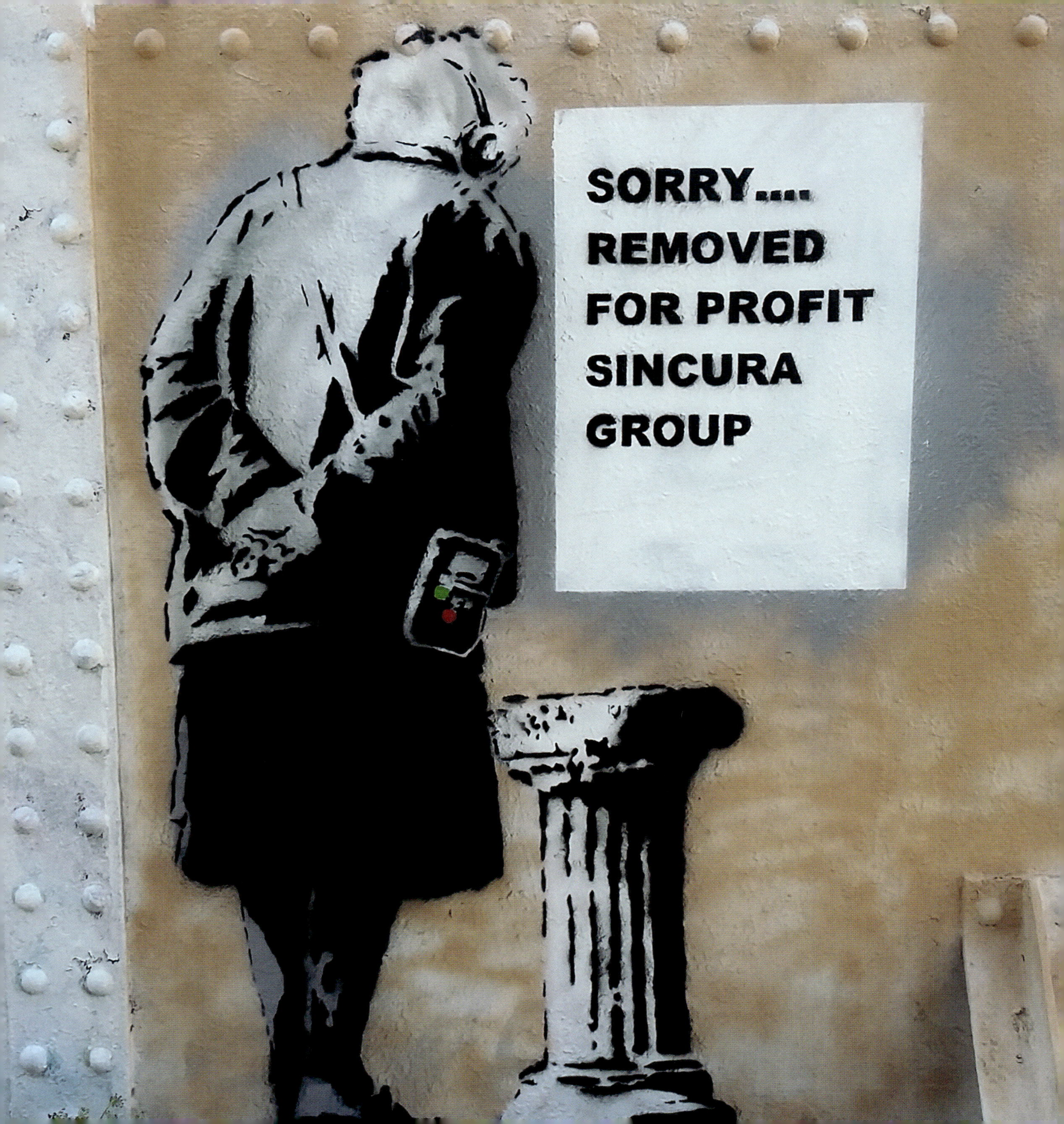
SORRY....
REMOVED
FOR PROFIT
SINCURA
GROUP

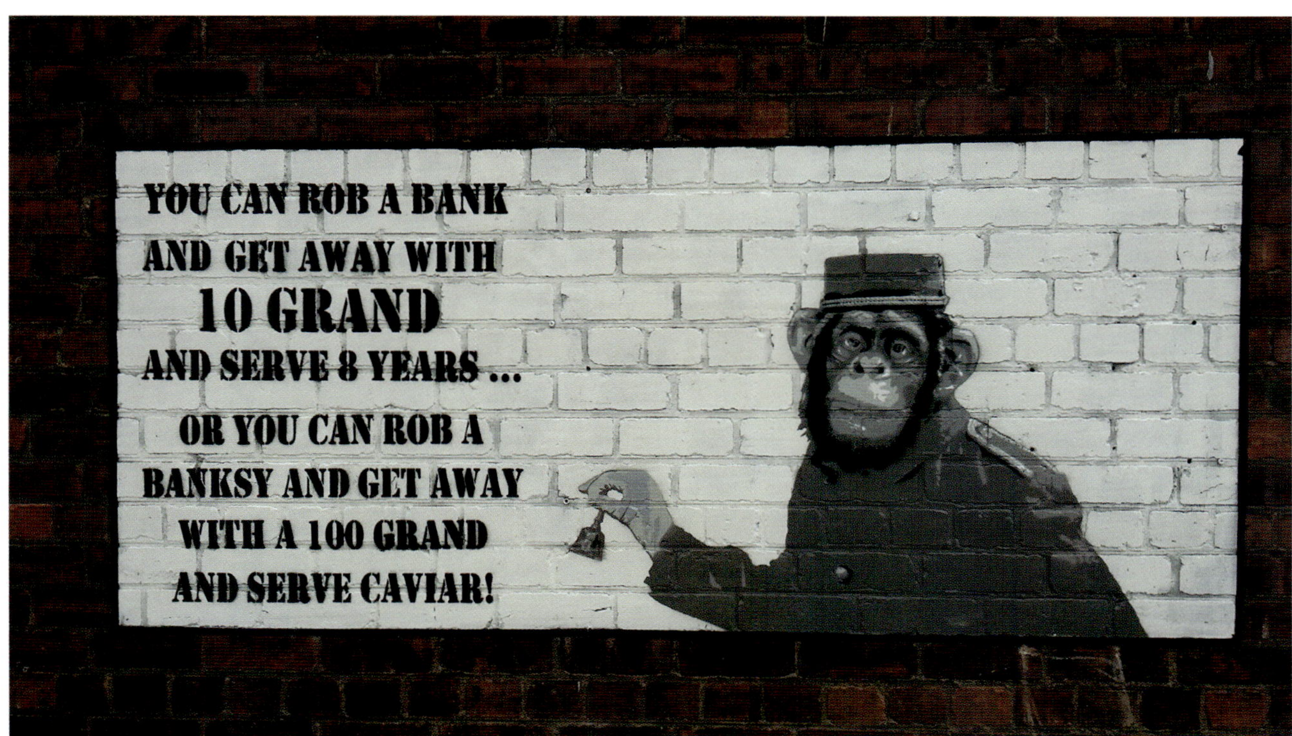

most museums, has a long-term investment potential. Not sure if I will feature in this Museum – especially after the annoyance I caused them! – but I find that completely understandable and did enjoy reading the book.

The protest and artwork was painted during 23-25 August 2017, which was a low point in my personal and private life. All of it was painted in plain daylight and, letting my emotions get the best of me, I made no attempt to hide. The *Rob a Bank* piece in the Baltic Triangle of Liverpool (just around the corner from where the Sincura Group Street Art Museum was going to be built) really started to draw a crowd and, even though I was telling people I was not Banksy, the Bristolian accent did not help.

At the time there were reporters and even a news crew going around the Baltic Triangle doing a negative exposé about North Point Global ltd and the Sincura Group. Silent Bill (who is generally not very silent) took them on a tour of the artwork that had been painted in

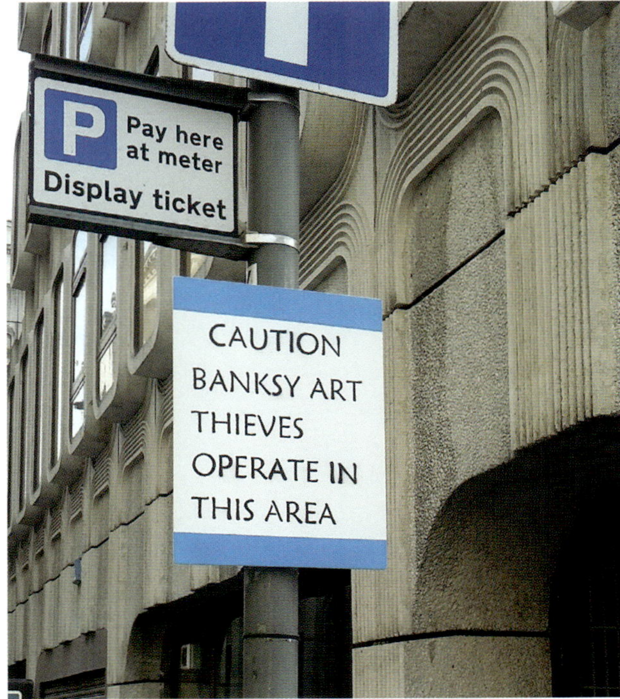

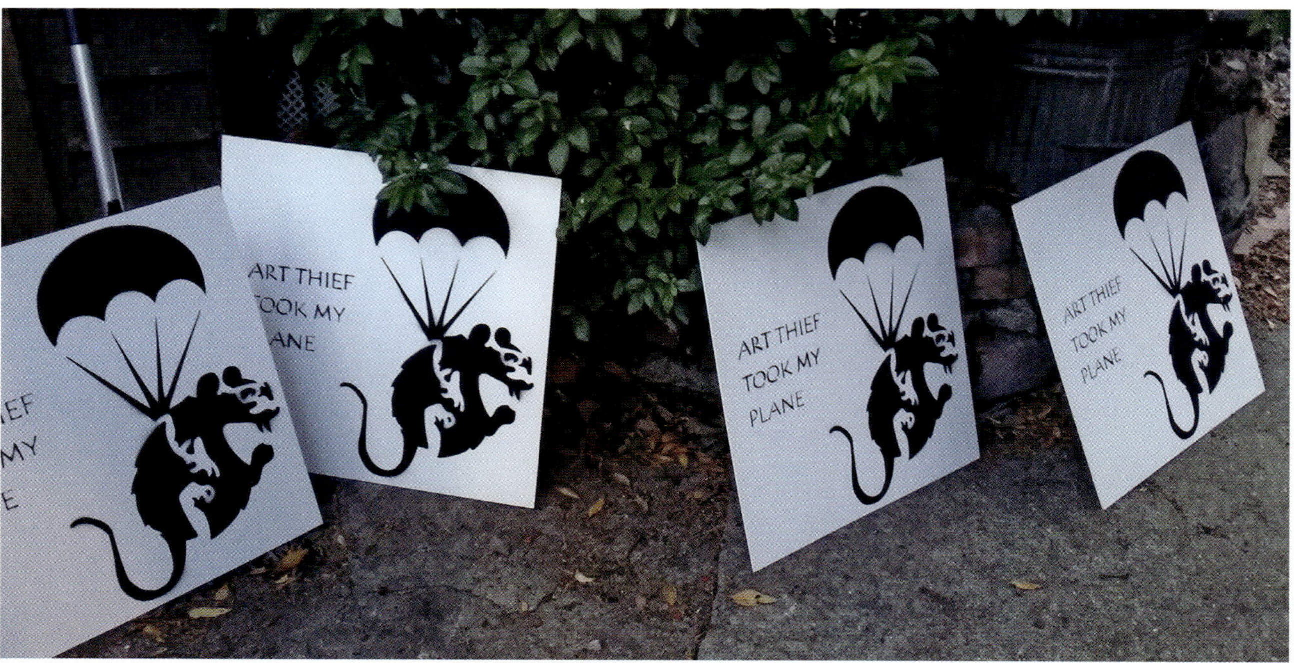

protest and it was featured in a short news story which was featured on west midlands TV I believe.

The Love Plane

A public notice was installed in the place of the removed artwork which said Banksy's *Love Plane* will be put on display at a Street Art Museum by developers North Point Global. The website, which was included on the notice, read:

The Banksy Love Plane artwork has removed. With this building due to be refurbished, the piece has been salvaged and is now being restored under management of the Sincura Group.

The artwork will be returned to Liverpool looking better than ever to hang alongside other Banksy pieces at the Gallery at Berry House Baltic Triangle, due to launch in Liverpool shortly.

Courtesy of North Point Global Group, this will be the first ever art museum anywhere in the world and will showcase to the public an exclusive collection of original Banksy artworks painted as part of Liverpool's art programme. With so many Banksy artworks disappearing from public view this will ensure your city preserves its street art heritage and showcases future talent.

The first piece of art that I painted in protest against the removal of street art in Liverpool was done on the same wall of Banksy's *Love Plane* in Rumford Street in Liverpool. It was painted on the Perspex that was protecting what was left of the piece as only the plane had been removed. From start to finish the piece took under three minutes to paint, including walking over to the wall, attaching the stencils, spraying, removal of stencil and photographing. The process can be done quicker but I can be a bit OCD about overspray and neatness even when possibly breaking the law. But technically I had not damaged the wall or the building itself. I certainly caused less damage to the building or artwork than the removal had done. In addition to this I also put up a number of signs which I attached to lamp posts with cable ties. This guerrilla campaign highlighted the removal of the art which didn't take the local press long to pick up on.

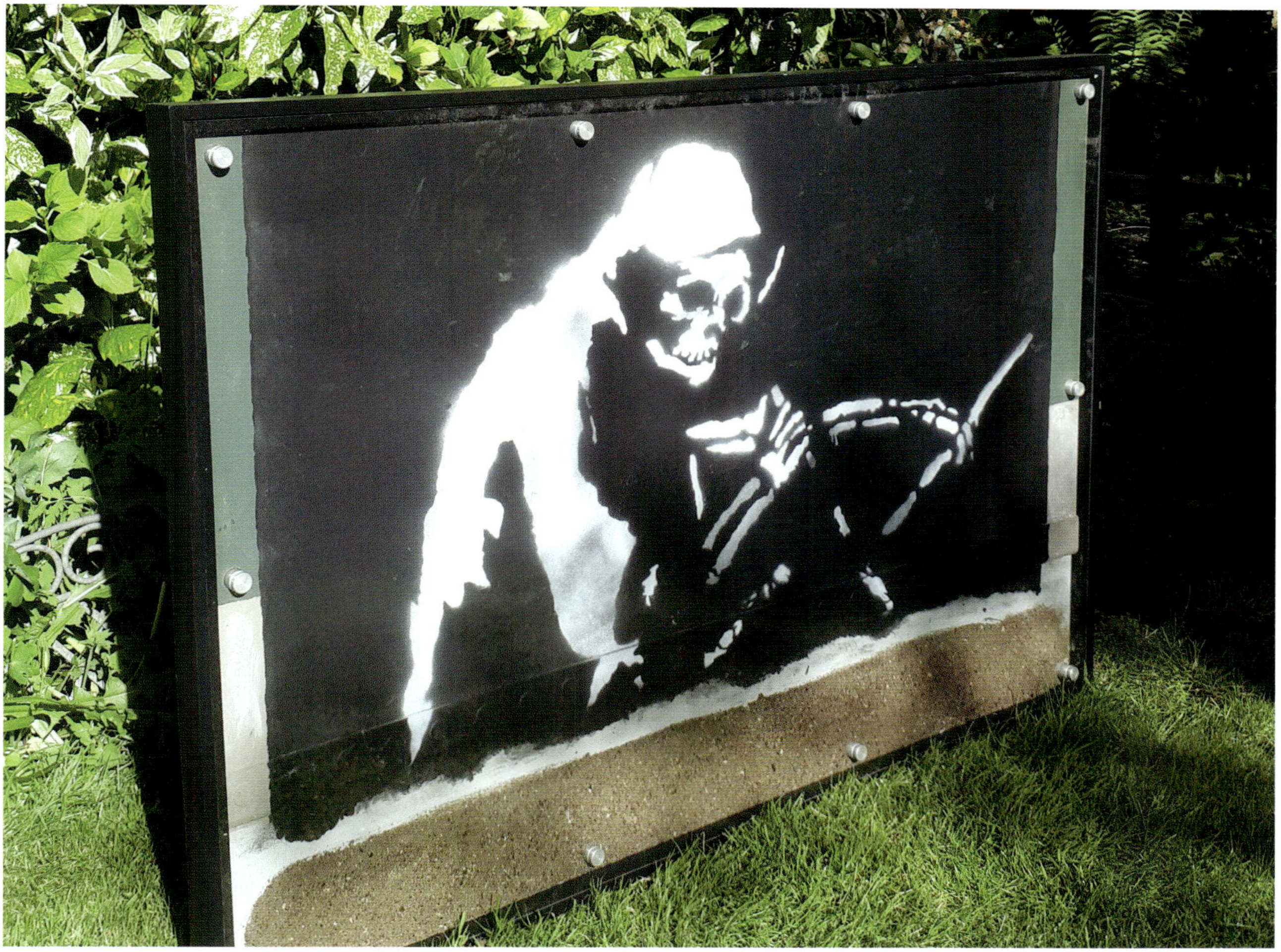

Replica of
Thekla Reaper
produced as a
prop for the
launch of this
book

Replica of
Love Plane
removed by the
Sincura Group
in Liverpool
produced as a
prop for book
launch

I Never liked
this Banksy.
A suspected
Banksy that
was done by
my friend
Silent Bill. So
a replica of
a Silent Bill
produced for
the book launch

Some or most
of the artwork
on show at the
book launch
focussed on
sections in
the book and
formed a mini
exhibition. The
artwork labels
carried small
stories and
information
about the art
or replicas
where required
and the story
behind the
removal

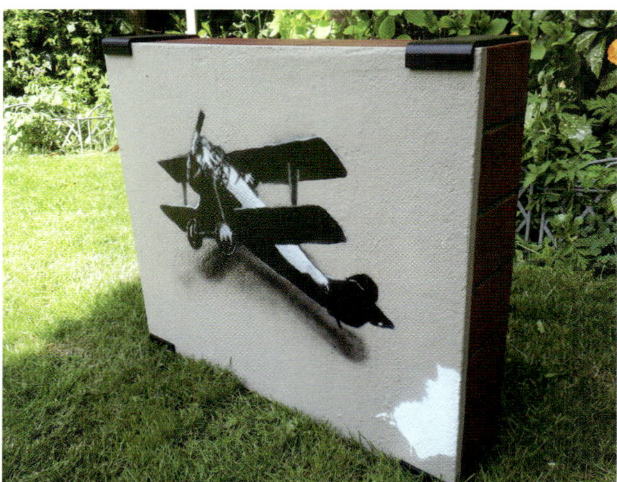

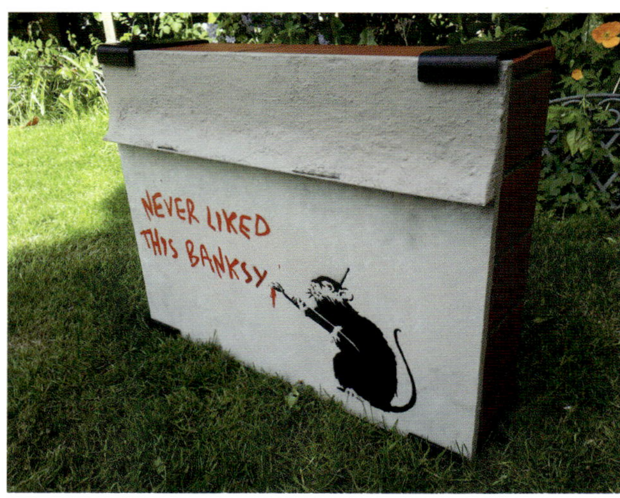

NEVER LIKED
THIS BANKSY

Painted at
various
locations
around
Liverpool
and Wirral
in protest
against the
removal of
Banksy Art
which was
later sold

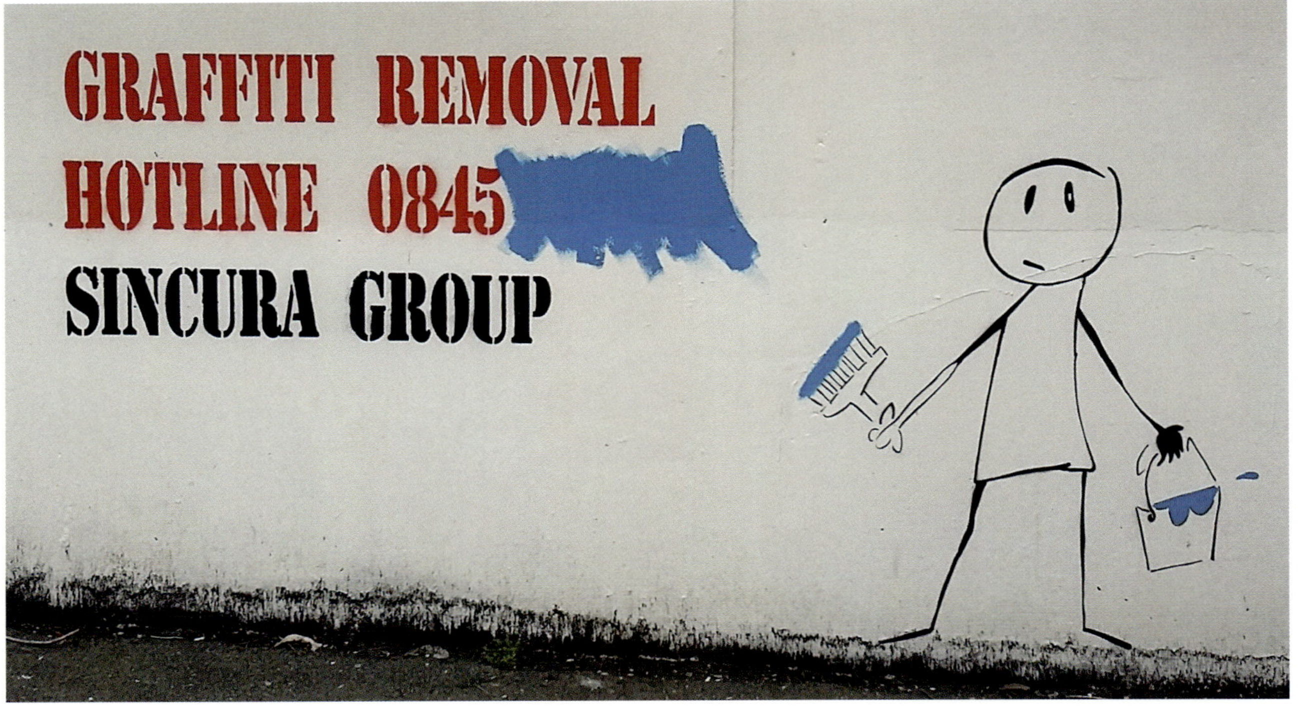
GRAFFITI REMOVAL
HOTLINE 0845
SINCURA GROUP

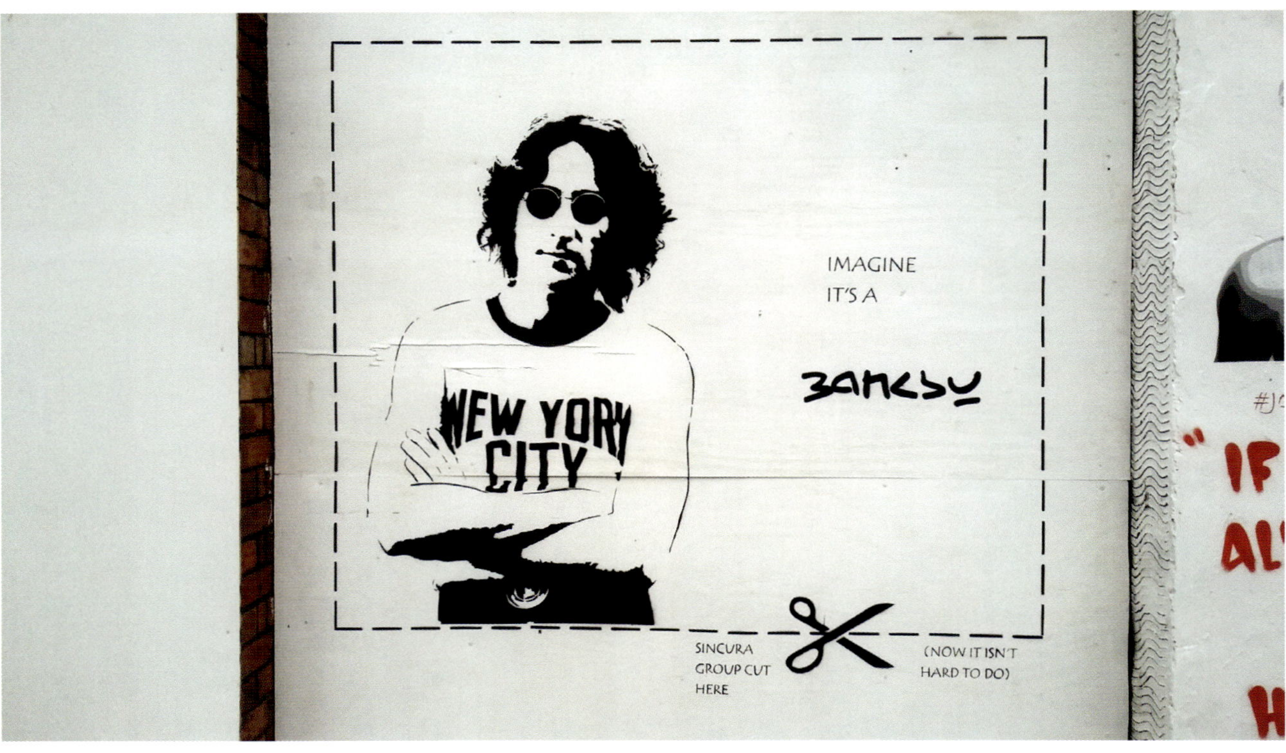
IMAGINE
IT'S A

Banksy

NEW YORK
CITY

SINCURA
GROUP CUT
HERE

(NOW IT ISN'T
HARD TO DO)

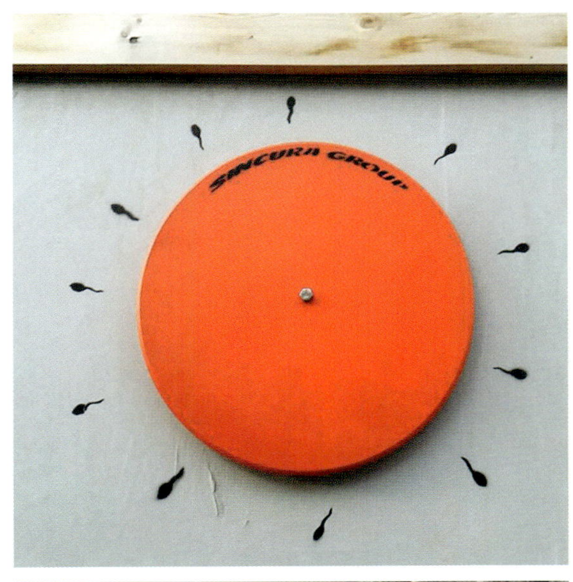

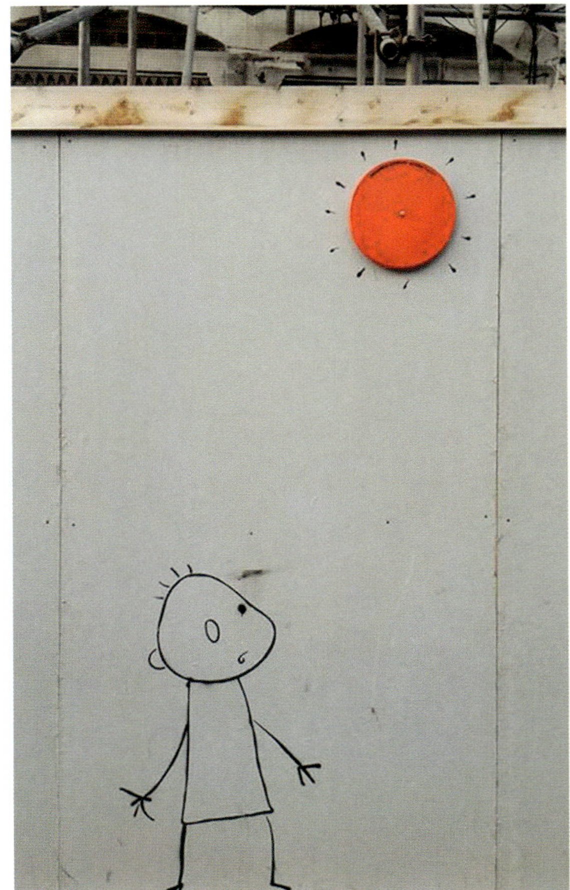

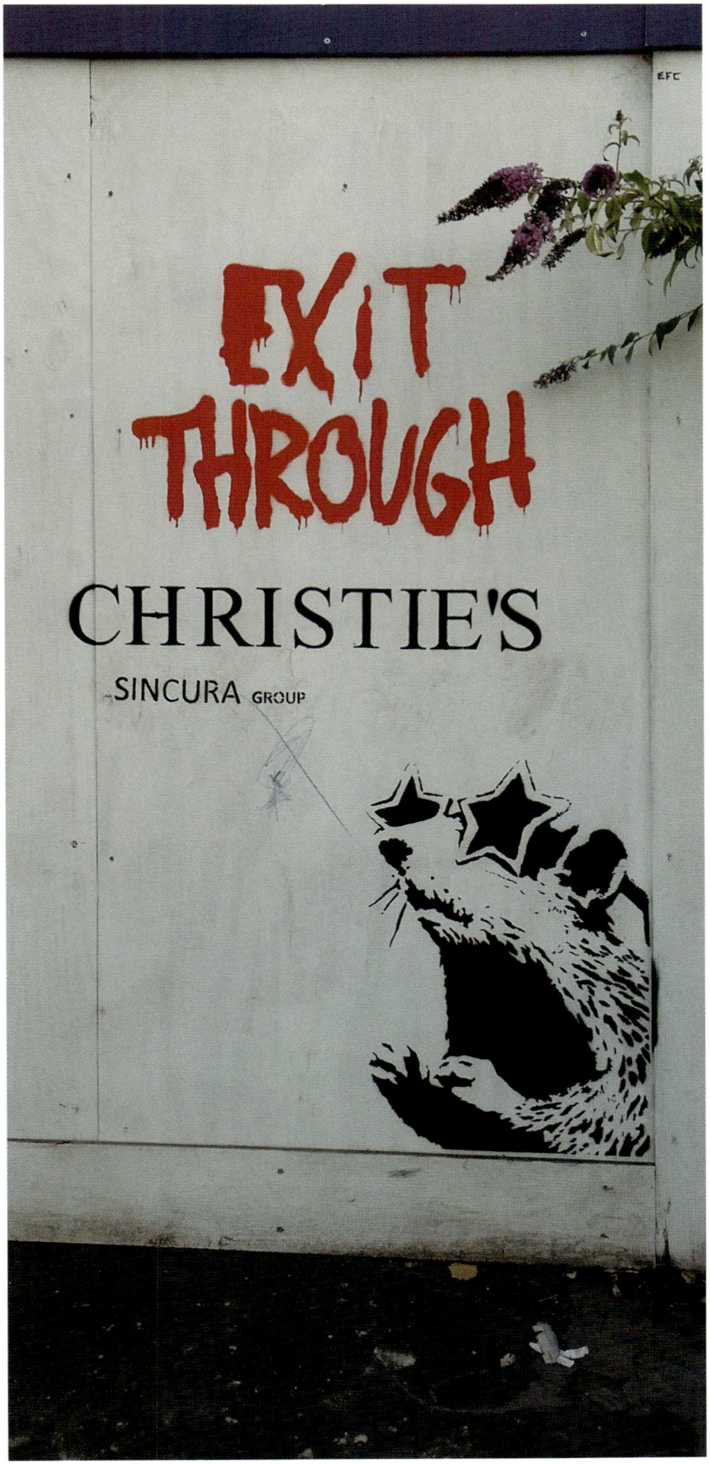

EXIT THROUGH

CHRISTIE'S

SINCURA GROUP

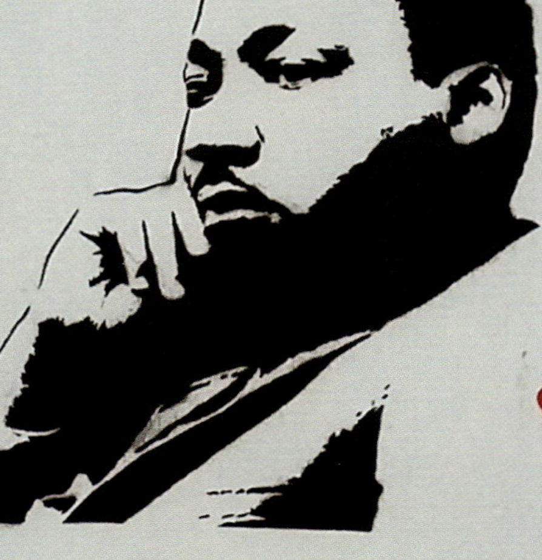

from dreams to...

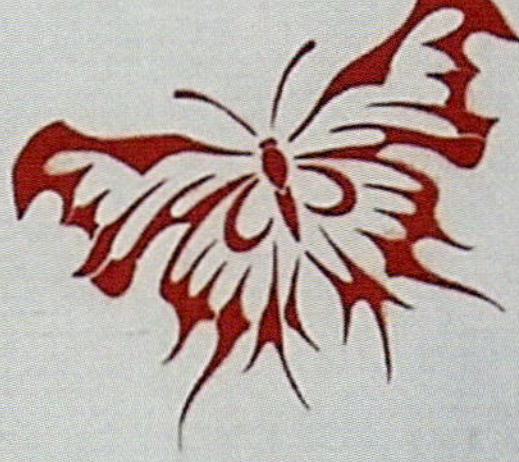

NIGHTMARES

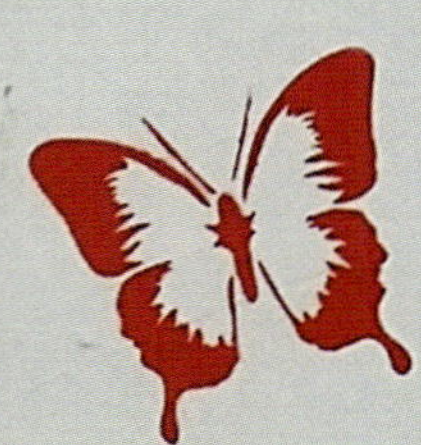

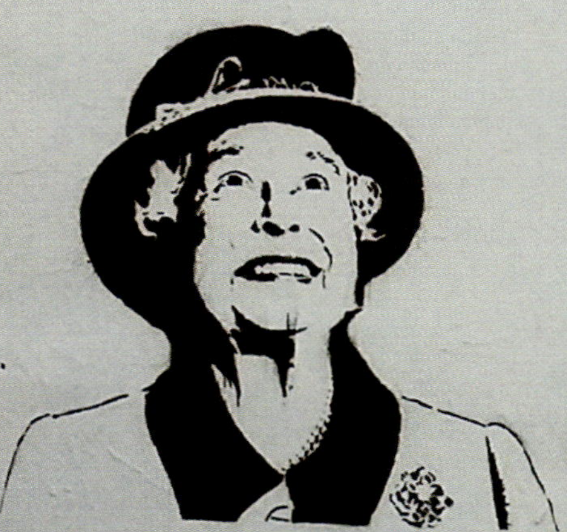

STRAIGHT
OUTTA
EUROPE

JOHN D'OH

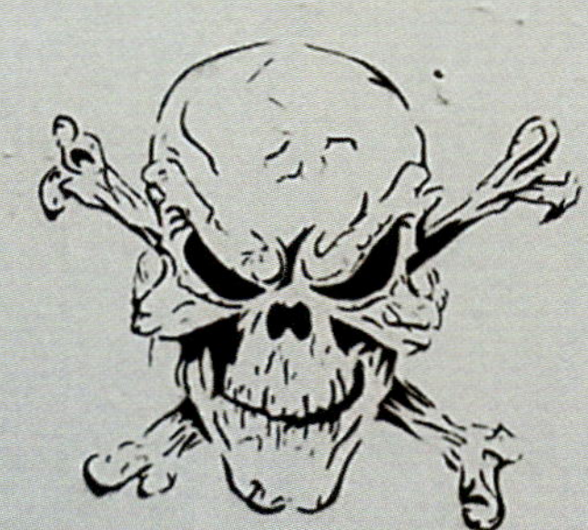

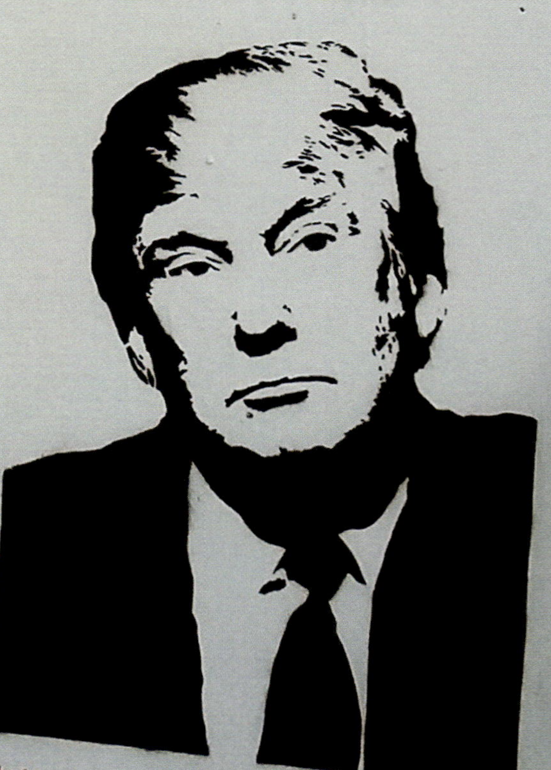

WWW.JOHN-DOH.CO.UK

My Personal Politics

If a work of art has one meaning it is propaganda, if it has no meaning it is just decoration.

Politics in street art is something a lot of artists try to avoid now for a number of different reasons, such as a lack of knowledge and interest or a concern that political bias may lead to a loss of popularity and art sales. I have experienced this reluctance and disinterest personally when, for instance, I tried to organise an art event for the general election in 2017 and had artists respond negatively to the idea. It's not for everyone.

I'm not sure if art changes people's minds on how they vote, but hopefully it might inspire the public to look into the policies or manifesto pledges of each party leader before putting a cross in a box – as that one mark can affect everything around you that you depend upon, including health care, infrastructure and education.

The size of the audience you can reach with just a bit of street art or graffiti is amazing. For example, I painted some pro-Labour street art on a subway in Exeter which was being renovated by fellow artists that I had been invited to attend, Exeter City Council

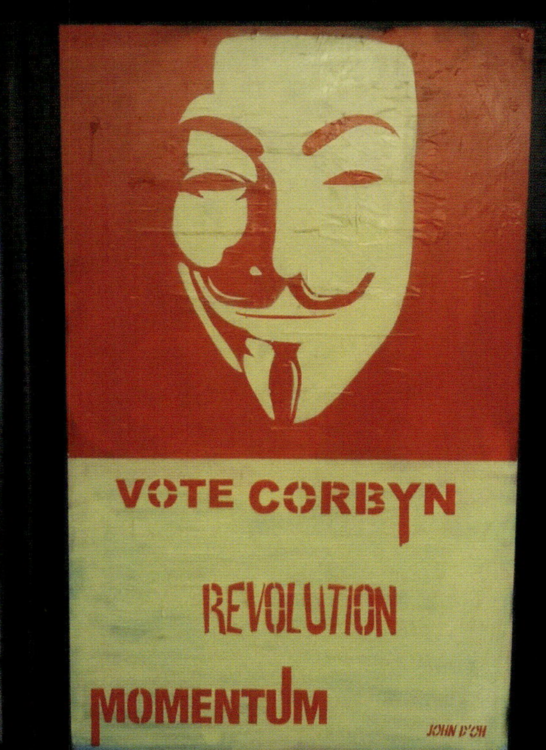

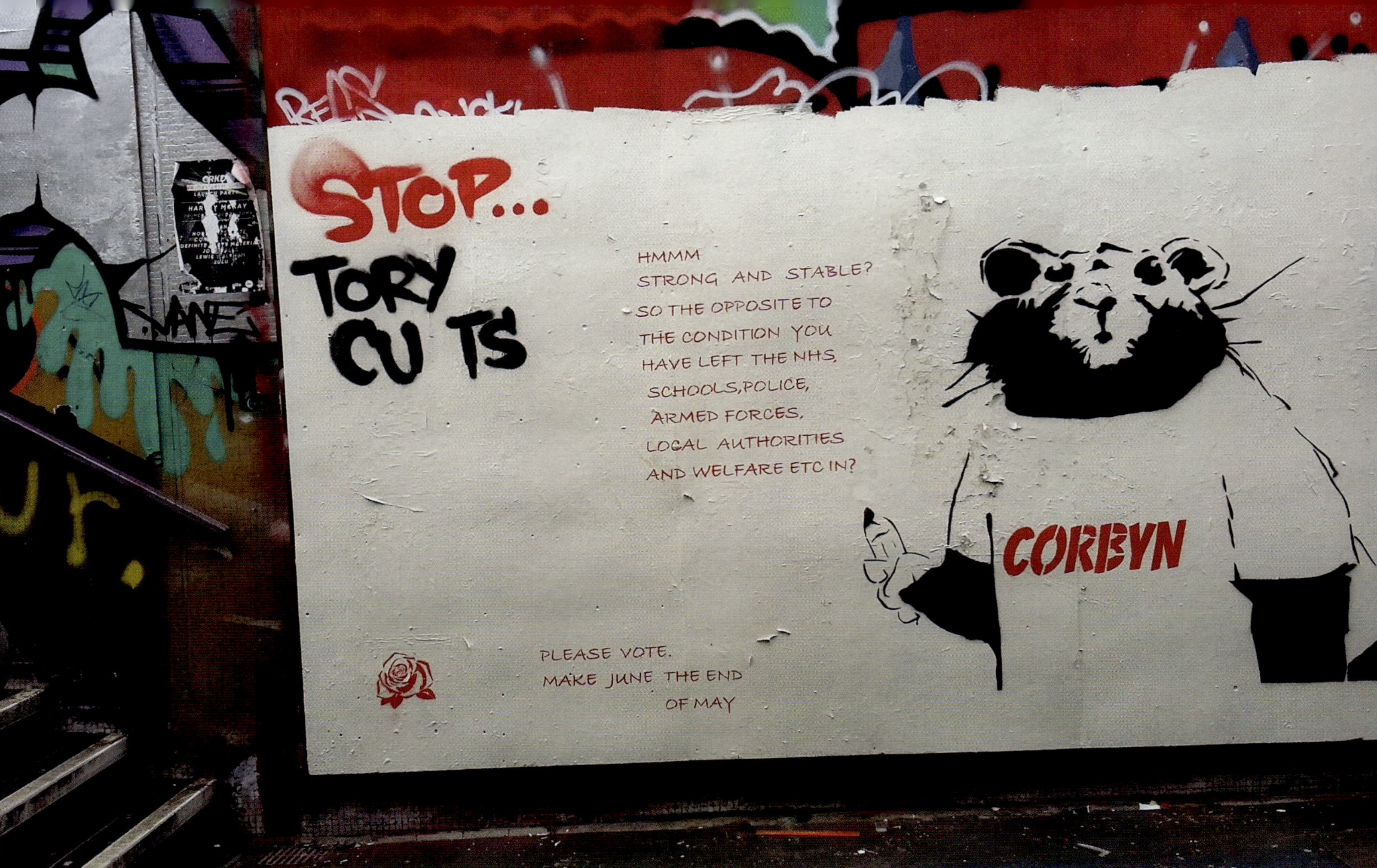

offence to it and it was jet washed within 24 hours. Admittedly, I was not surprised the wall was buffed, as there was a brief on what subjects I was allowed to paint that I deliberately ignored. But it is astonishing how quickly local politicians can act when it suits their personal needs or when they simply require your votes to keep them in a job. Ironically, the controversies around removing political street art actually end up causing more people to see the very message or image the council were originally trying to hide. The news of its removal and photos of the art appeared in the *Bristol Post* and *Devon Live*.

Sometimes, however, you just have to be flexible and work with the brief. When painting in Gloucester, I was told I could paint something on the wall but it had to be specifically Gloucester-related. This was at the time of the David Cameron Piggate scandal, where the former Prime Minister was claimed to have put a "private part of his anatomy" into a dead pig's mouth as part of an initiation ceremony for a "dining club" at Oxford University. So I combined the local requirements with national politics, painting David Cameron holding a Gloucestershire Old Spots pig with the wording "Got to love a Gloucester Old Spot" and "you can put lipstick on a pig". The piece was painted on the weekend and lasted until the Monday morning when, apparently, the leader of the Gloucester City Council drove by at 9am and it was buffed by 10am.

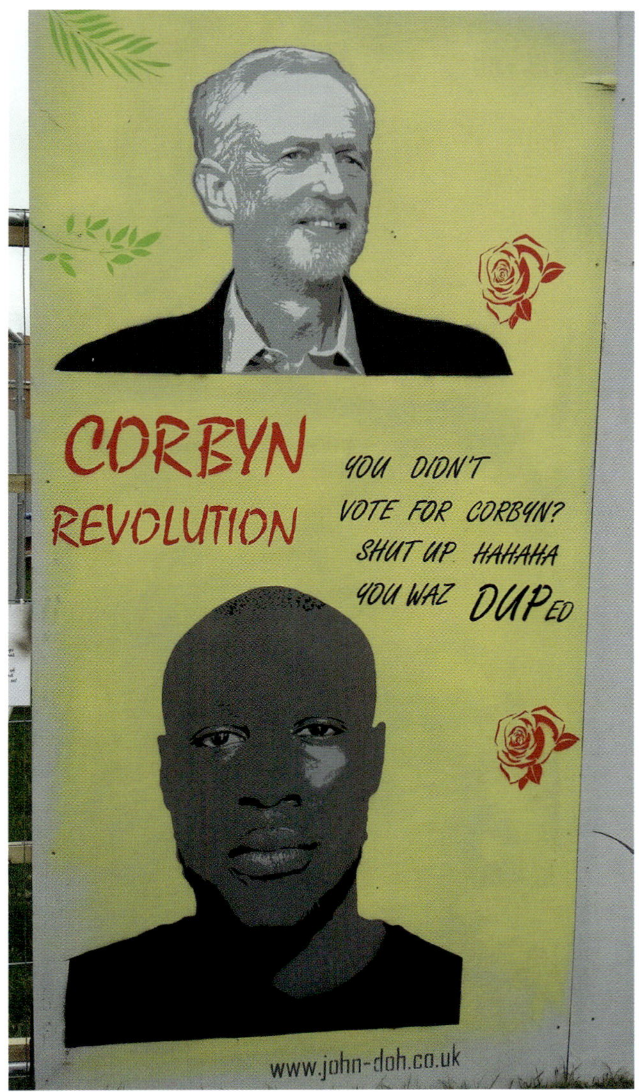

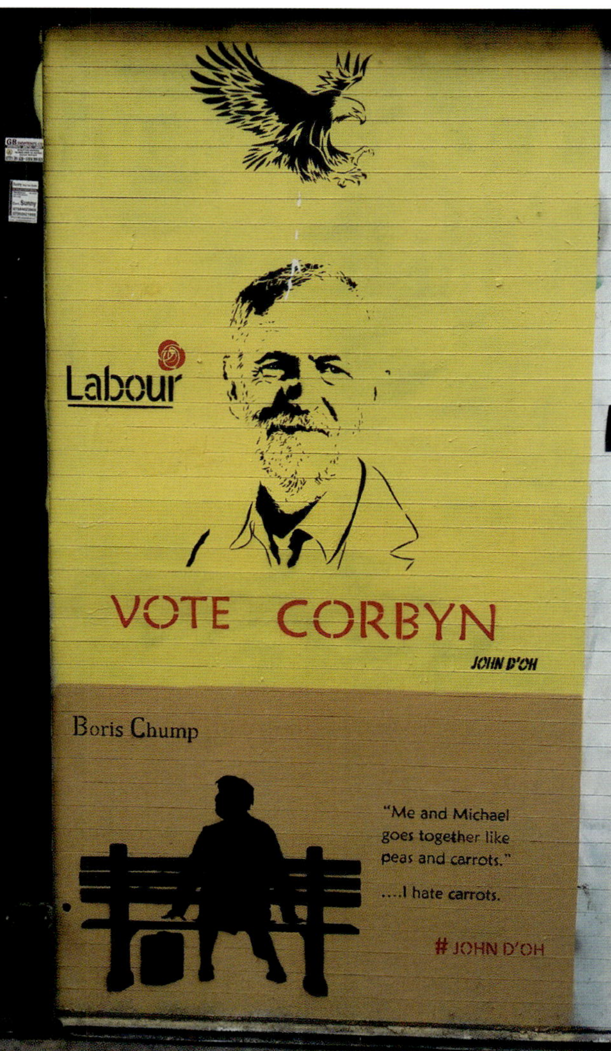

I have painted Jeremy Corbyn quite a few times even adding Stormzy, a rapper who has also shown support for the Labour leader

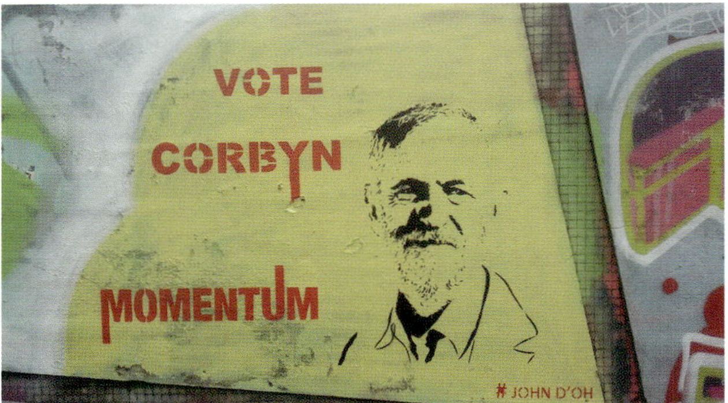

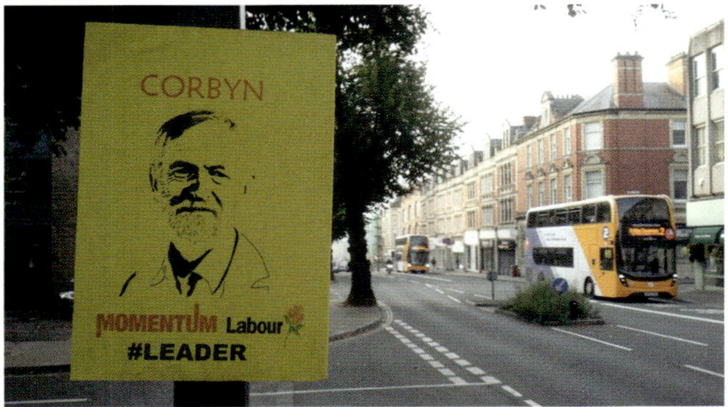

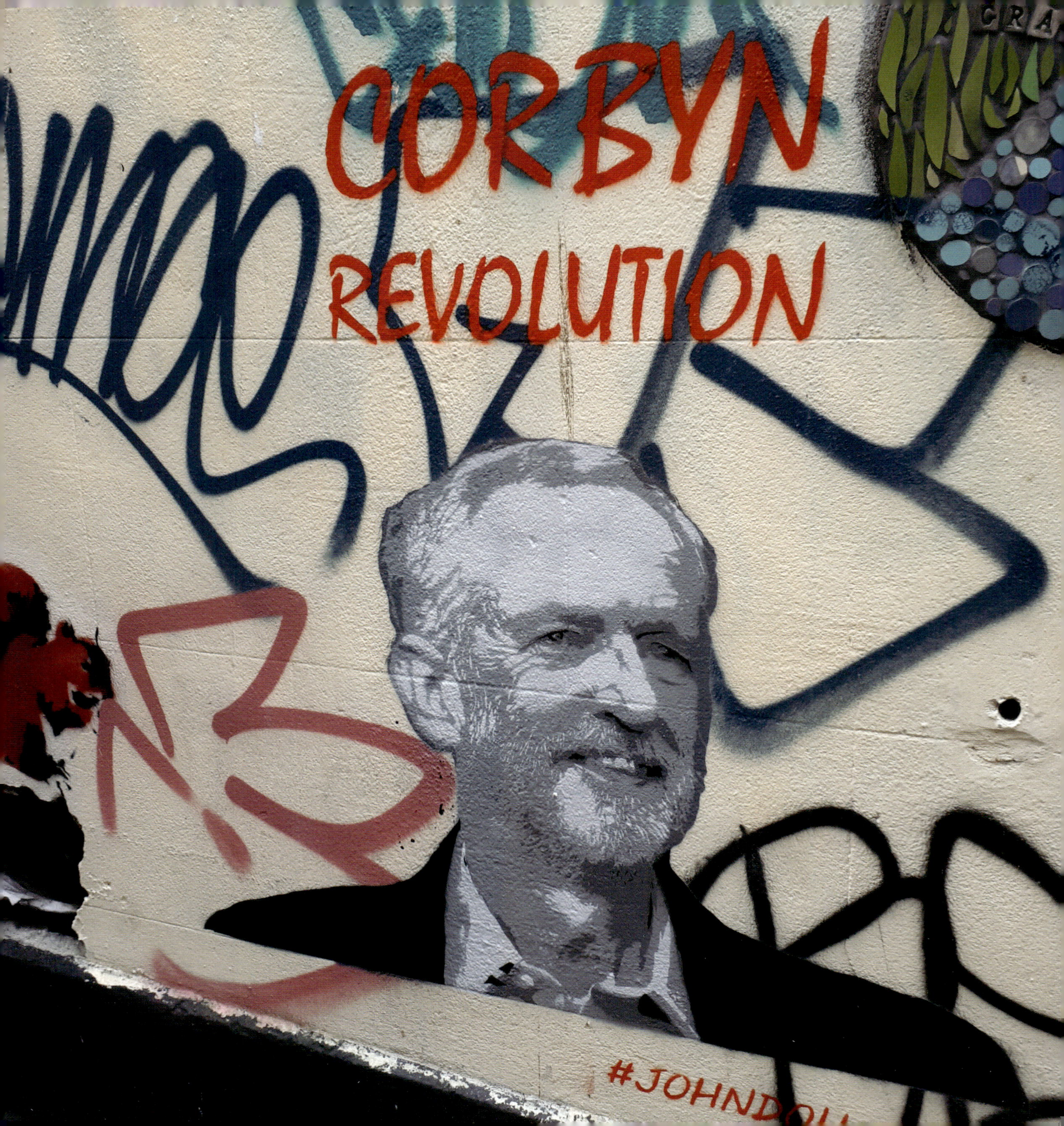

CORBYN
REVOLUTION
#JOHNDOH

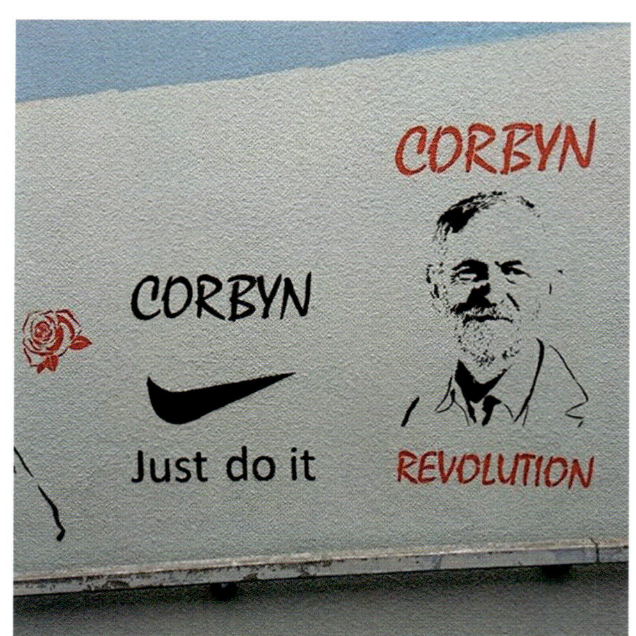
CORBYN
CORBYN
Just do it
REVOLUTION

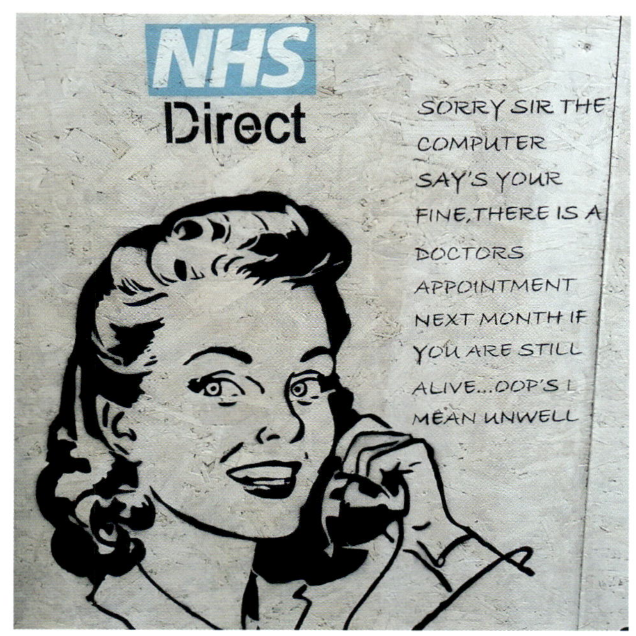
NHS
Direct
SORRY SIR THE
COMPUTER
SAY'S YOUR
FINE, THERE IS A
DOCTORS
APPOINTMENT
NEXT MONTH IF
YOU ARE STILL
ALIVE...OOP'S I
MEAN UNWELL

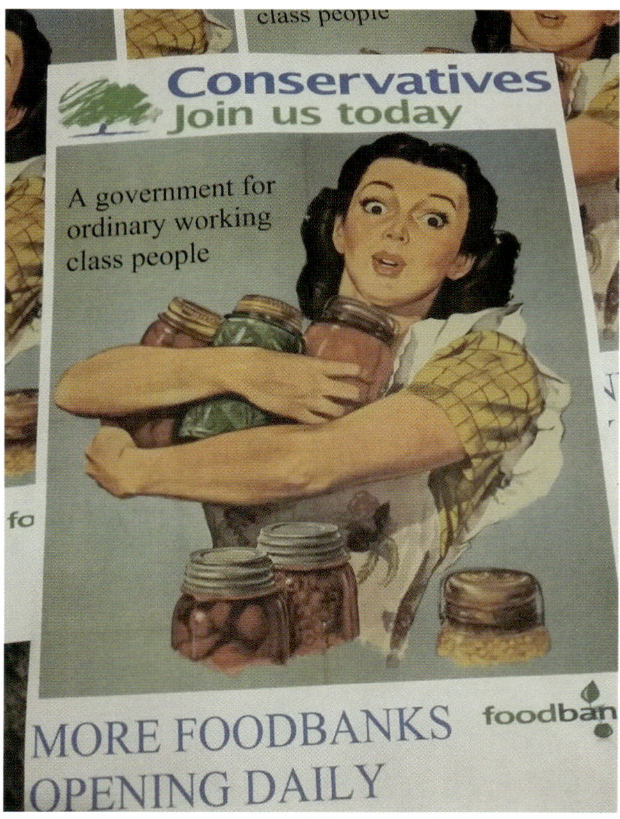
Conservatives
Join us today
A government for
ordinary working
class people
MORE FOODBANKS
OPENING DAILY
foodban
class people

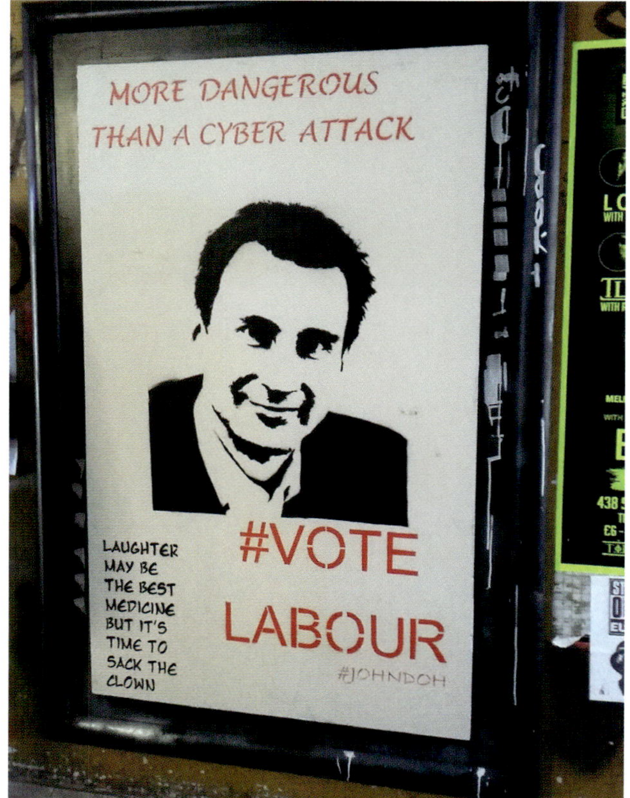
MORE DANGEROUS
THAN A CYBER ATTACK
#VOTE
LABOUR
#JOHNDOH
LAUGHTER
MAY BE
THE BEST
MEDICINE
BUT IT'S
TIME TO
SACK THE
CLOWN

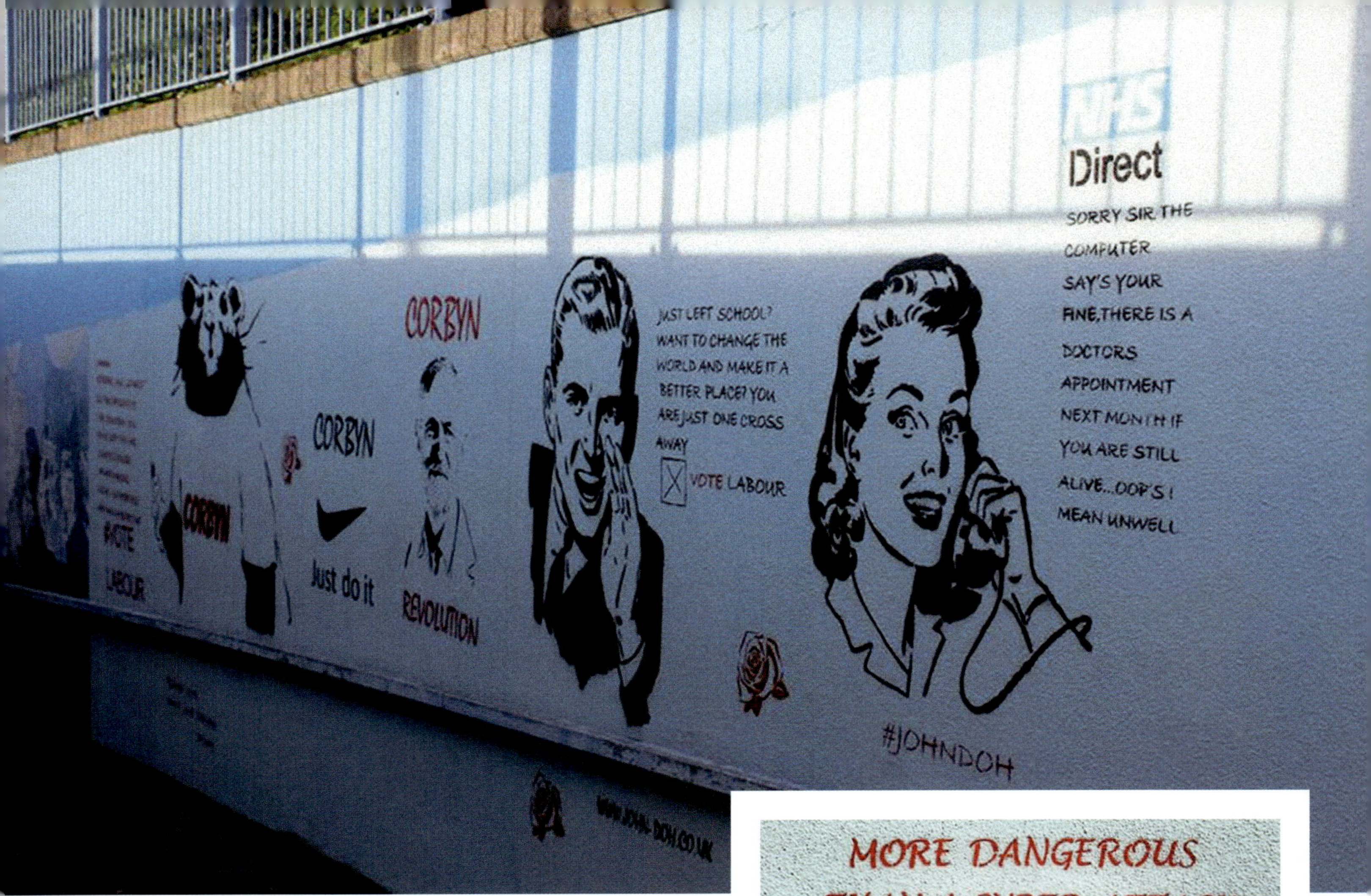

Painted in Taunton. The council took offence and the artwork seen here was jet washed away shortly after

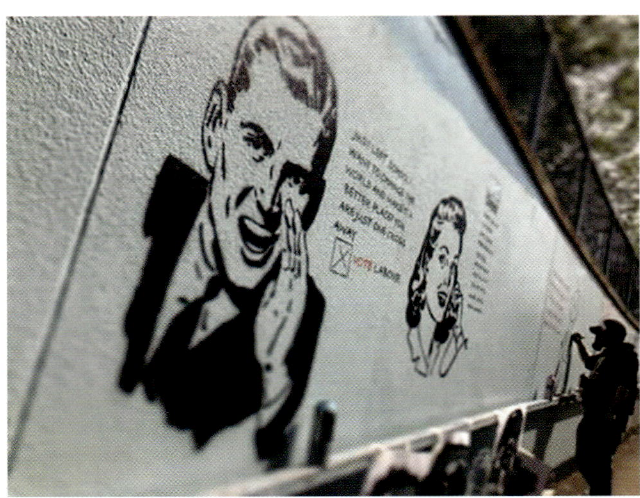

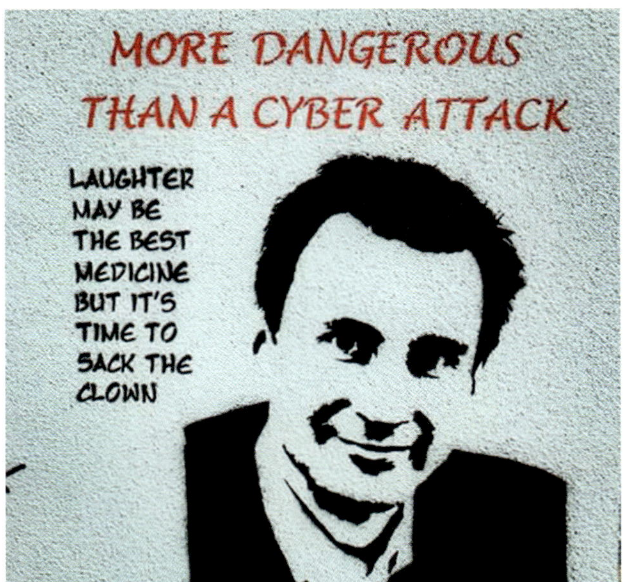

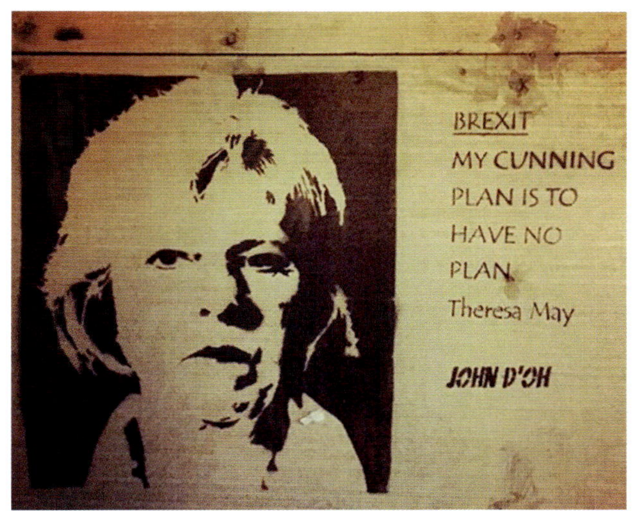
BREXIT
MY CUNNING
PLAN IS TO
HAVE NO
PLAN.
Theresa May
JOHN D'OH

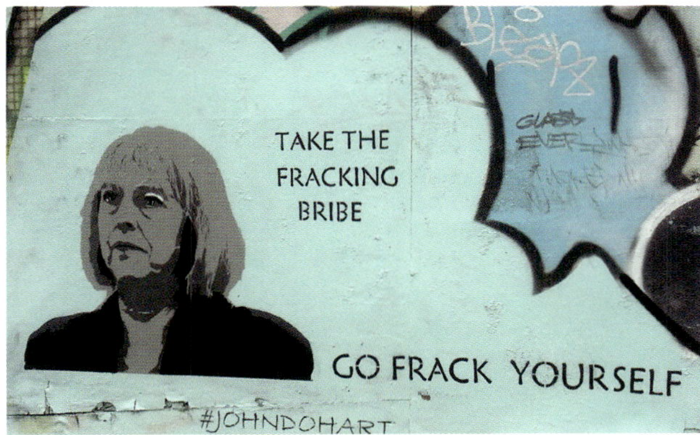
TAKE THE
FRACKING
BRIBE
GO FRACK YOURSELF
#JOHNDOHART

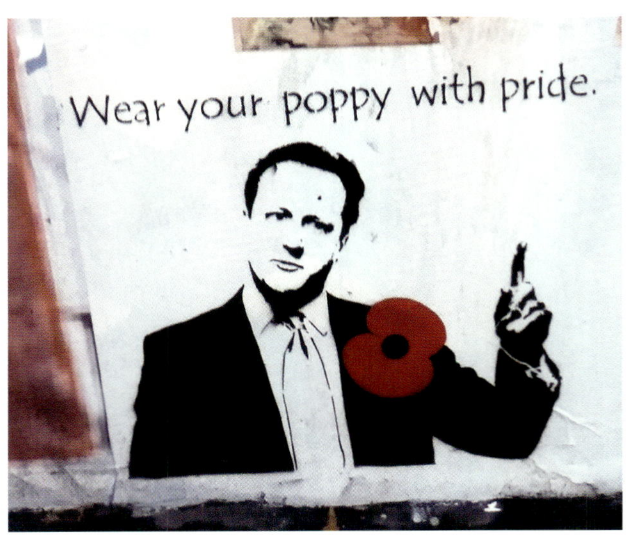
Wear your poppy with pride.

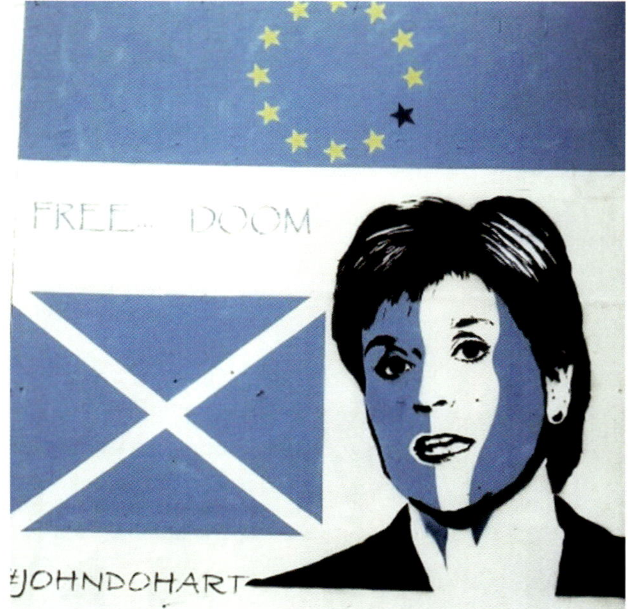
FREE... DOOM
#JOHNDOHART

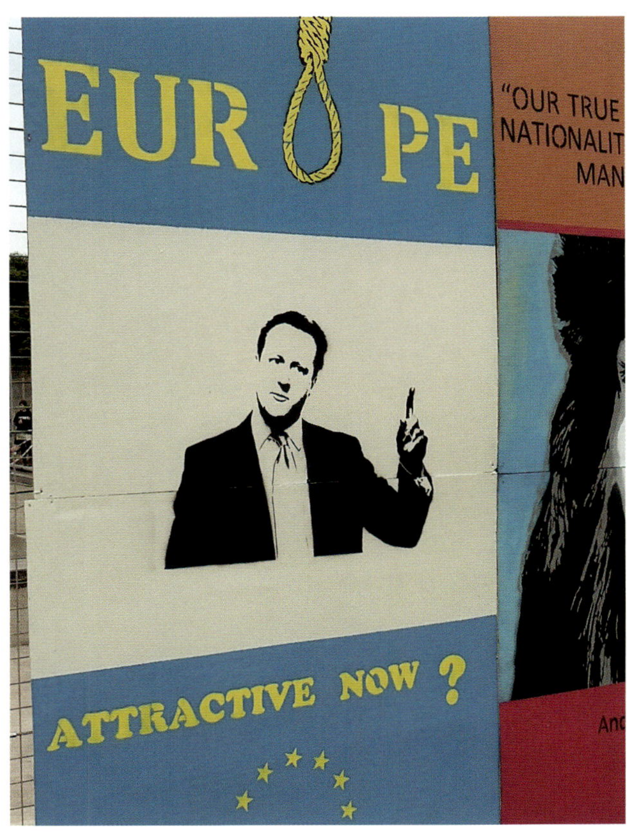
EUR PE
"OUR TRUE
NATIONALIT
MAN
ATTRACTIVE NOW ?
An

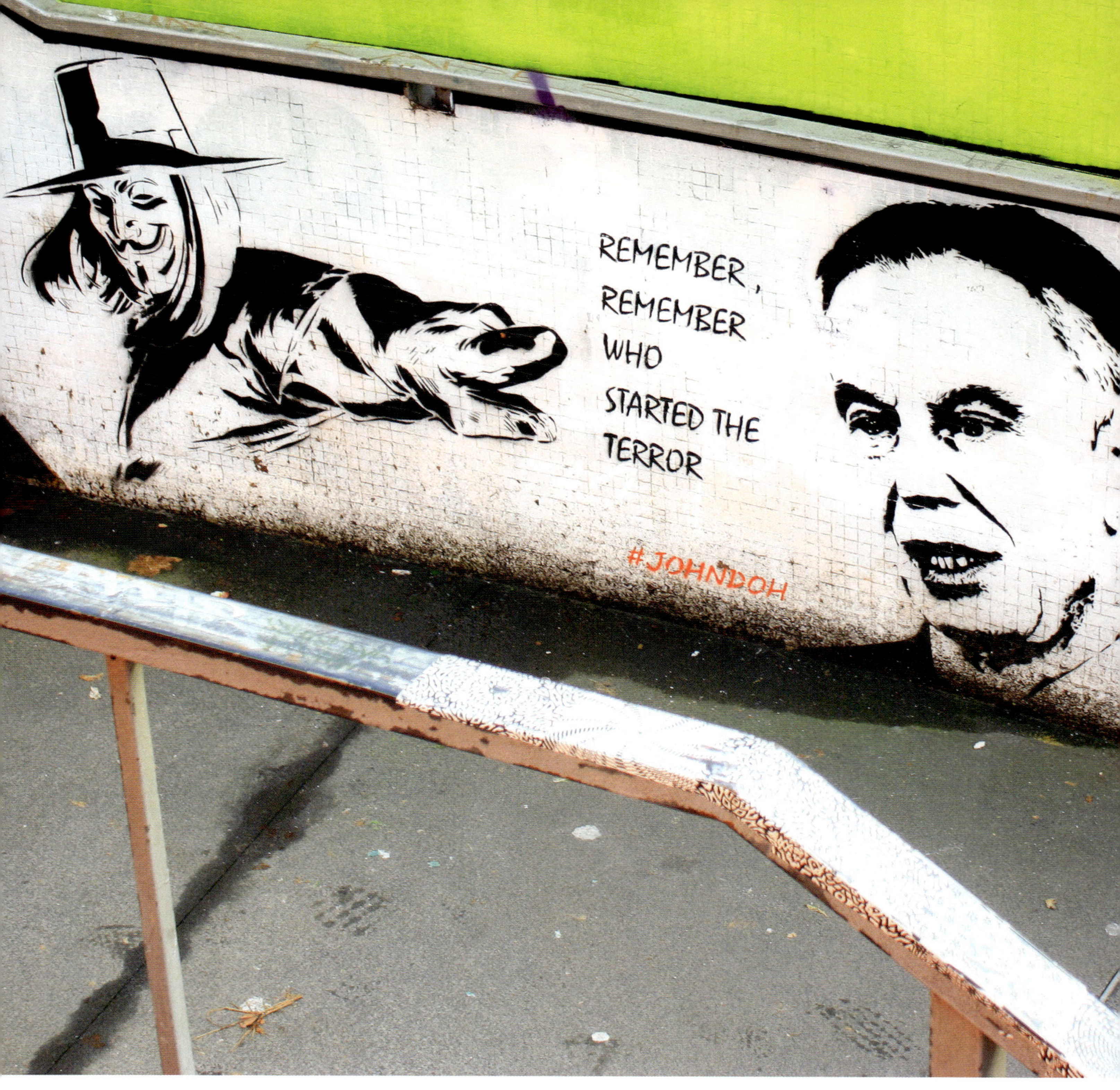

REMEMBER,
REMEMBER
WHO
STARTED THE
TERROR
#JOHNDOH

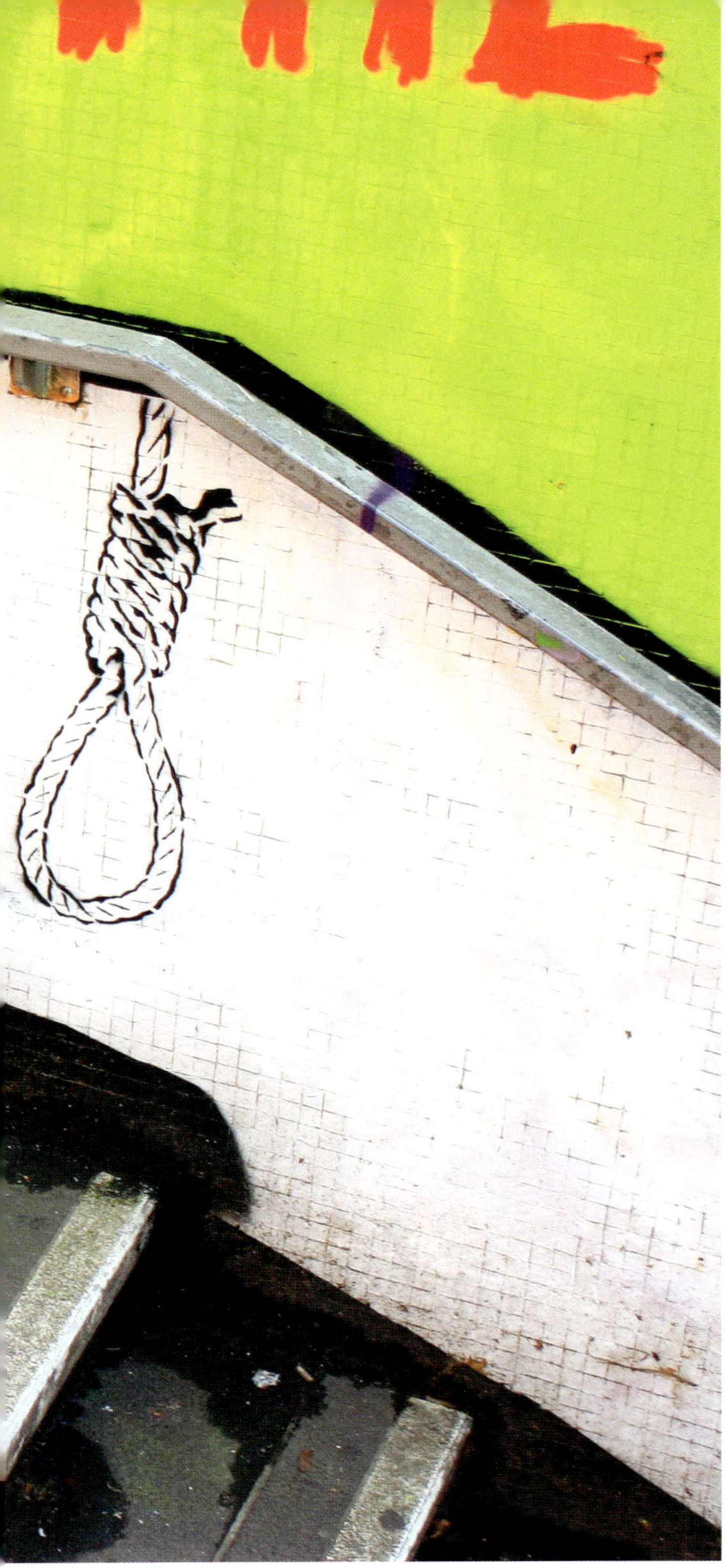

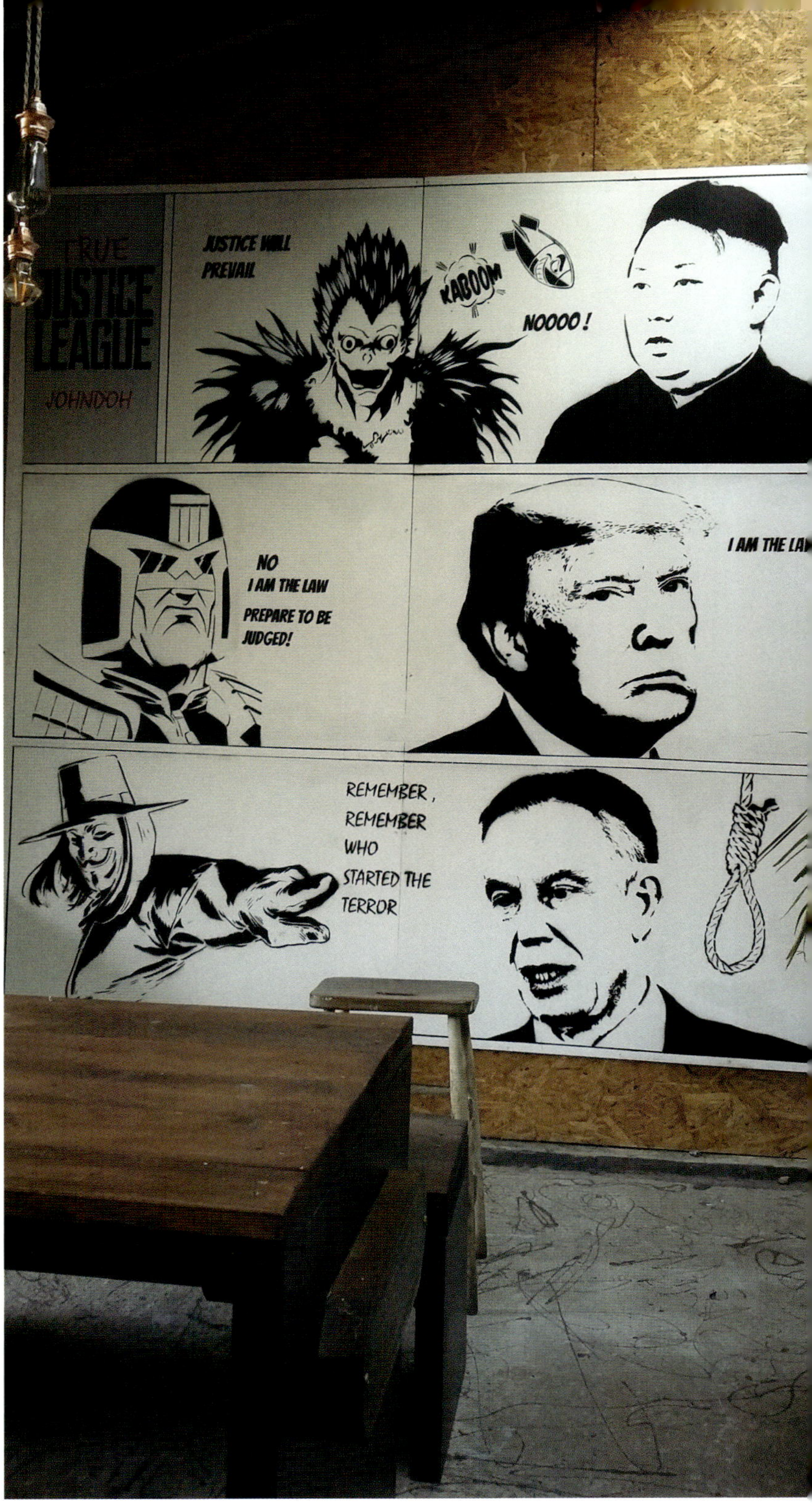

TRUE
JUSTICE
LEAGUE
JOHNDOH
JUSTICE WILL PREVAIL
KABOOM
NOOOO !
NO
I AM THE LAW
PREPARE TO BE
JUDGED!
I AM THE LAW
REMEMBER,
REMEMBER
WHO
STARTED THE
TERROR

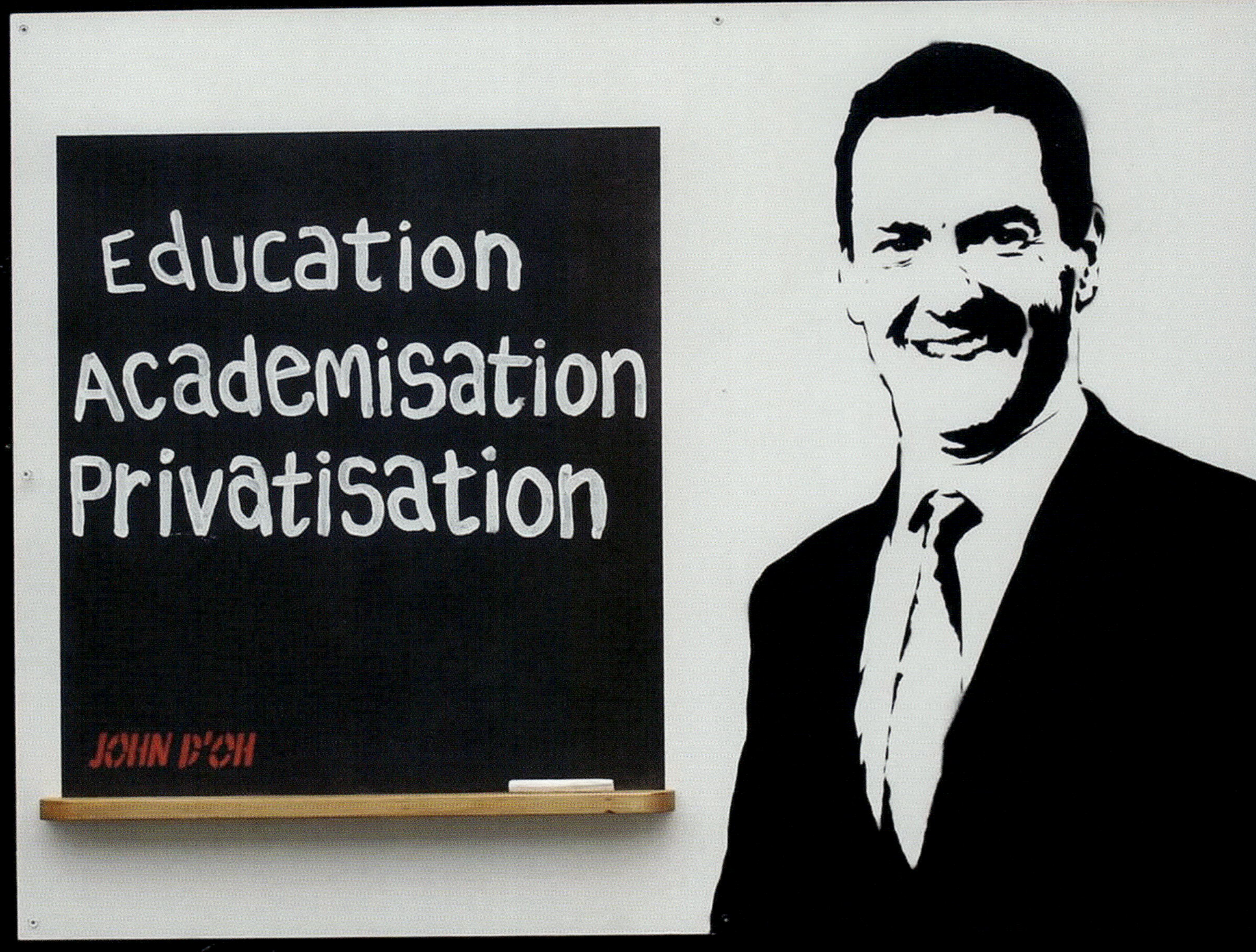

Education
Academisation
Privatisation
JOHN D'OH

Academy schools are state-funded schools in England which are directly funded by the Department for Education and independent of local authority control. Academy trusts use public money without transparency and often pay incredibly high salaries to bosses, without high standards of governance, accountability and financial management. It was under Tony Blair and Lord Adonis that academies were established with the apparent aim of improving pupil performance and breaking the cycle of low expectations and low social mobility. The Conservatives and the Liberal Democrats sought to increase the number of academies by enabling all maintained schools to convert to academy status and redirected funding in a move that pressurised schools into academisation. Moreover, Conservatives wanted to pass legislation that would force all schools to become academies, but retracted in 2016 after opposition from rural areas, which are one of their main voting bases.

I made a piece protesting the academisation of English schools in 2016 which featured a painting of Chancellor George Osborne stood next to a wooden, three-dimensional blackboard with the words "Education, academisation, privatisation" written in white chalk. Alluding back to Tony Blair's famous 1997 "Education, education, education" speech, it was not just a way of criticising this Conservative focus on the systematic funding, independence and autonomy of schools as opposed to the education of actual children, it was also a way of reminding people that this entire process began under Thatcherite economic policies of New Labour. Another similar piece showed Osborne in a dunce's cap with a bright red "D". This was because the adoption of this controversial extension in academisation was ideological and against a lot of the evidence about the proclaimed "successes" of academies.

In fact, according to papers such as the *Guardian* and the Independent, the lack of strong regulation and scrutiny has allowed many academies to become targets for nepotism and profit-making, with some academy trustees billing schools massive amounts of money in related-party transactions for minor tasks. When a trust fails, as many have subsequently done, schools may even be "asset stripped" by transferring millions of pounds of the schools' savings into different accounts before collapsing. And while some academy trusts have achieved 'outstanding' status and become 'energised' as a result of the changed school system, according to Ofsted the overall programme has resulted in nearly a hundred other schools loosing their status of 'good' or 'outstanding' educational facilities after converting into academies. It is no wonder, then, that the *Bristol Post* reported on my work and raised additional awareness about the problems of the academy system.

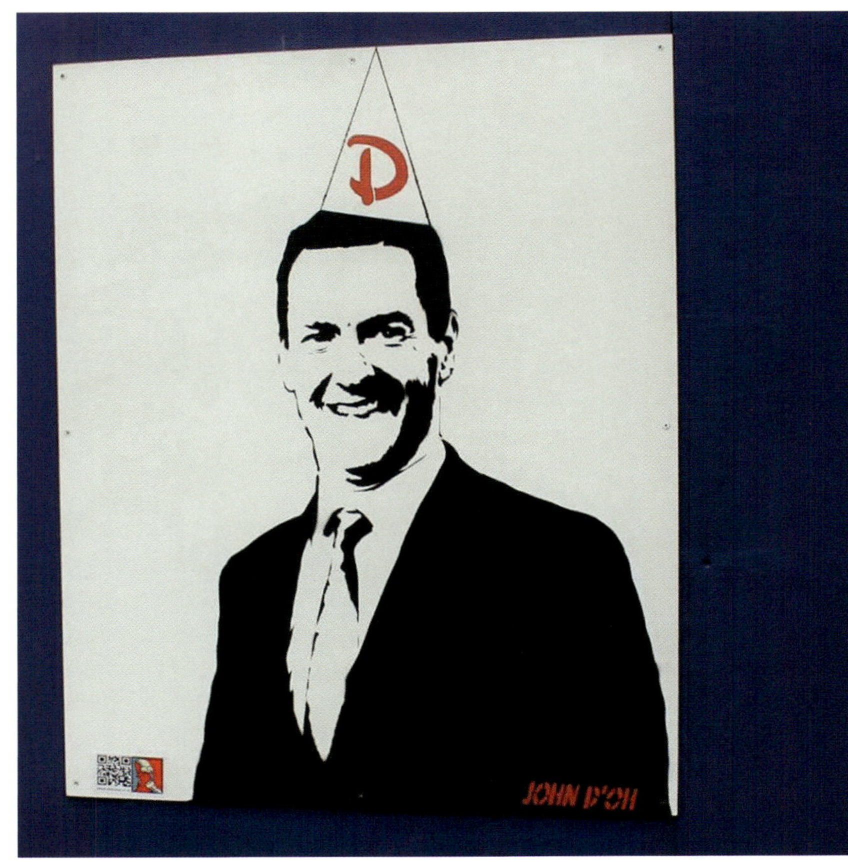

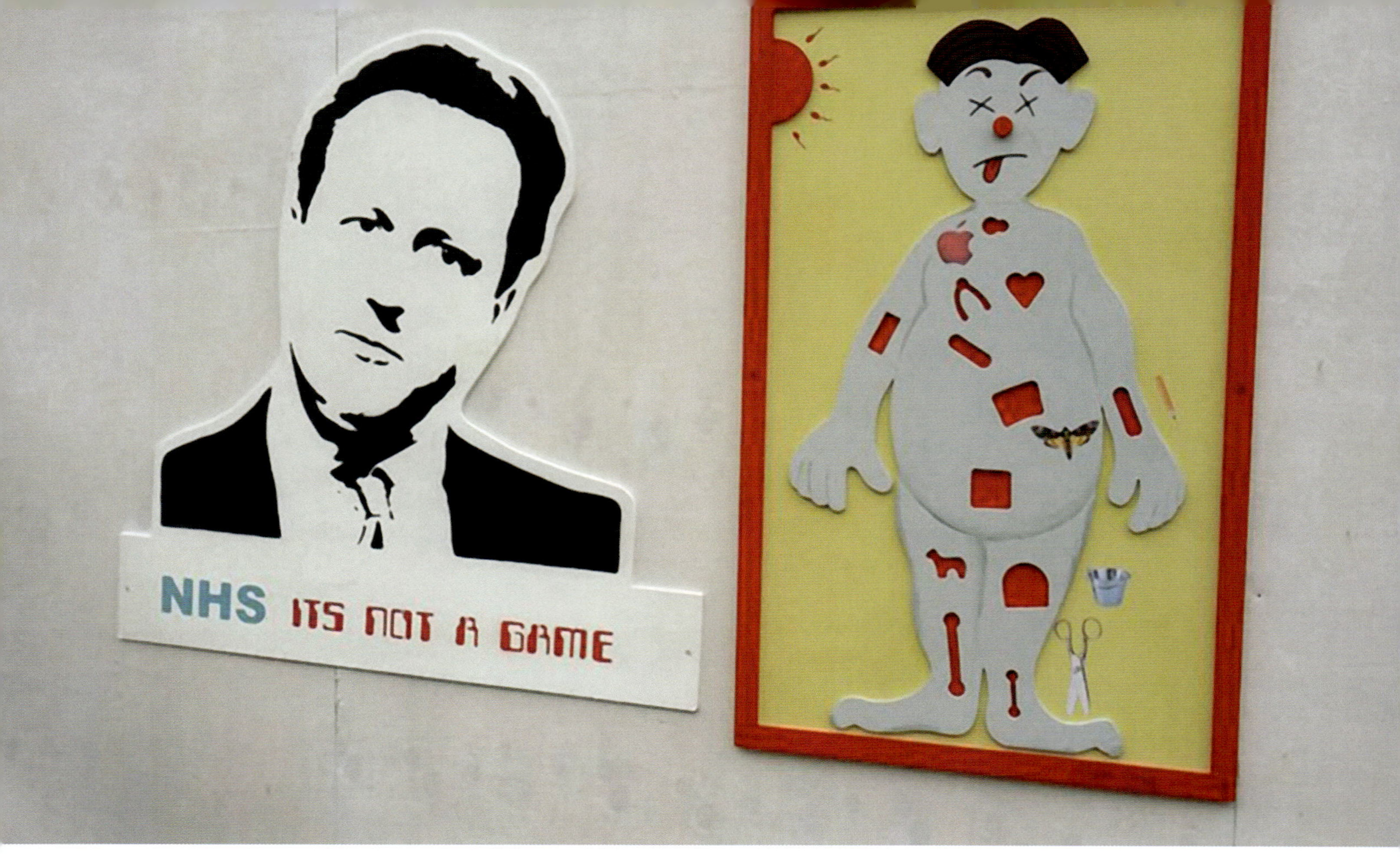

THE JUNIOR DOCTORS' STRIKE AND OPERATION: "IT'S NOT A GAME"

In response to contractual changes forced through under the Conservative government, junior doctors went on strike repeatedly throughout 2015 and 2016. In Bristol, passers-by cheered, honked their car horns or signed petitions in support of the doctors. It was in this situation that I did a piece comparing the actions of Prime Minister David Cameron and Health Secretary Jeremy Hunt to playing a losing round of the widely-sold *Operation* board game, highlighting that this increasingly monetary and politicised attitude towards the National Health Service by the Conservative Government raised serious concerns about patient safety and privatisation.

Placing my brightly-painted pieces of MDF outside the Bristol Royal Infirmary on Upper Maudlin Street helped contextualise the work and intensify its concerns about the NHS, something that should be especially relevant for those who depend on a publicly-funded health service. In the political atmosphere, my work was well received on social media and the *Bristol Post* featured it in their report on the strikes.

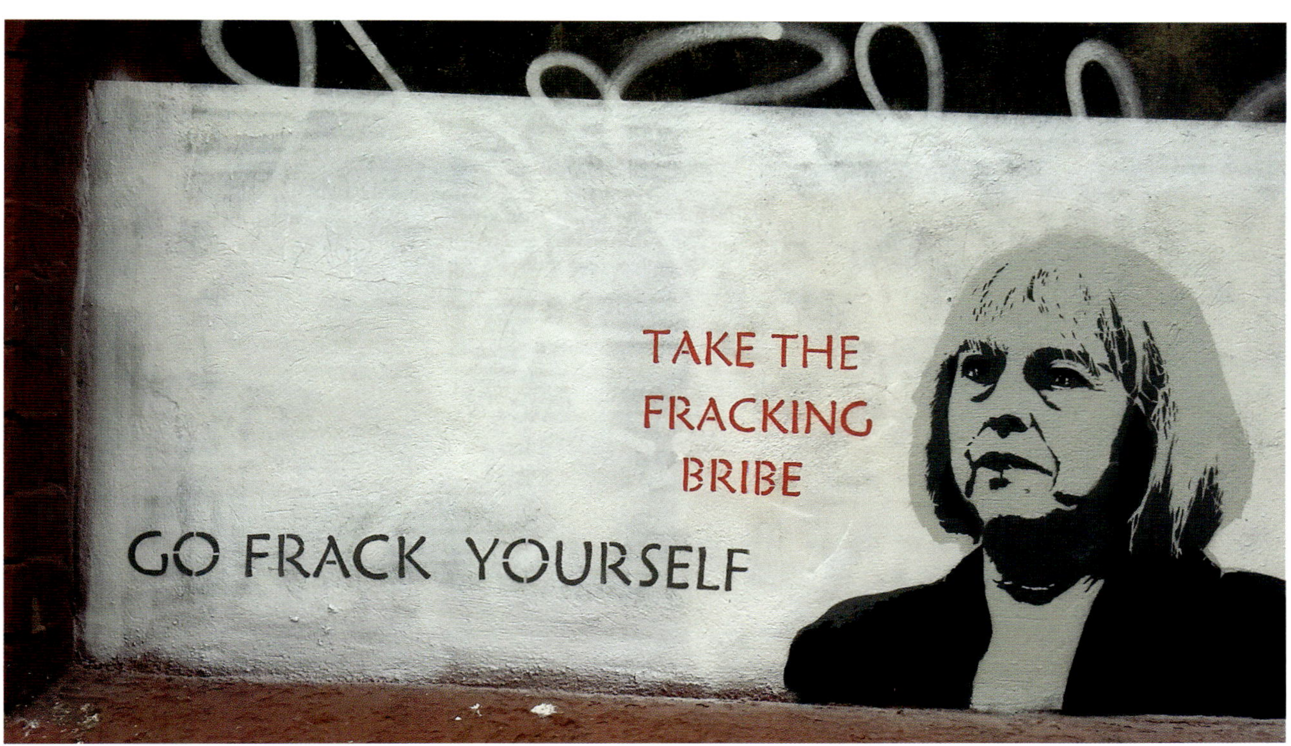

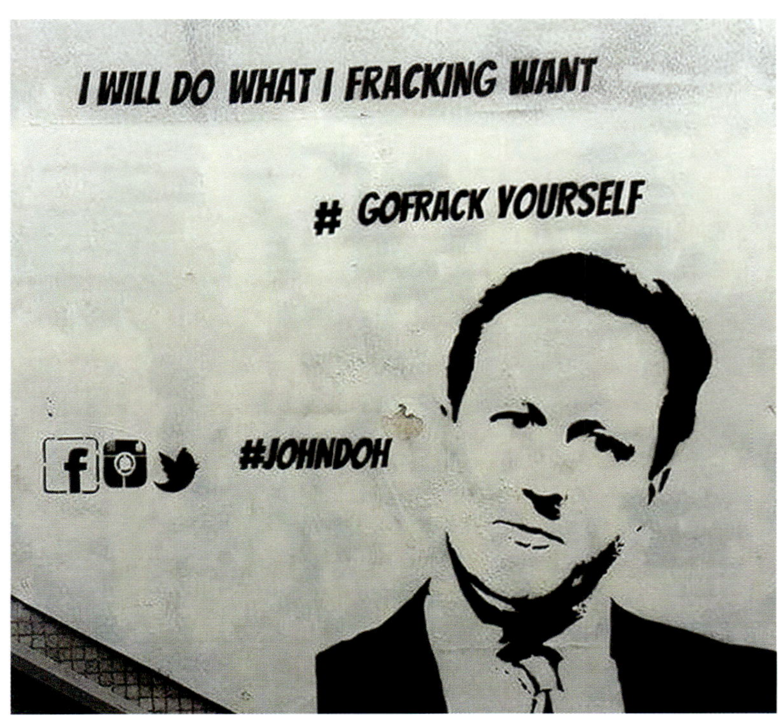

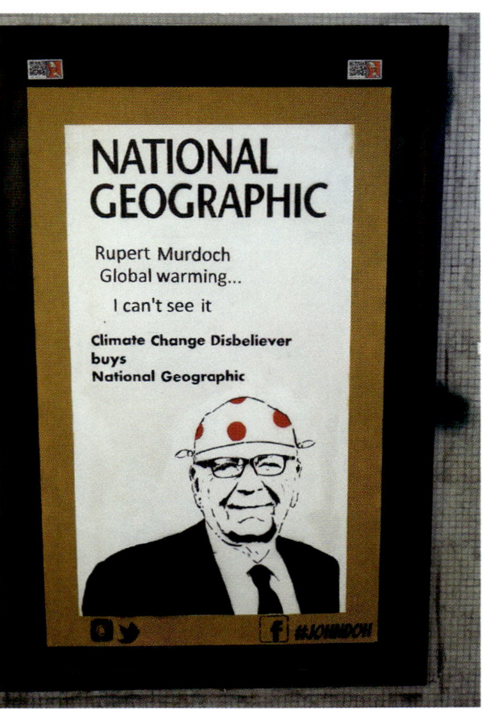

Environmental issues are also very important to me and often feature heavily in my artwork

Go Frack Yourself featuring Theresa May

Go Frack Yourself featuring David Cameron 15/08/2015

My response on 20/09/2015 to Rupert Murdoch (a well-known climate change denier) purchasing the National Geographic magazine

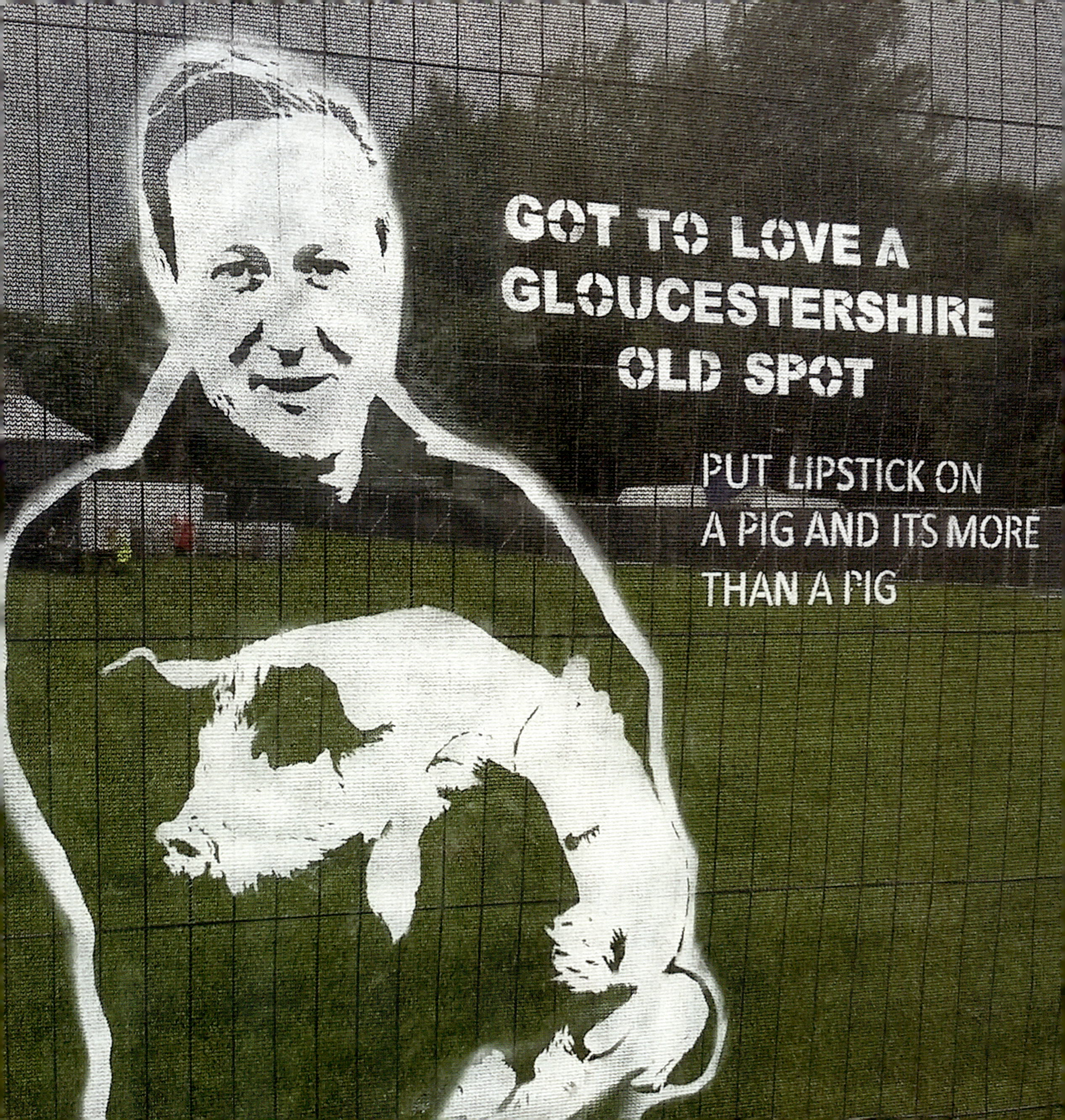

GOT TO LOVE A
GLOUCESTERSHIRE
OLD SPOT
PUT LIPSTICK ON
A PIG AND ITS MORE
THAN A PIG

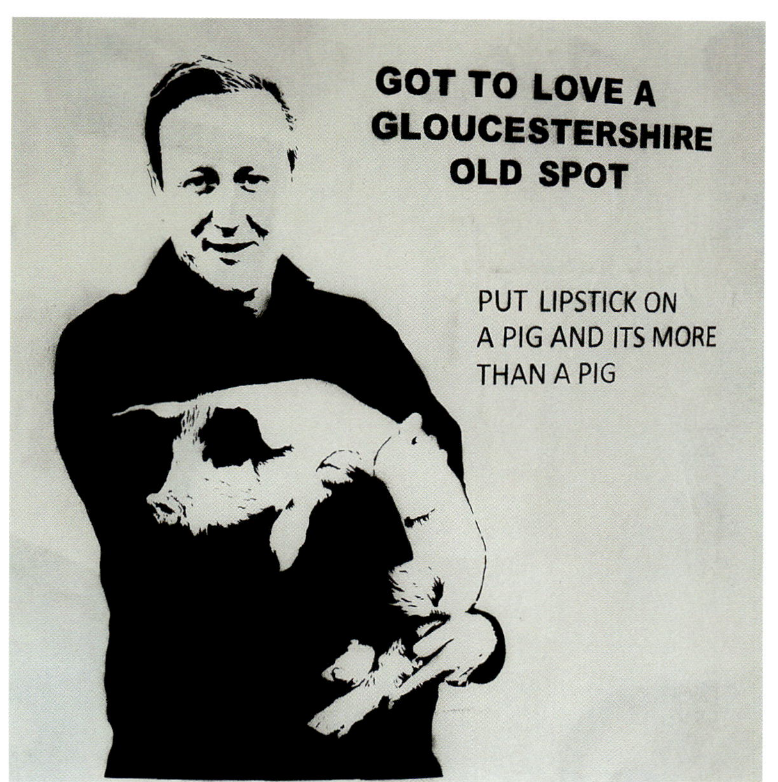
GOT TO LOVE A
GLOUCESTERSHIRE
OLD SPOT

PUT LIPSTICK ON
A PIG AND ITS MORE
THAN A PIG

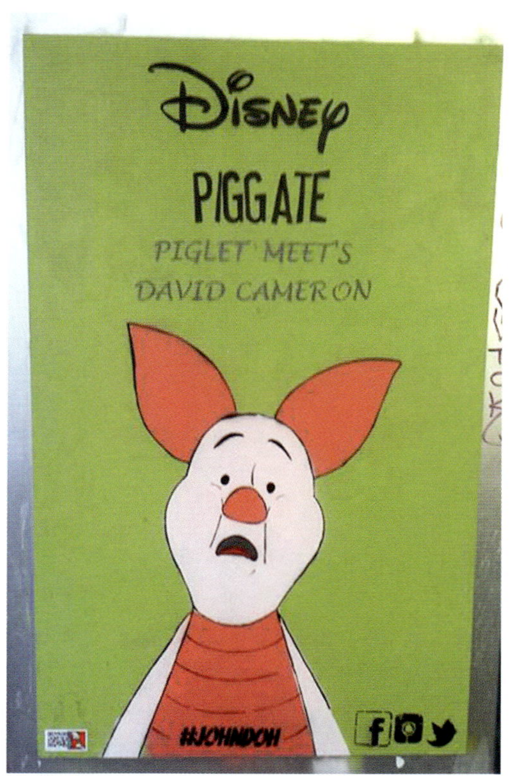
Disney
PIGGATE
PIGLET MEET'S
DAVID CAMERON
#JOHNDOH

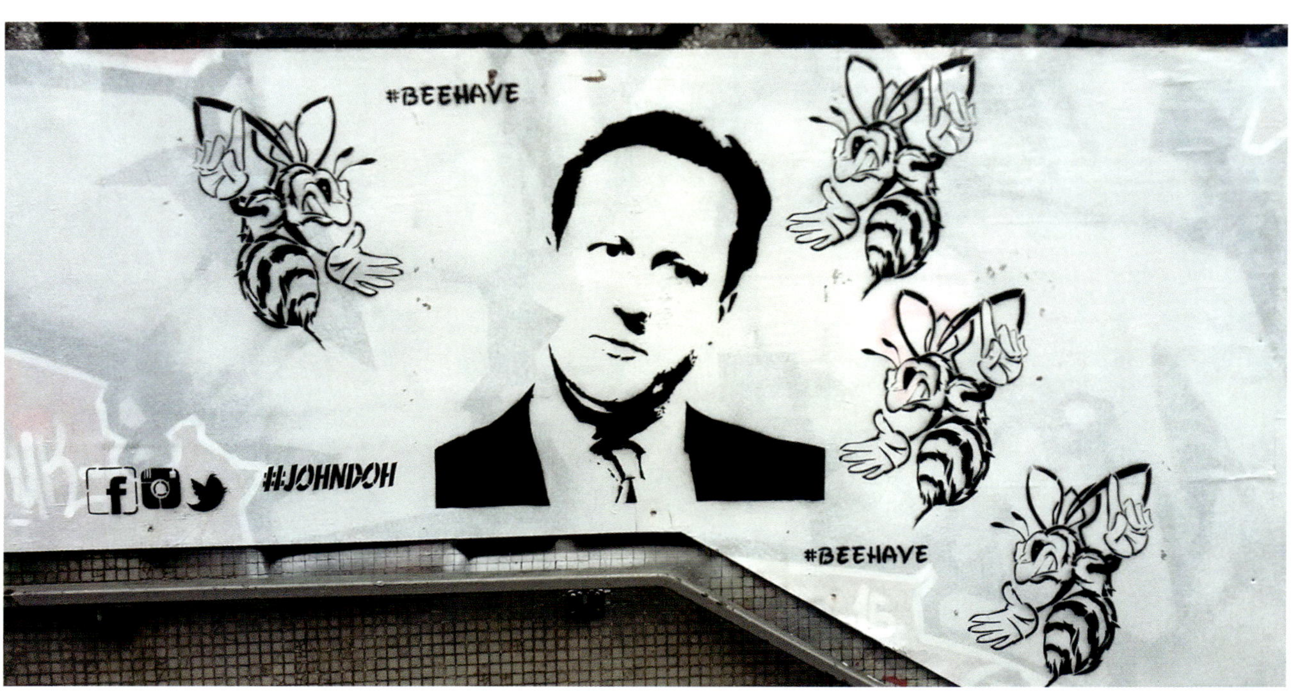
#BEEHAVE
#JOHNDOH
#BEEHAVE

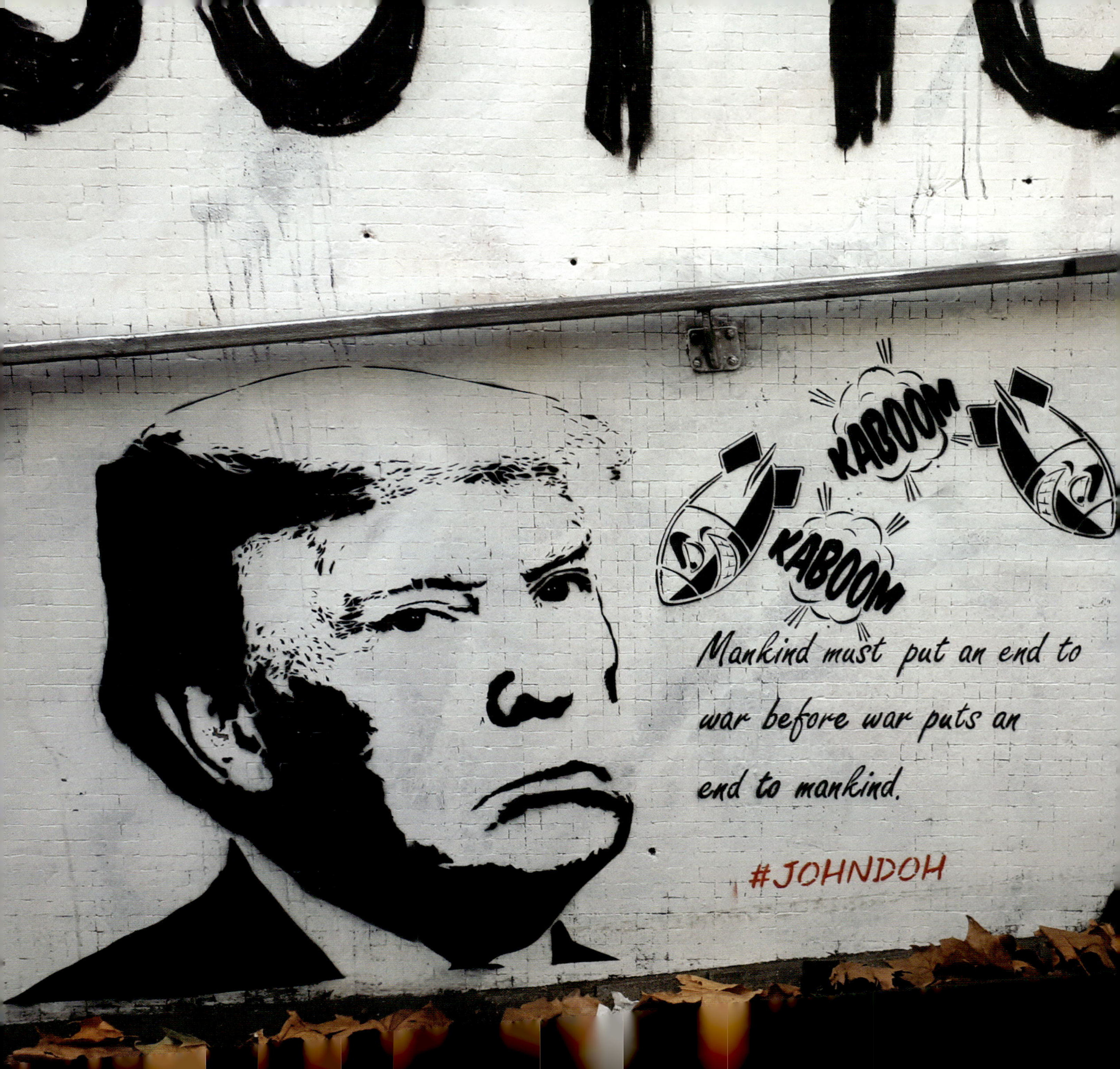

KABOOM
KABOOM
Mankind must put an end to war before war puts an end to mankind.
#JOHNDOH

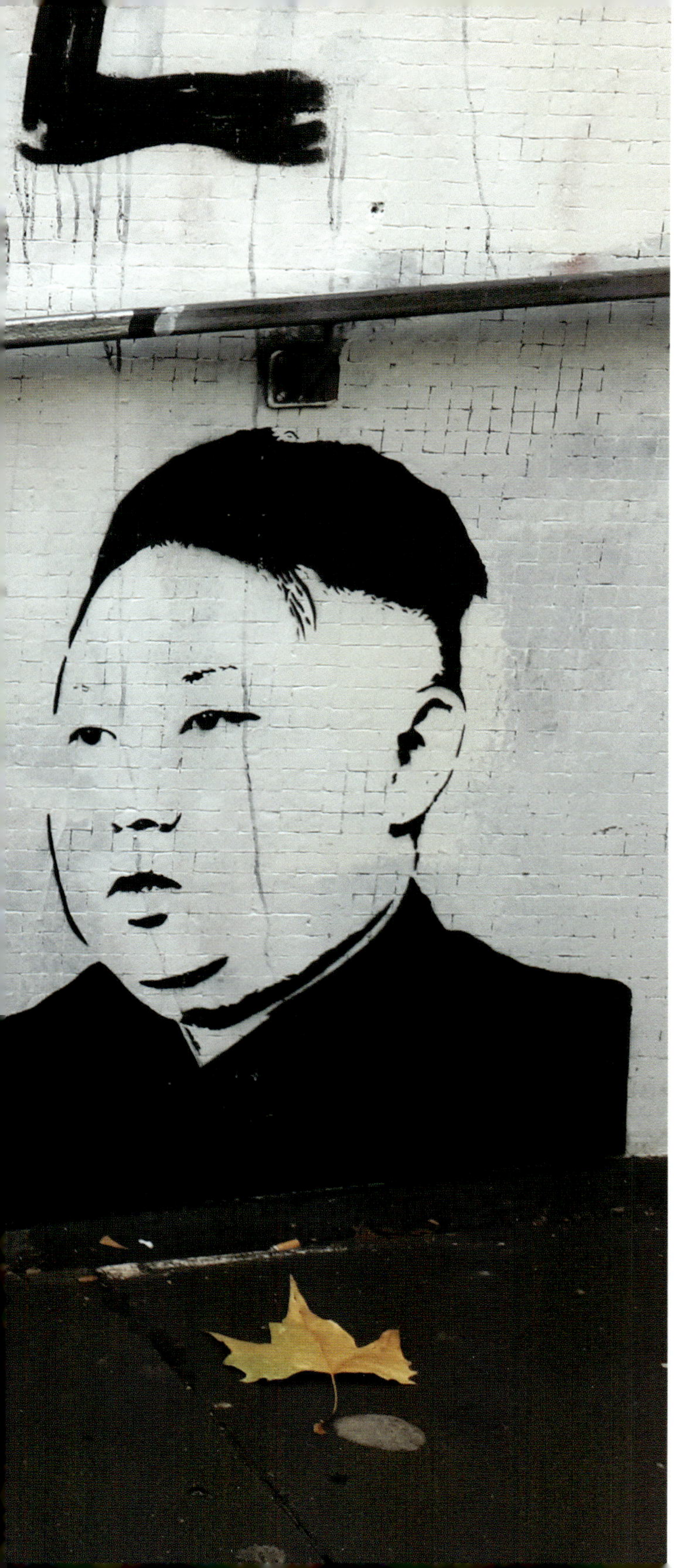

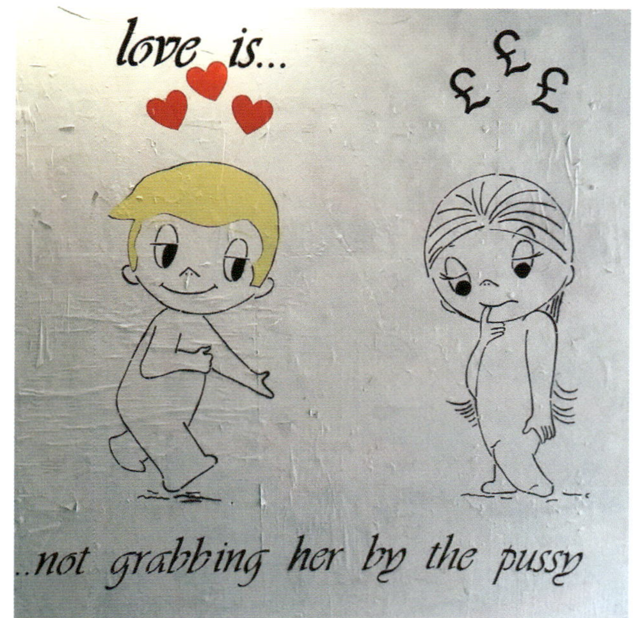

love is...
£ £ £
...not grabbing her by the pussy

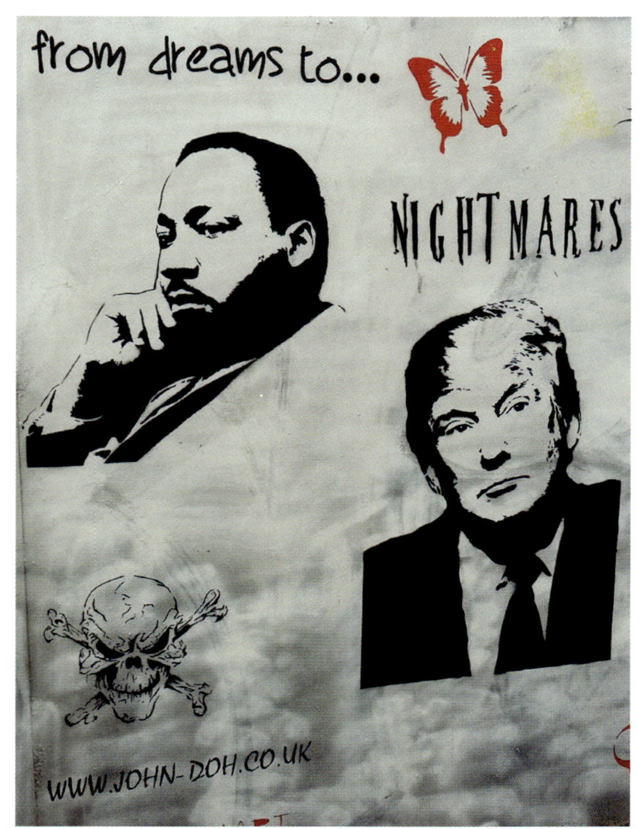

from dreams to...
NIGHTMARES
WWW.JOHN-DOH.CO.UK

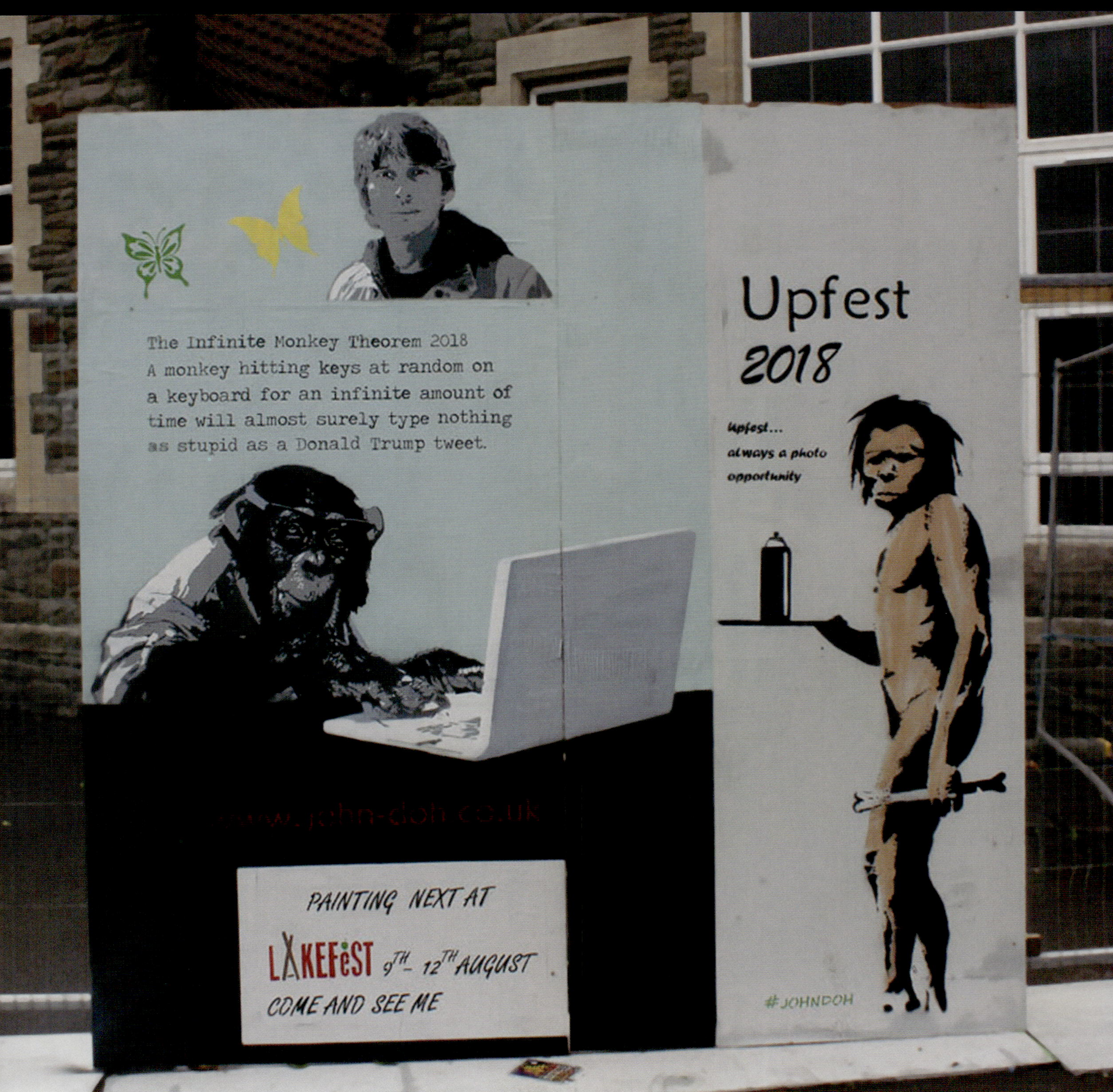
The Infinite Monkey Theorem 2018
A monkey hitting keys at random on
a keyboard for an infinite amount of
time will almost surely type nothing
as stupid as a Donald Trump tweet.
www.john-doh.co.uk
PAINTING NEXT AT
LAKEFEST 9TH - 12TH AUGUST
COME AND SEE ME
Upfest
2018
upfest...
always a photo
opportunity
#JOHNDOH

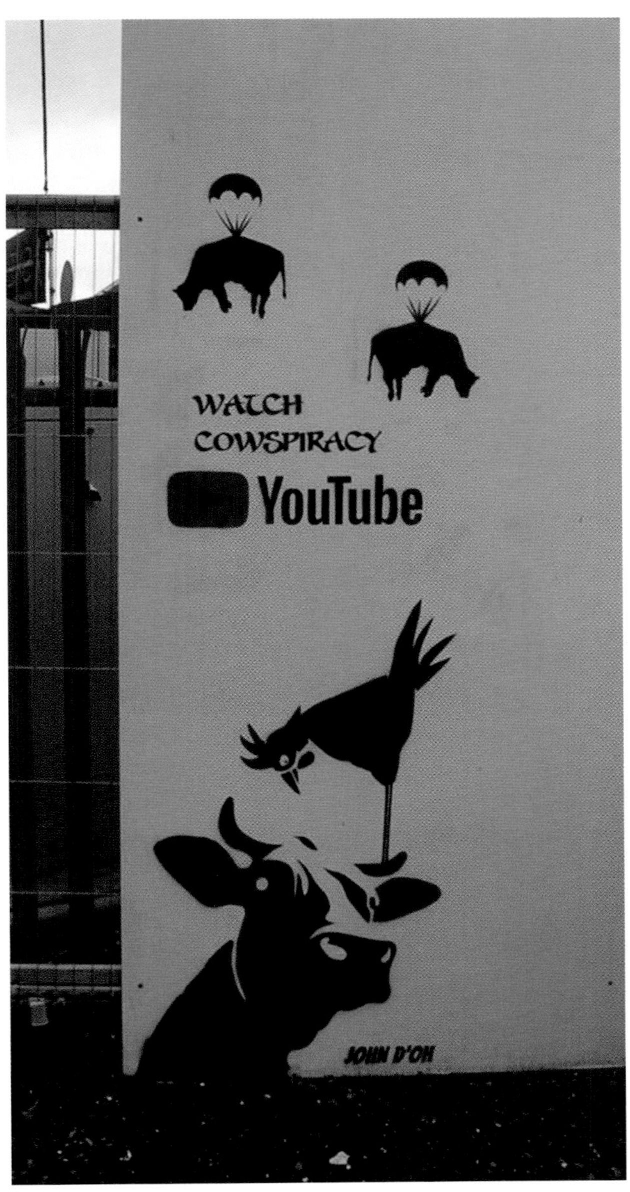

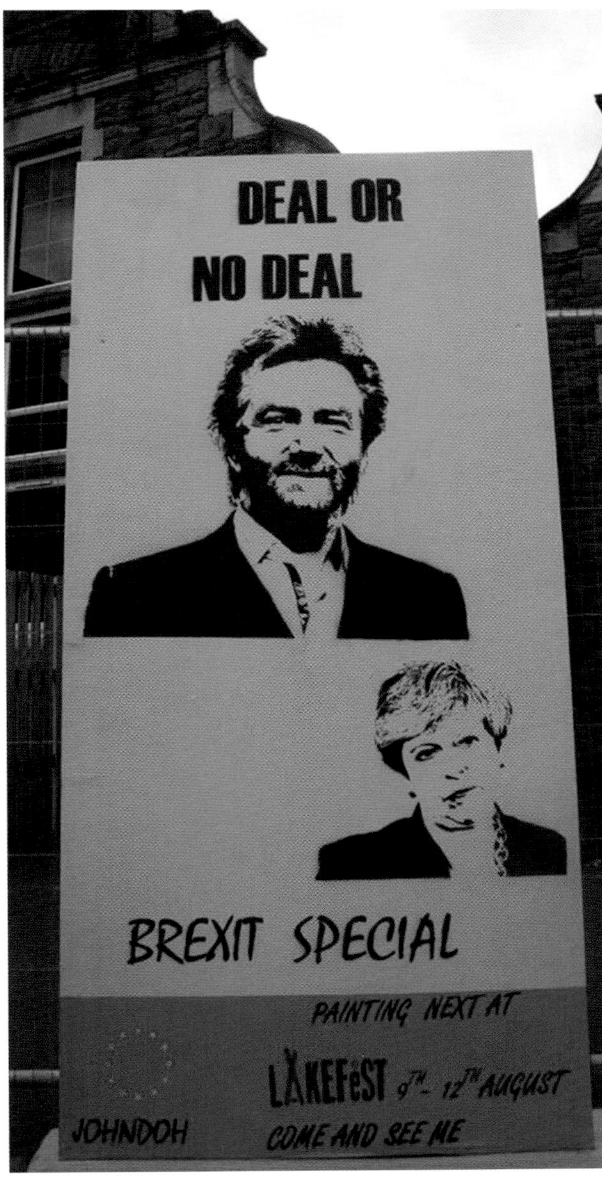

That page:
Infinite
Monkey Theorem
2018. My
contemporary
take on the
famous thought
experiment
incorporating
tweets from
the orangutan
currently in
charge of the
United States

This page:
Watch
Cowspiracy
painted
at Upfest
28/7/2018
promoting the
YouTube video
of the same
name

Deal or No
Deal painted
at Upfest
28/7/2018. As
Theresa May
continues to
struggle for a
deal on Brexit,
I felt a spot on
the television
gameshow Deal
or No Deal with
Noel Edmonds
would be
appropriate

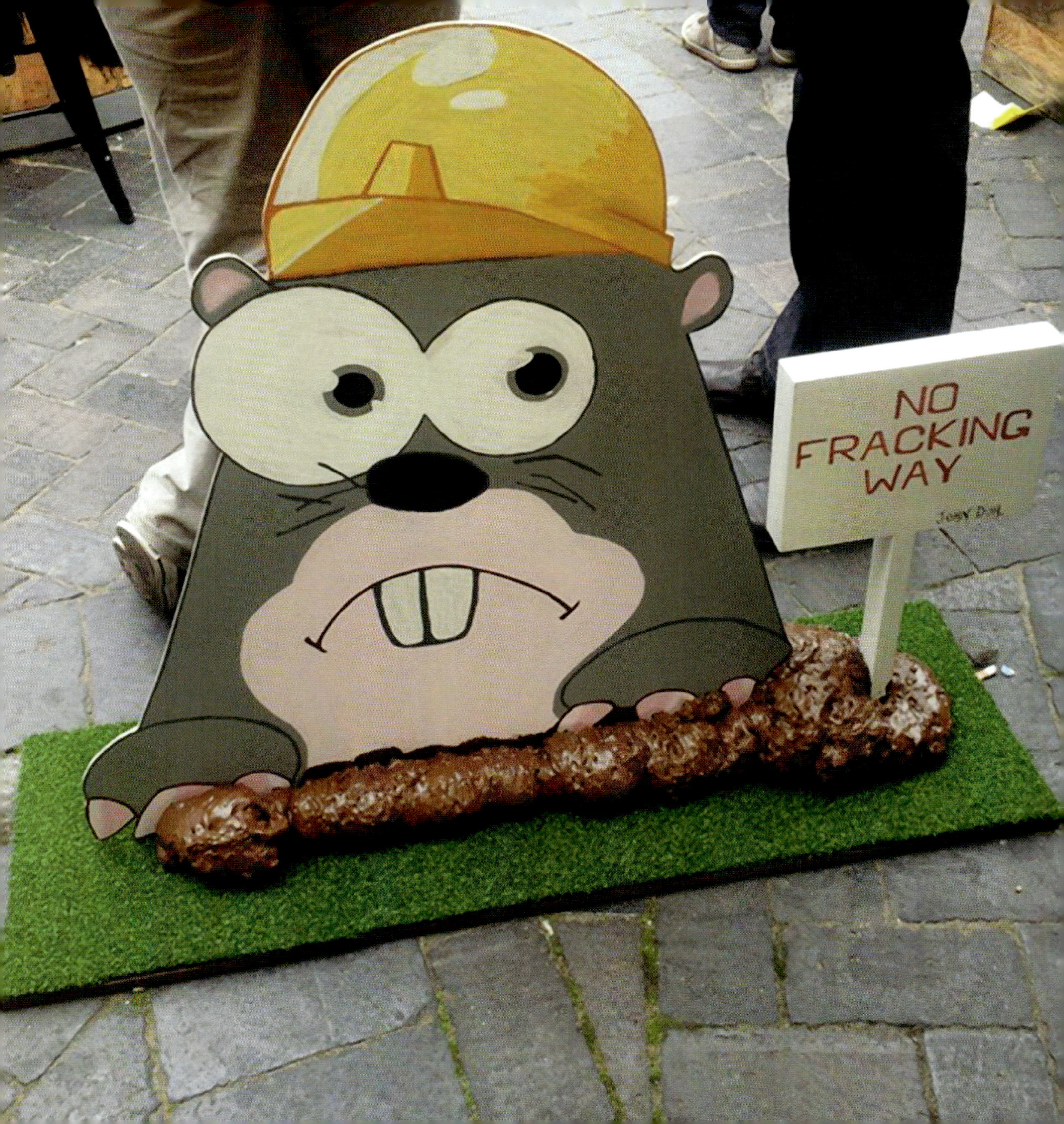

NO
FRACKING
WAY

Installations and Woodcut Art

I have been doing art installations for many years and as far as I know I was the first artist to start to do what I refer to as woodcut images, but many more artists have since started replicating it. I'm quite humbled. After all, I consider imitation as the biggest form of flattery and it's nice to leave a little something in street art history.

It all started when I wanted to put art in areas that were heavily populated by CCTV cameras and I just needed to reduce the installation time by coming up with something even quicker than stencils. By pre-painting and cutting out images and applying high bond tape and no-nails adhesive to the back I could drop the installation time considerably. Often, the work would be completed without the need to have a spray can at all, which not only made the process easier but meant that I had no incriminating paint on my person. It was a foolproof way to get art on the street in areas that were more well-defended with surveillance cameras, lights and physical security. These prohibitive measures made many other artists more reluctant to paint there, which had the added advantage of making my own work stand-out in areas with much less graffiti.

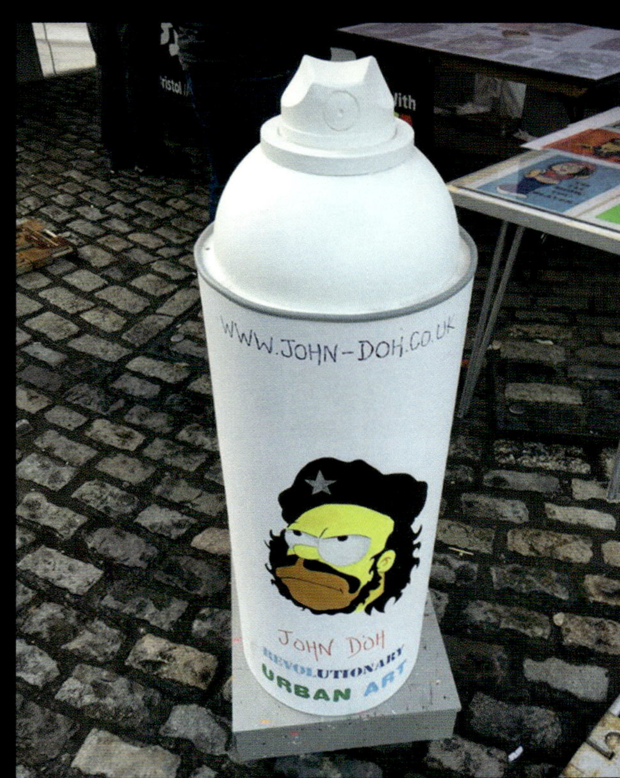

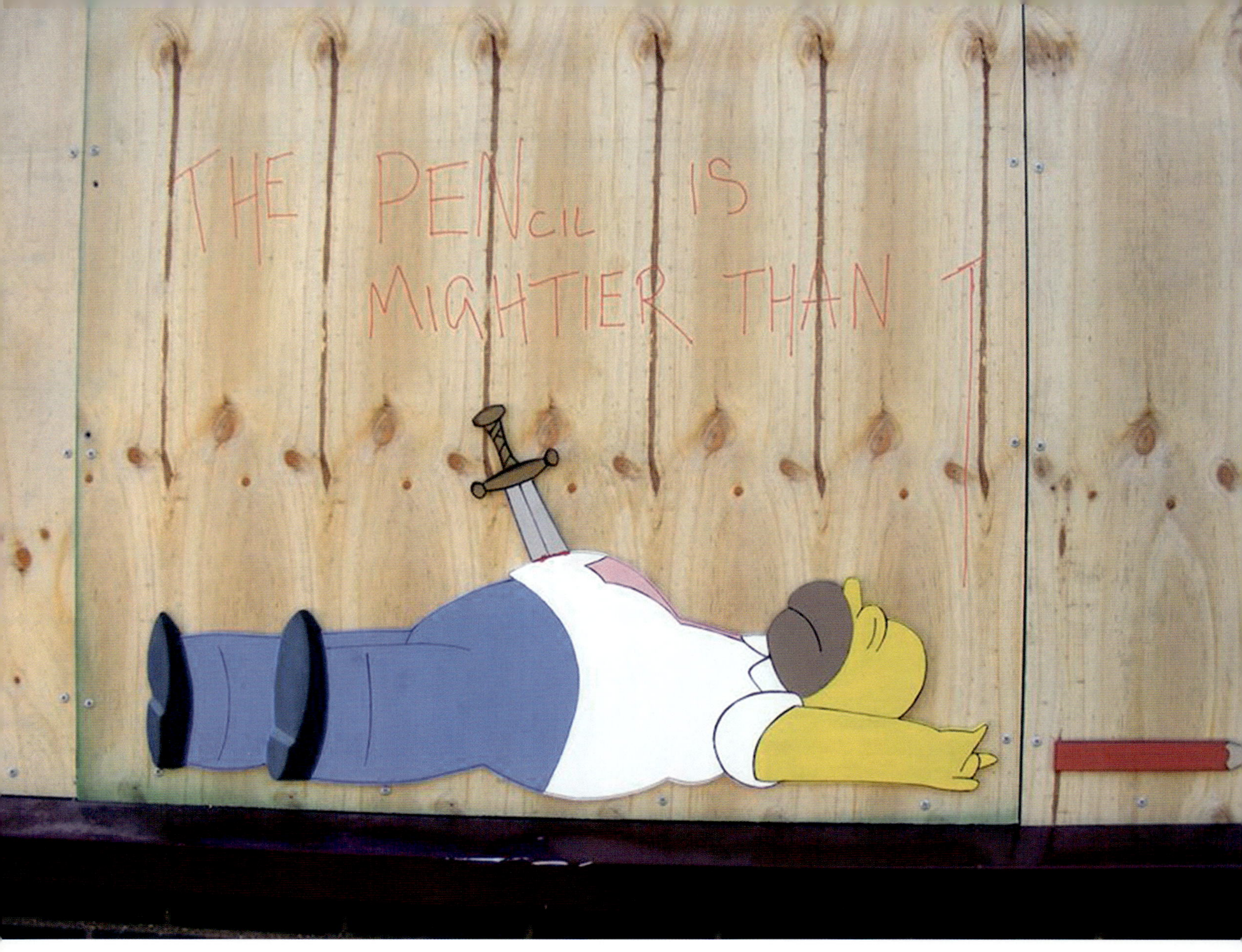

From then on it evolved and I would make wooden sculptures and cut-outs to adorn the street, things that you would be more accustomed to seeing in an art gallery or museum I suppose. As for me, the art was all about the street and it wasn't meant to be taken and hung on somebody's wall. Although that doesn't mean I expect it not to be taken, moved or damaged in some way. In fact, while I always tried to create artwork that was pleasing to the eye, I try not to overinvest hours of my time building something to the best of my ability when it may only survive on the streets for a couple of hours. This is why photography is almost a necessary part of street art, it records an image of an artwork or sculpture that will probably be painted over, destroyed or removed by the end of the day.

Back in 2013 I was the first artist at Upfest to do

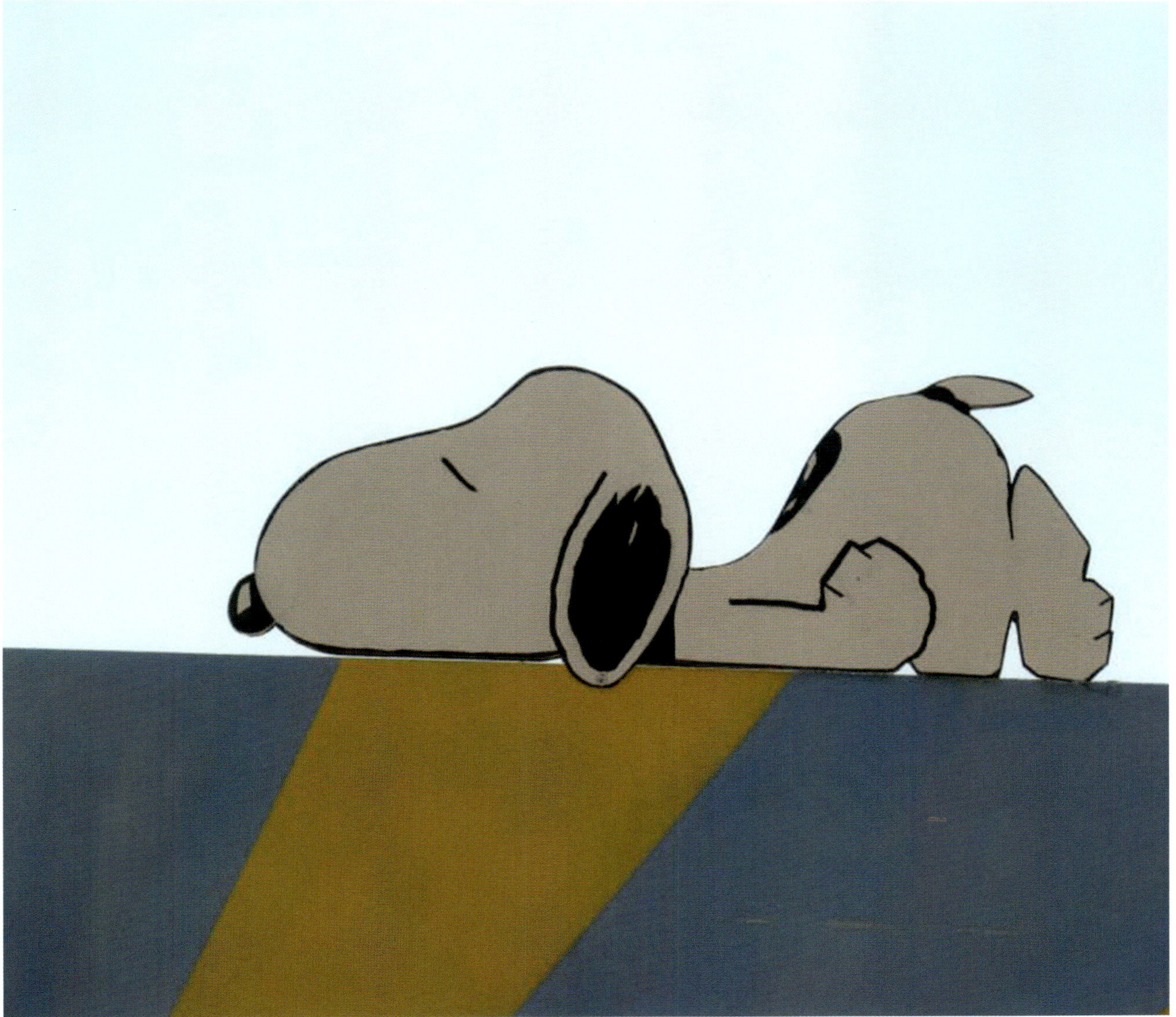

3D art installations, it was a bit quirky and different from the norm but gradually more and more artists are creating sculptures for the streets. I have done many installations over the years but try to normally tie them in with news stories, things I am passionate about or just something I find humorous.

I have done installations in various locations around the country and I find normally they are quite well received by the general public and often make social media and local news. It is probably what I am better known for along with my stencil work.

Installations can also be a lot more fun to do and I have many favourite pieces that bring back good memories. Among them are attaching art to the Thekla, fastening giant love locks to Pero's Bridge, placing a giant mole near Gardiner Haskins and, of course, the

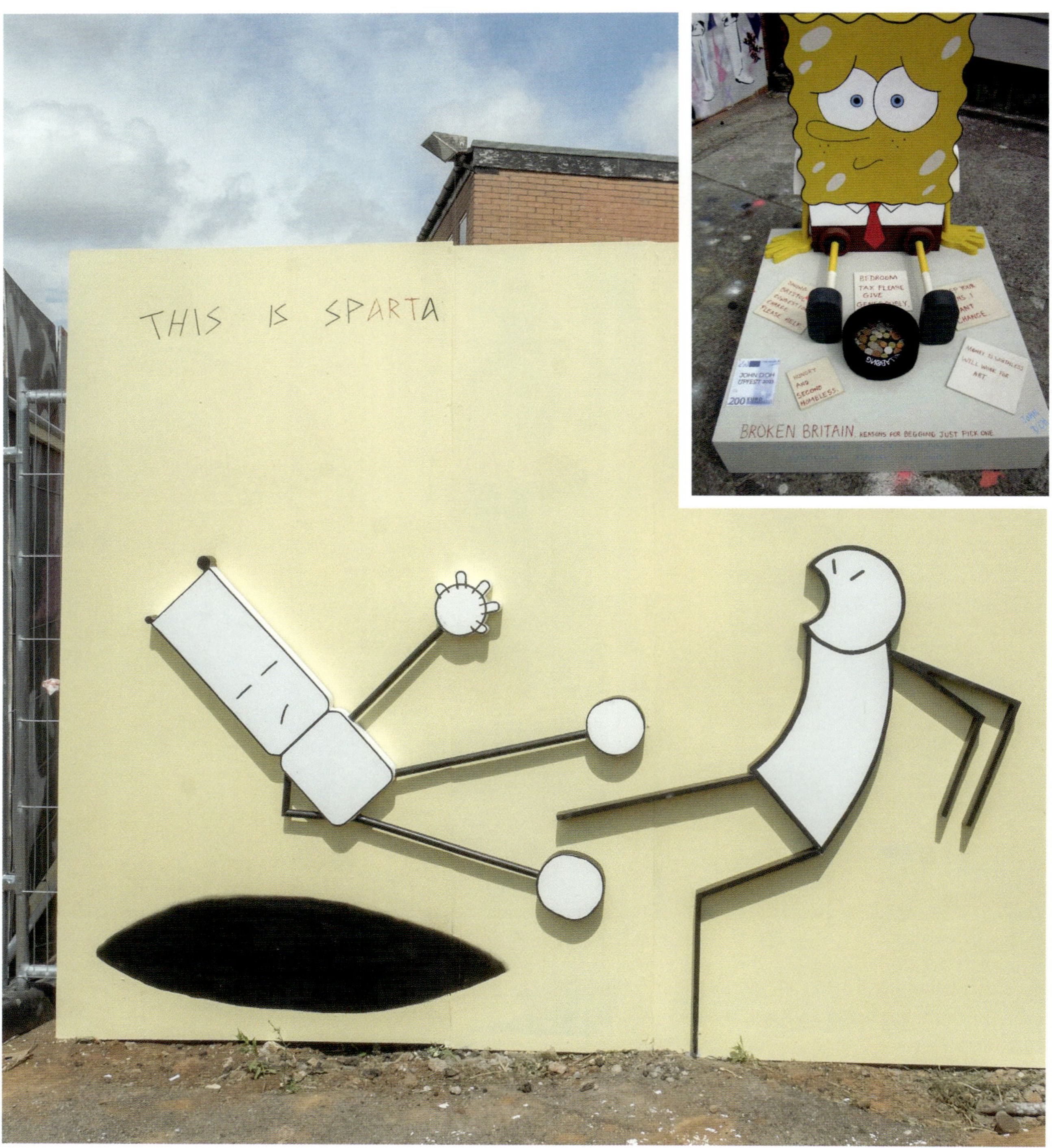
THIS IS SPARTA
BEDROOM TAX PLEASE GIVE GENEROUSLY
JOHN D'OH OFFEST 2013
200
HUNGRY AND SECOND HOMELESS
WILL WORK FOR ART
BROKEN BRITAIN. REASONS FOR BEGGING JUST PICK ONE

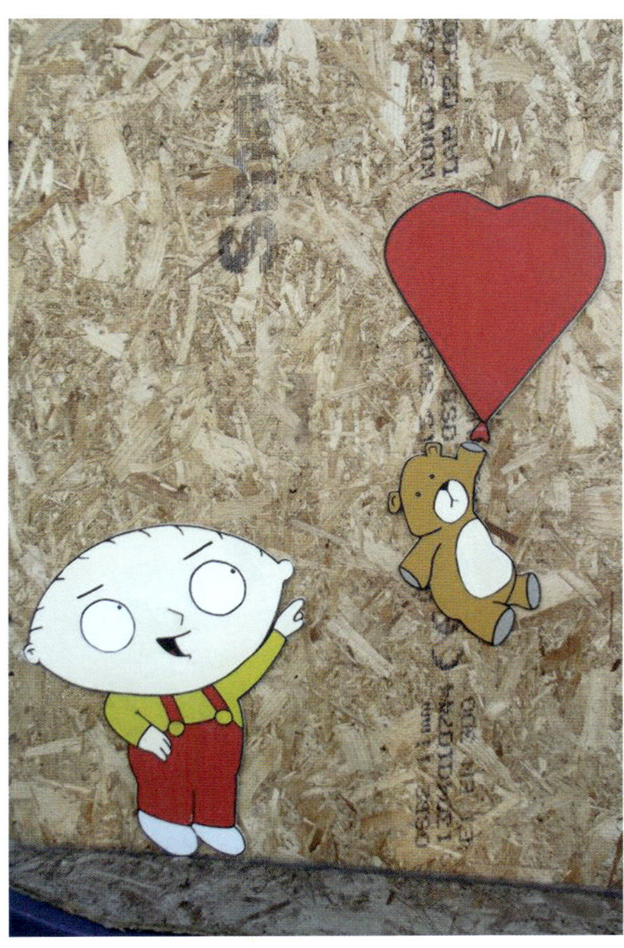

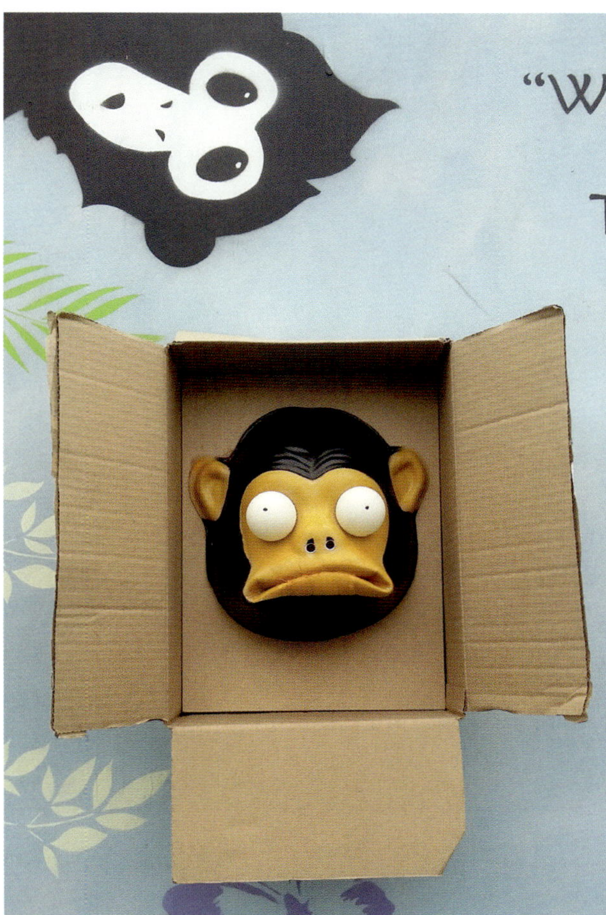

many skeletons I have put out.

One of the favourites with some of my followers is the *This is Sparta* piece. It was a 3D cut-out of two figures from two well-known street artists My Dog Sighs and Stik mashed into a movie scene. Stik even contacted me after seeing the piece on social media and said he loved it. To a certain extent, it can be seen as an inside-joke that only people who are generally aware of the urban art scene could fully enjoy. The mock-battle parallels critical comparisons made between their respected characters. But for many, simply posing and taking selfies by these life-size and three-dimensional cartoonish figures was enjoyment enough.

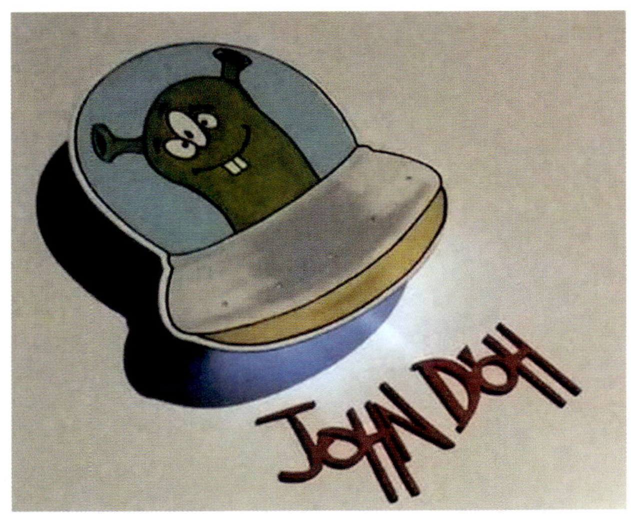

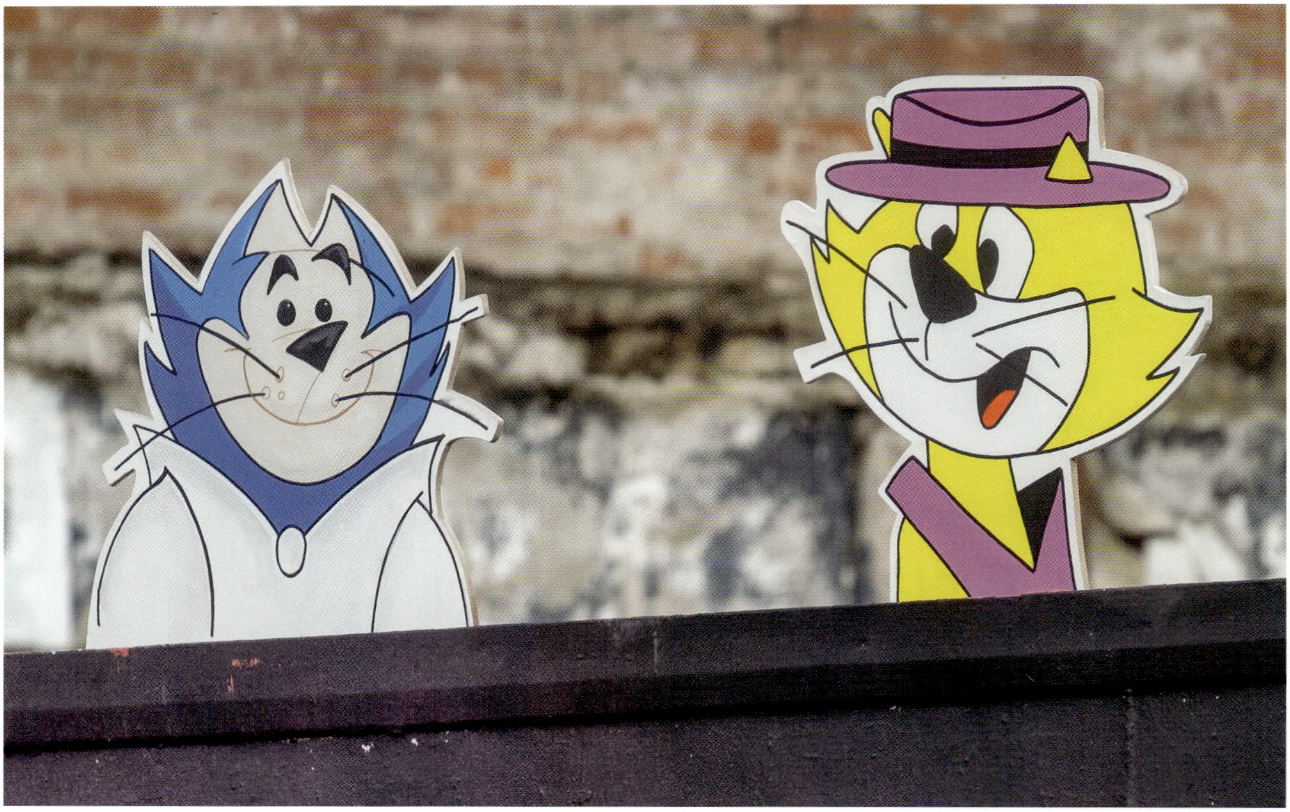

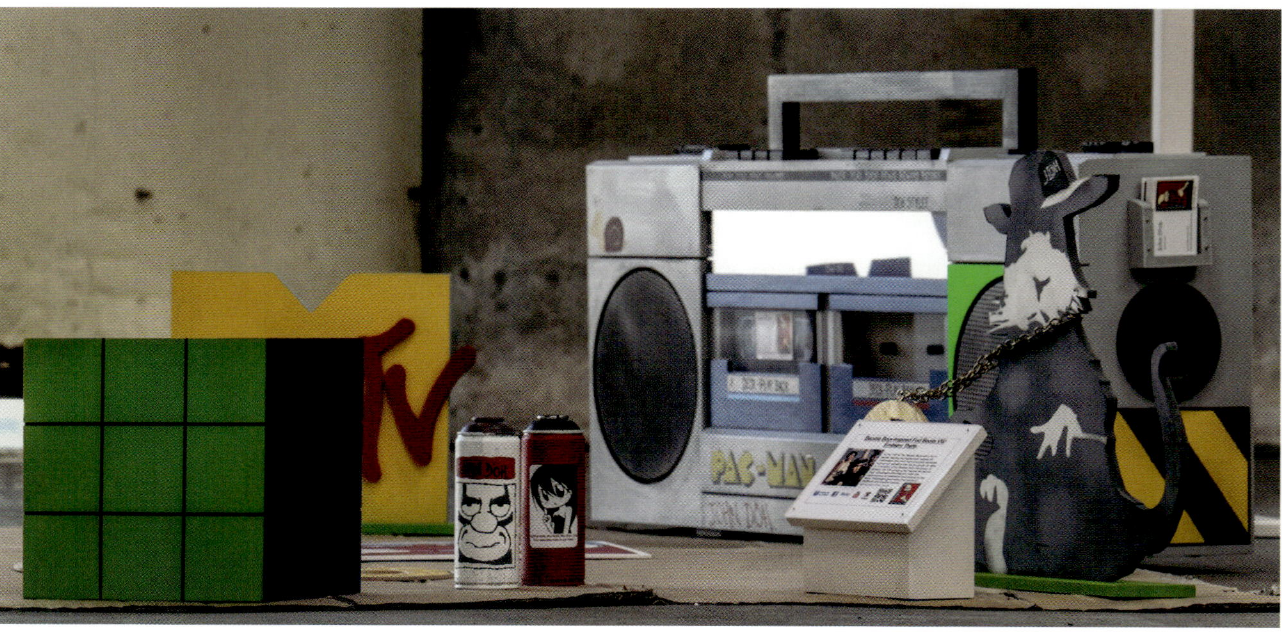

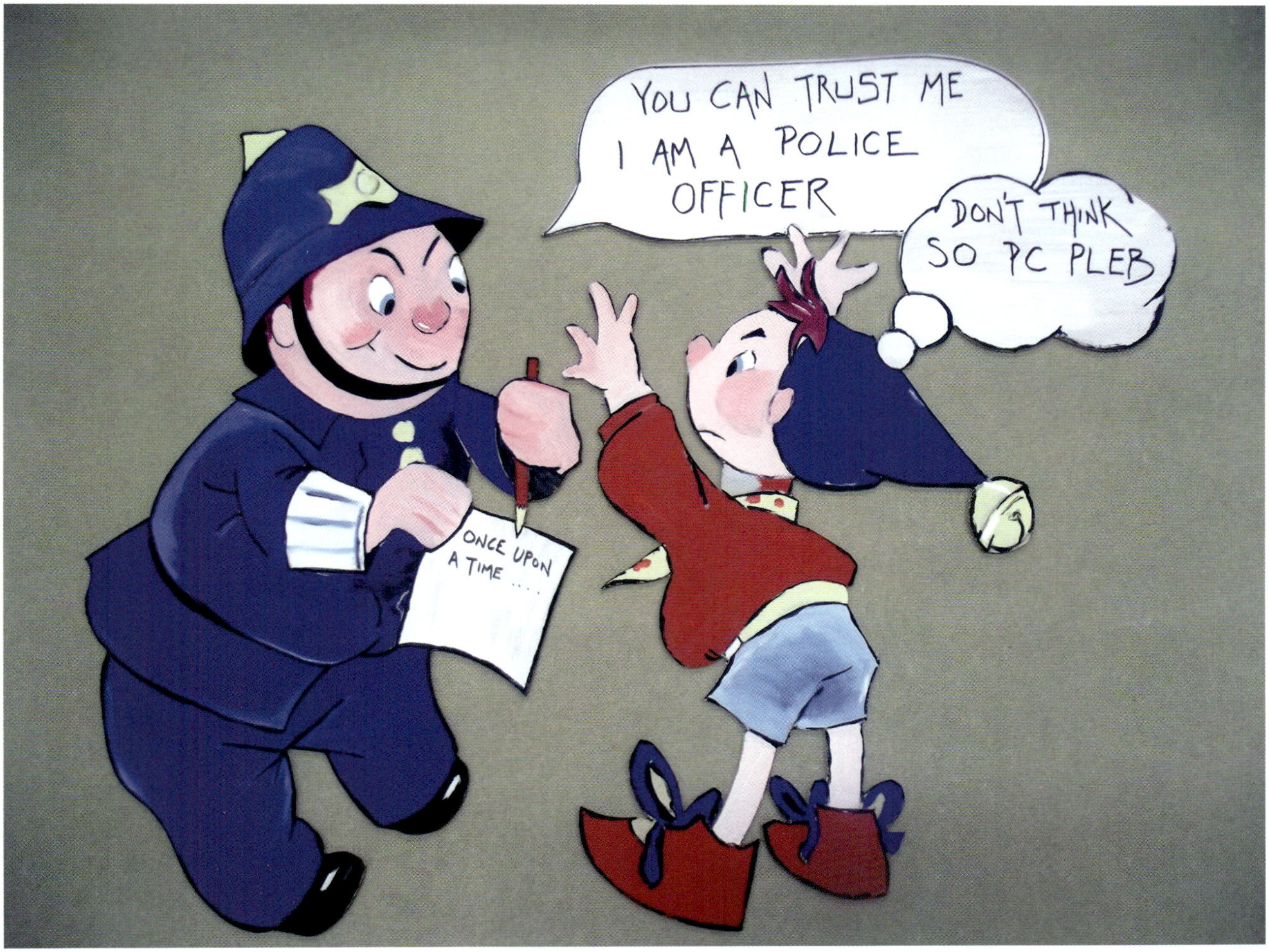

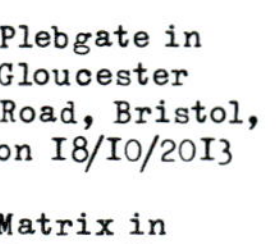

YOU CAN TRUST ME I AM A POLICE OFFICER
DON'T THINK SO PC PLEB
ONCE UPON A TIME . . . .

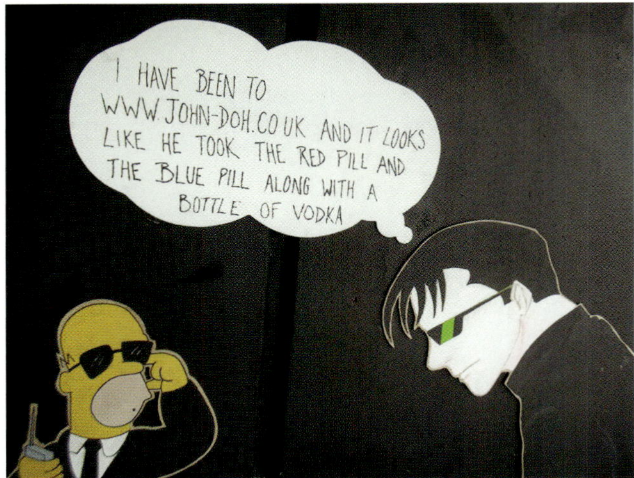

I HAVE BEEN TO WWW.JOHN-DOH.CO.UK AND IT LOOKS LIKE HE TOOK THE RED PILL AND THE BLUE PILL ALONG WITH A BOTTLE OF VODKA

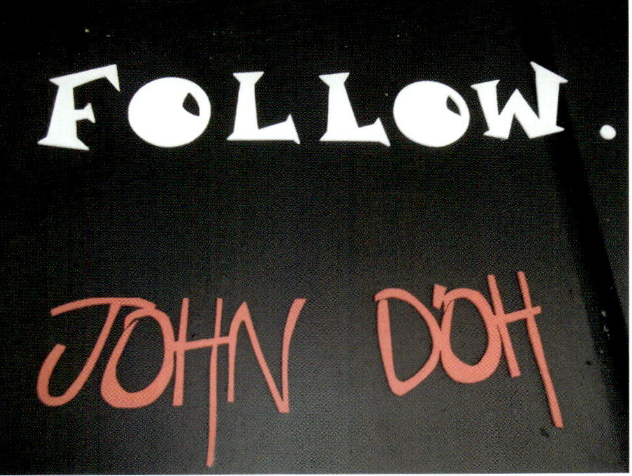

FOLLOW.
JOHN DOH

This page:

Roche Art
Laugh Now on
25/04/2013

Graffik Gallery
on 09/04/2013
Yate Sign on
14/02/17

That page:
Stik and My Dog
Sighs: "I Am
Your Father"
created for
Upfest on
26/07/2015

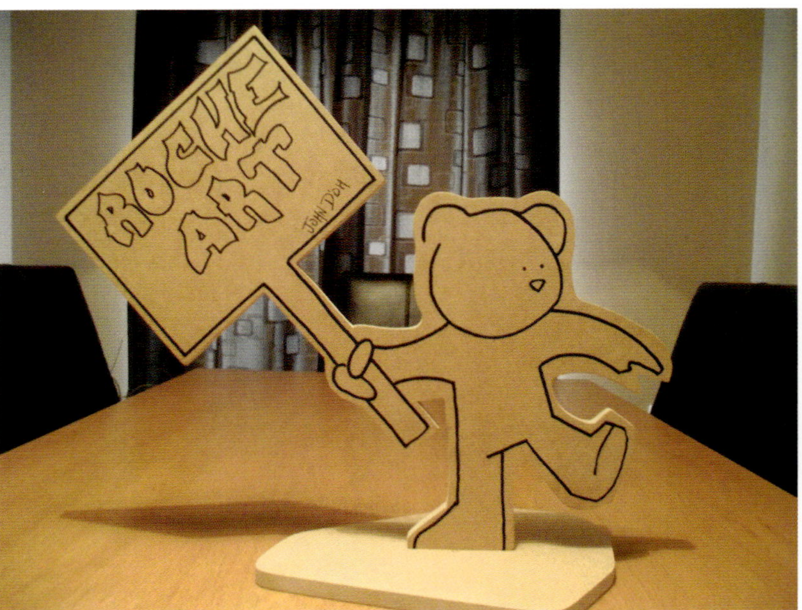

ROCHE ART
JOHN D'oh

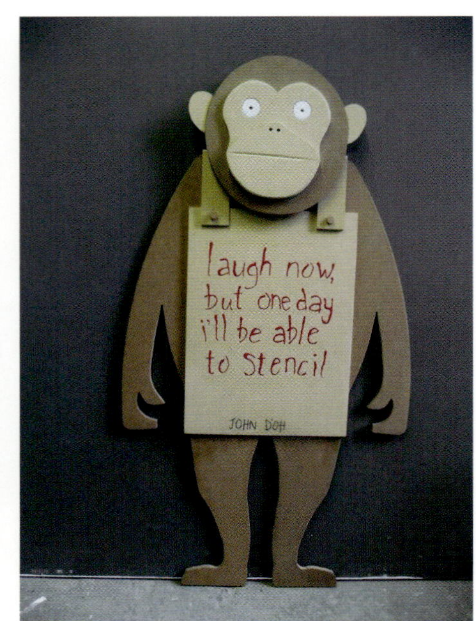

laugh now,
but one day
i'll be able
to stencil
JOHN D'oh

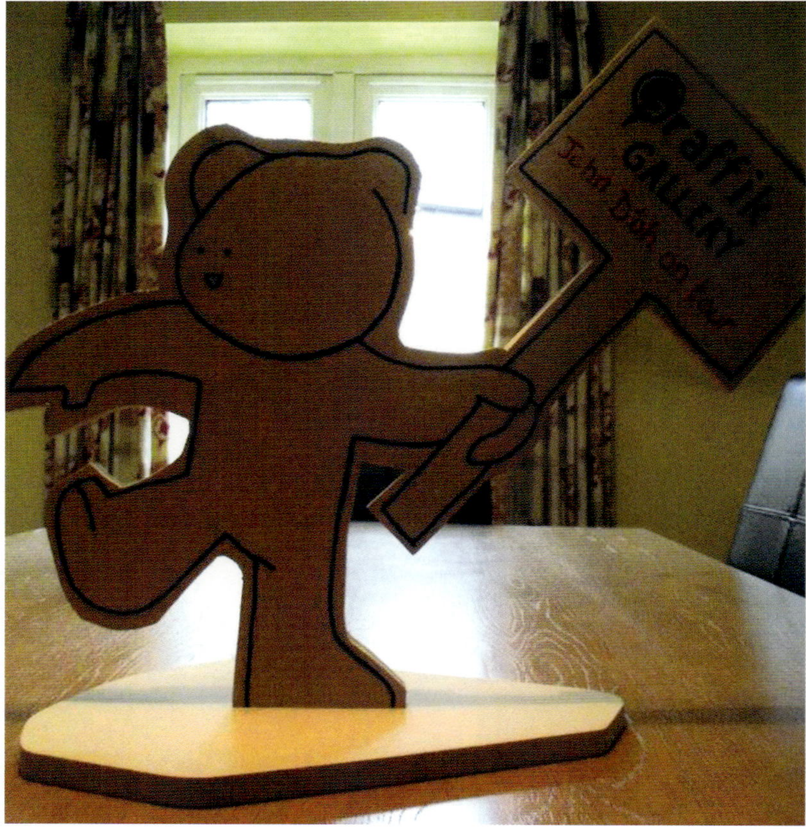

Graffik
GALLERY

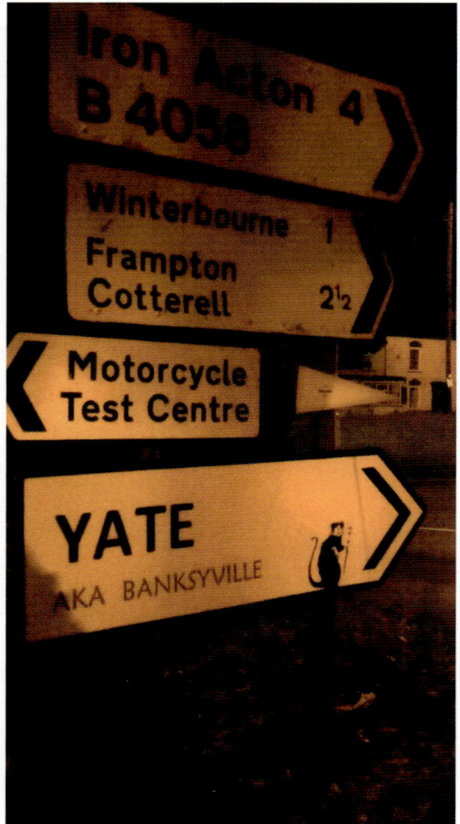

Iron Acton 4
B 4058
Winterbourne 1
Frampton
Cotterell 2½
Motorcycle
Test Centre
YATE
AKA BANKSYVILLE

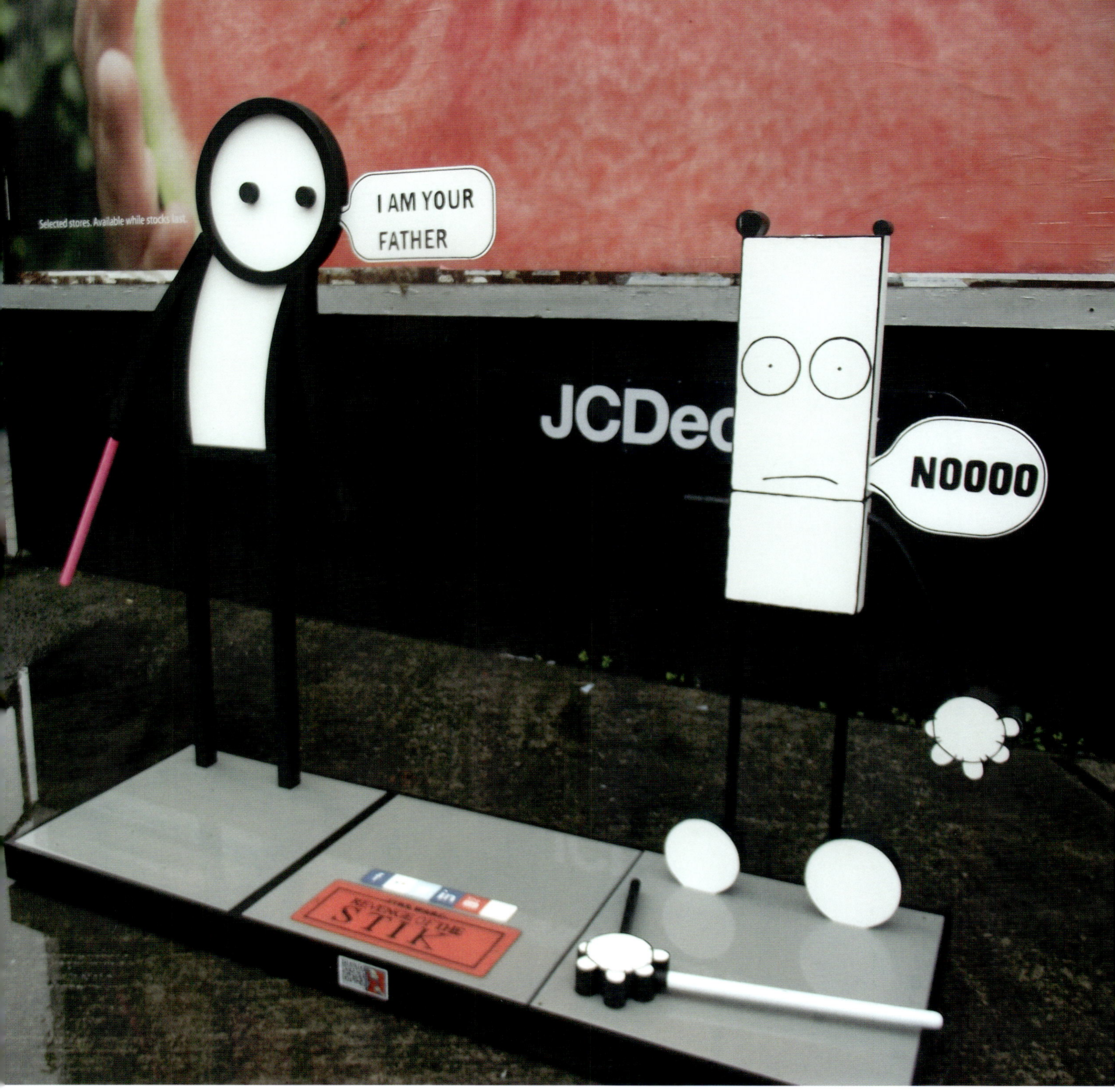
Selected stores. Available while stocks last.
I AM YOUR FATHER
JCDec
NOOOO
REVENGE OF THE STIK

Dambo Box
Man, "I won't
sell out to no
sponsor", at
Gloucester
Museum on
09/03/2018

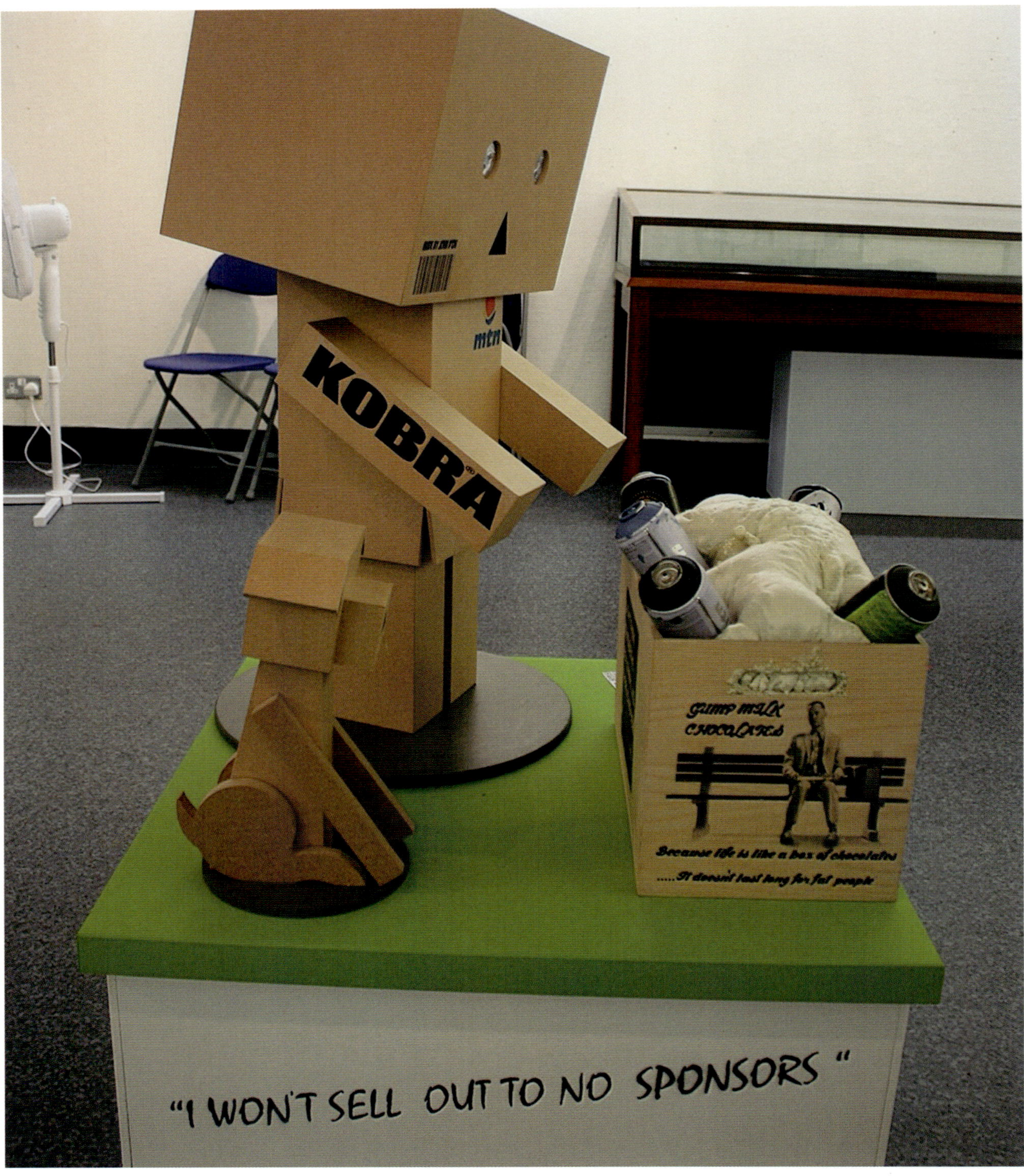

KOBRA
"I WON'T SELL OUT TO NO SPONSORS"

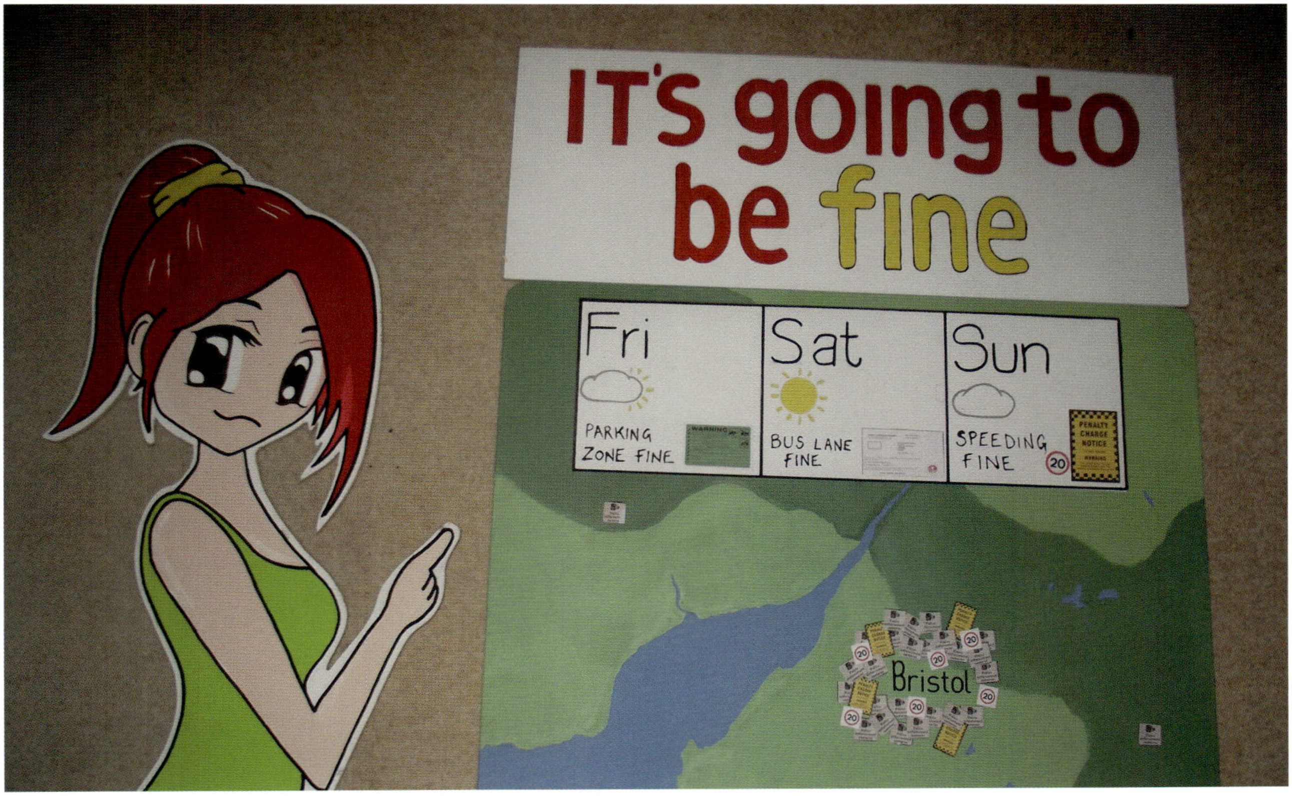

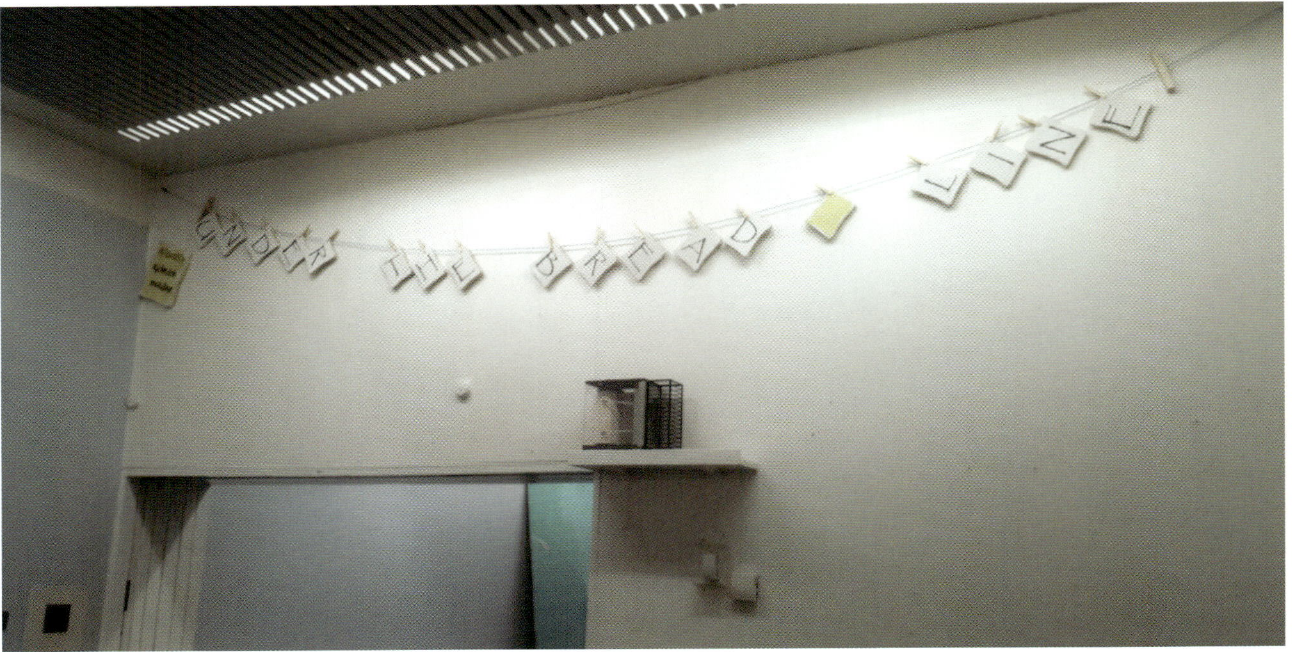

It's Going To Be Fine, a commentary on the increase of parking and travel fines by local councils in the UK, done on 17/04/2017

Under the Bread Line, a piece highlighting the increase of food poverty and the use of food banks in the country — something which has become increasingly normalised — at Gloucester Museum on 09/03/2018

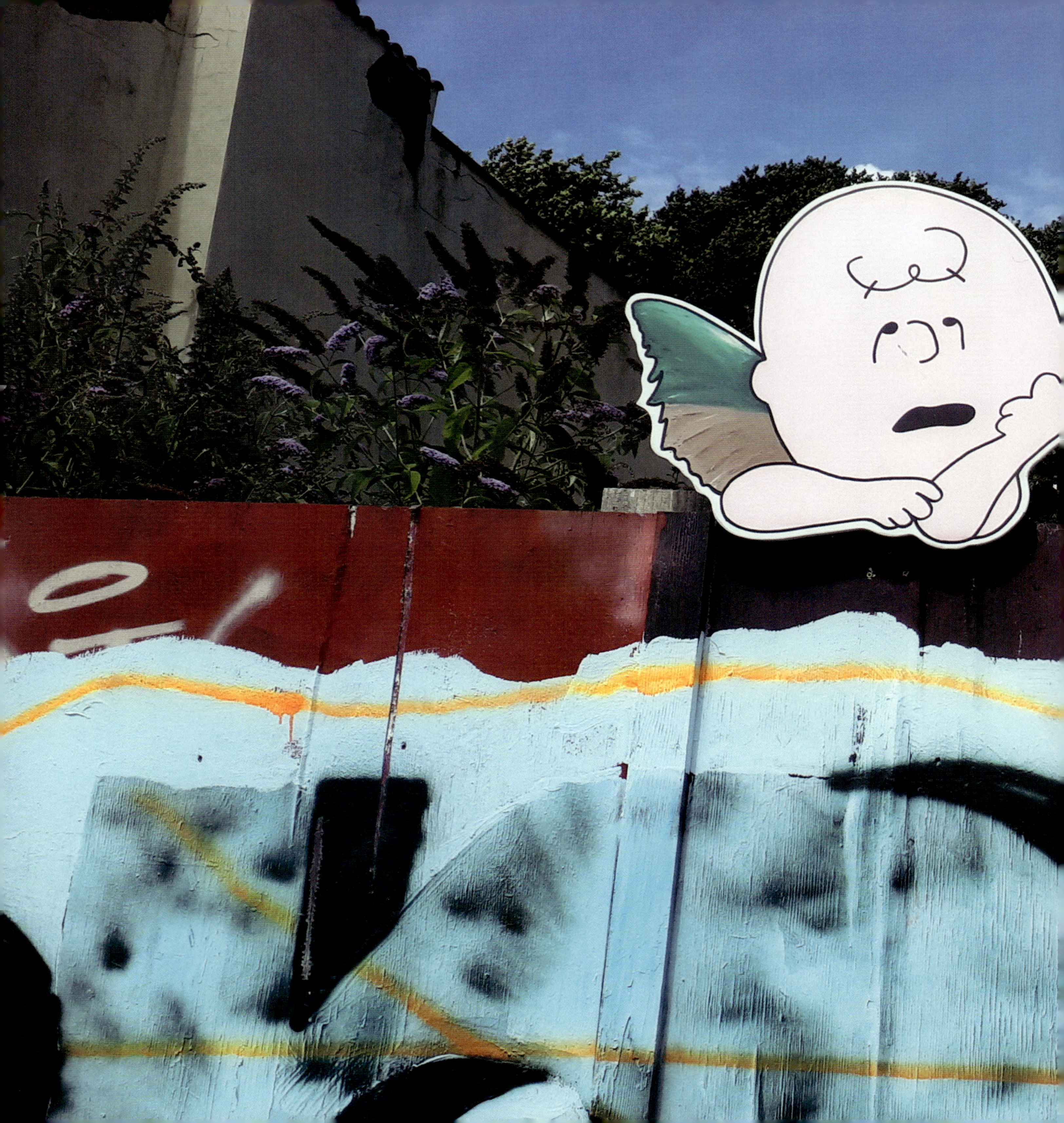

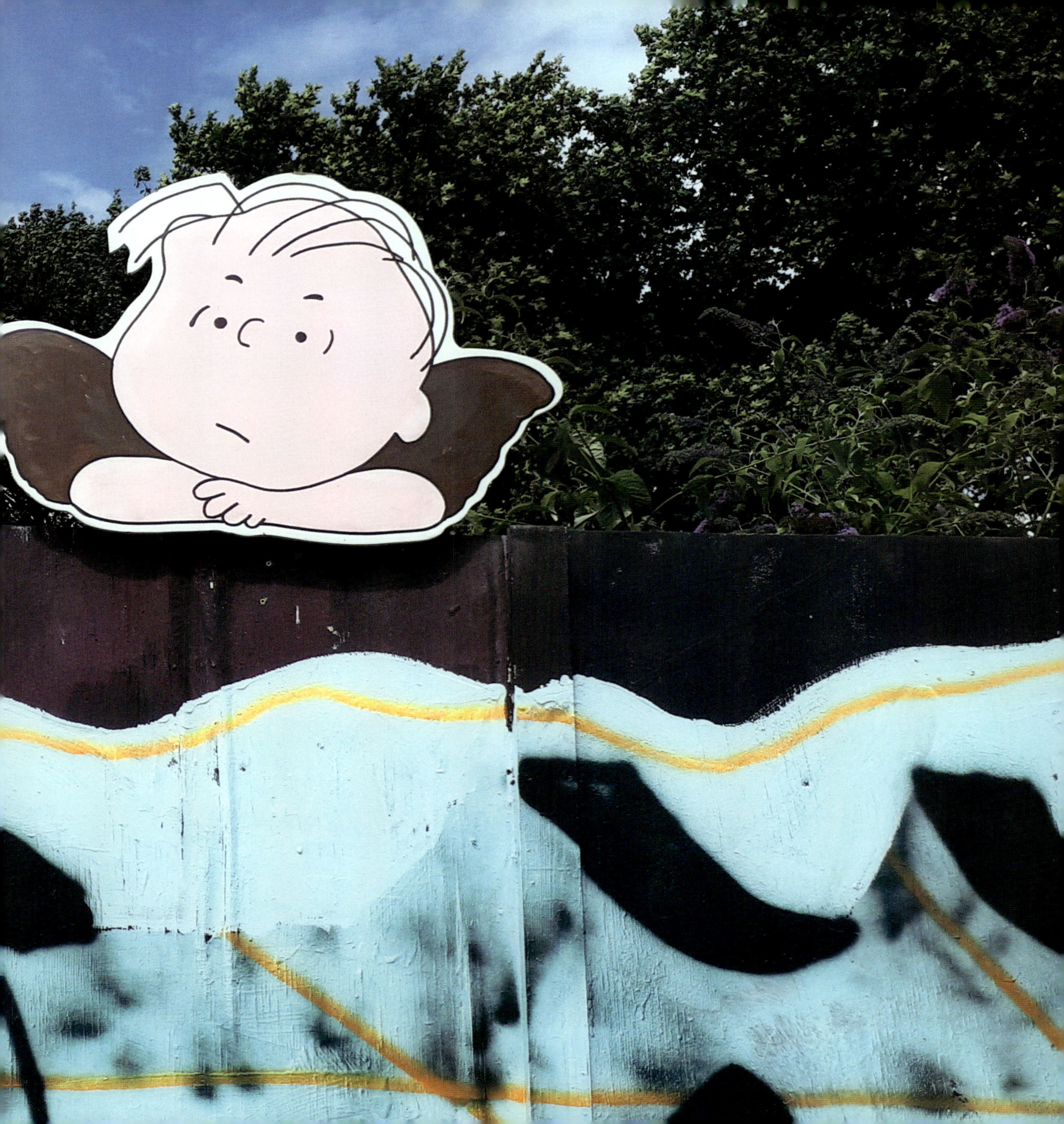

MAKING A MOLE HILL OUT OF A MOUNTAIN

(Installed on 08/02/2015)

This large mole was installed at the top of a mound of dirt at an undeveloped site by the Temple Way bridge in Bristol. It was probably one of my favourite installations. Having been on my mind every time I passed the mound of gravel for the last year or so, I finally got around to cutting and installing it. The timing also seemed right. The politics over fracking had become increasingly prevalent over the previous months, with the Conservative government voting to allow fracking for shale gas below national parks and other protected sites. This controversial industrial process uses huge amounts of water, can cause small earth tremors and potentially contaminates local groundwater with its carcinogenic chemicals, not to mention it can have a potentially negative-effect on house prices for the nearby residents. So putting the subterranean, digging animal at the top of a pile of industrial waste in unused, privately-owned land seemed to playfully speak to people's concerns and I would later do a series of different moles in mining gear to continue highlighting the issue.

The installation took two attempts. The first was simply to try and go through a hole in the fence but there were homeless people living in tents just inside and, with a few broken bottles and syringes littering the ground, I quickly decided to postpone the installation. Coming back the following day with a telescopic ladder, I abandoned all caution and just scaled the gates at the rear. What I didn't know was the mound of gravel was drastically steeper at the rear. The install was assisted by a friend of mine, the artist Rumple Stiltskin, who was equally as out of shape as I was. Every step was like being on a stair-climber at the gym as your feet would slide back as you pushed down into the gravel. Rumple was slightly in front of me carrying a couple of metal stays and a lump hammer. I followed behind dragging up the large wooden mole. As if reaching the peak of some mountain, we both had to stop and catch our breath once we reached the top of the heap.

There were great panoramic views of inner Bristol from the top, so fixing the mole in place here meant it would be seen by many pedestrians and commuters from a fair distance. Getting down was a lot quicker, but not necessarily easier. You had to try to stay upright and not fall the whole way. All we had to do then was jump the fence. I went over easily enough but Rumple wasn't so lucky, catching his trousers on a nail and tearing a massive hole. This left his arse exposed for all to see – not a pretty sight – especially for the passengers on the train he caught back to Swindon.

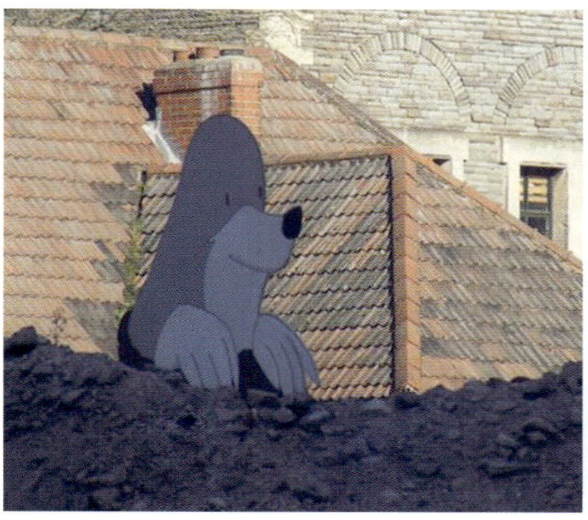

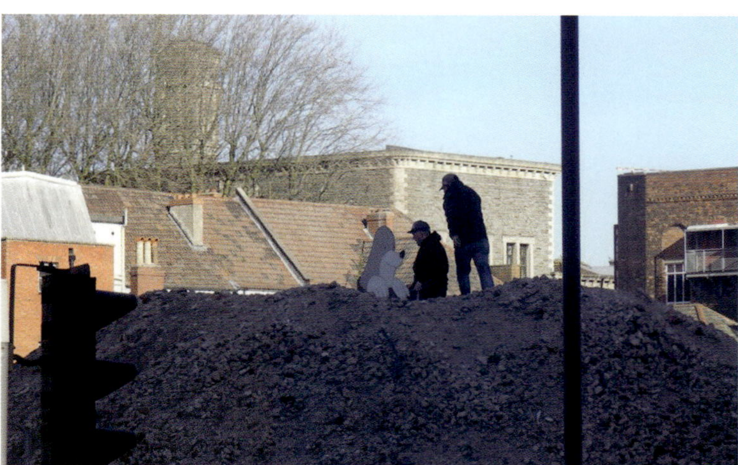

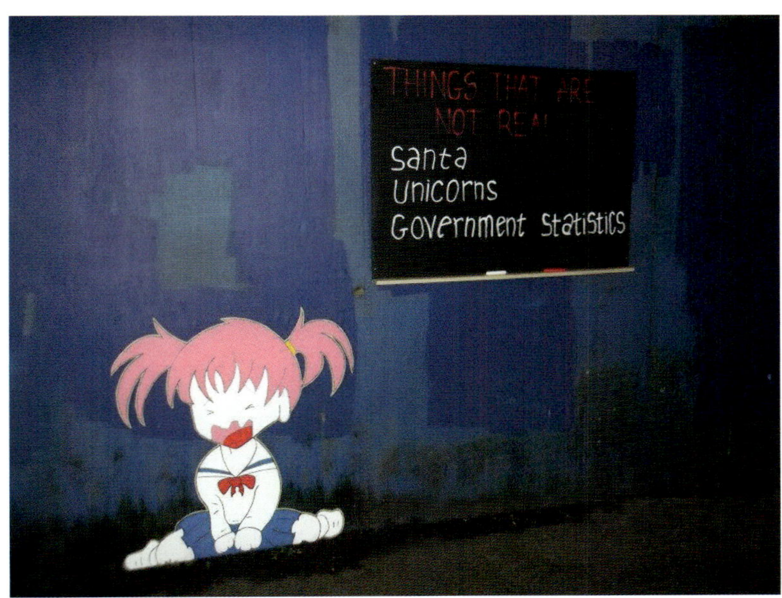

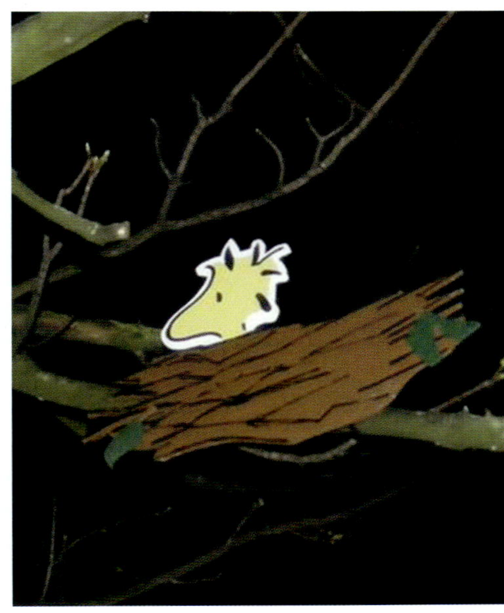

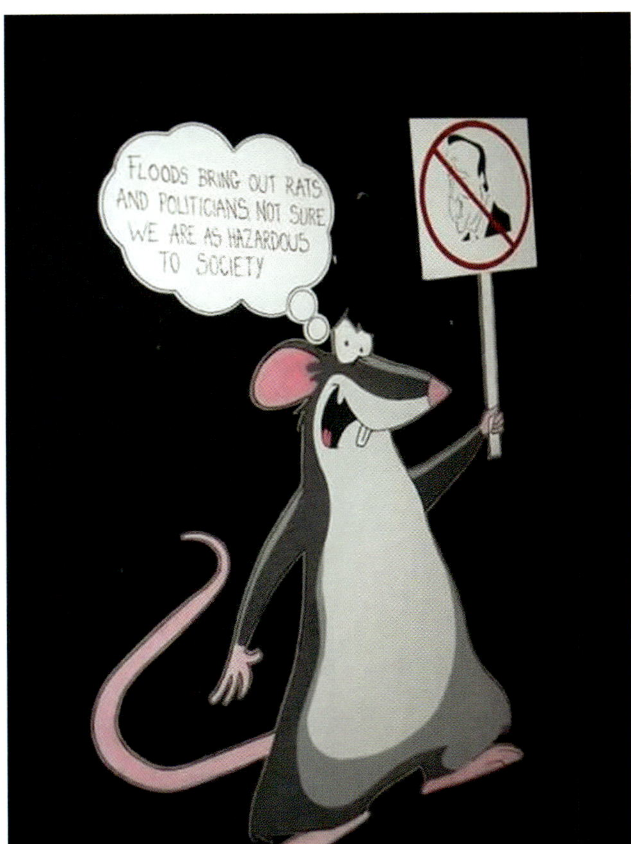

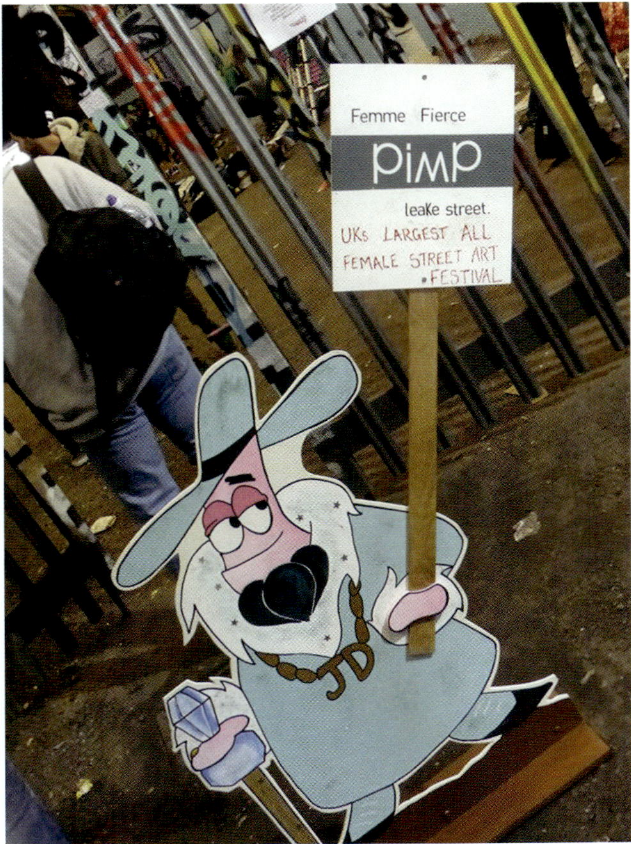

Government Statistics, a commentary on how seemingly objective and mathematical data can be made to support different political views, at Windmill Hill, Bristol on 02/03/2014

Woodstock outside the Tap and Barrel pub in Bristol on 02/04/2015

Floods, done in the Clifton Triangle, Bristol, as a response to the floods in 2015, where the lack of funding for defences and the absence of politicians or environmental agency staff on the scene were heavily-criticised

Pimp, done for an all female paint festival in Leake Street, London on 08/03/2015

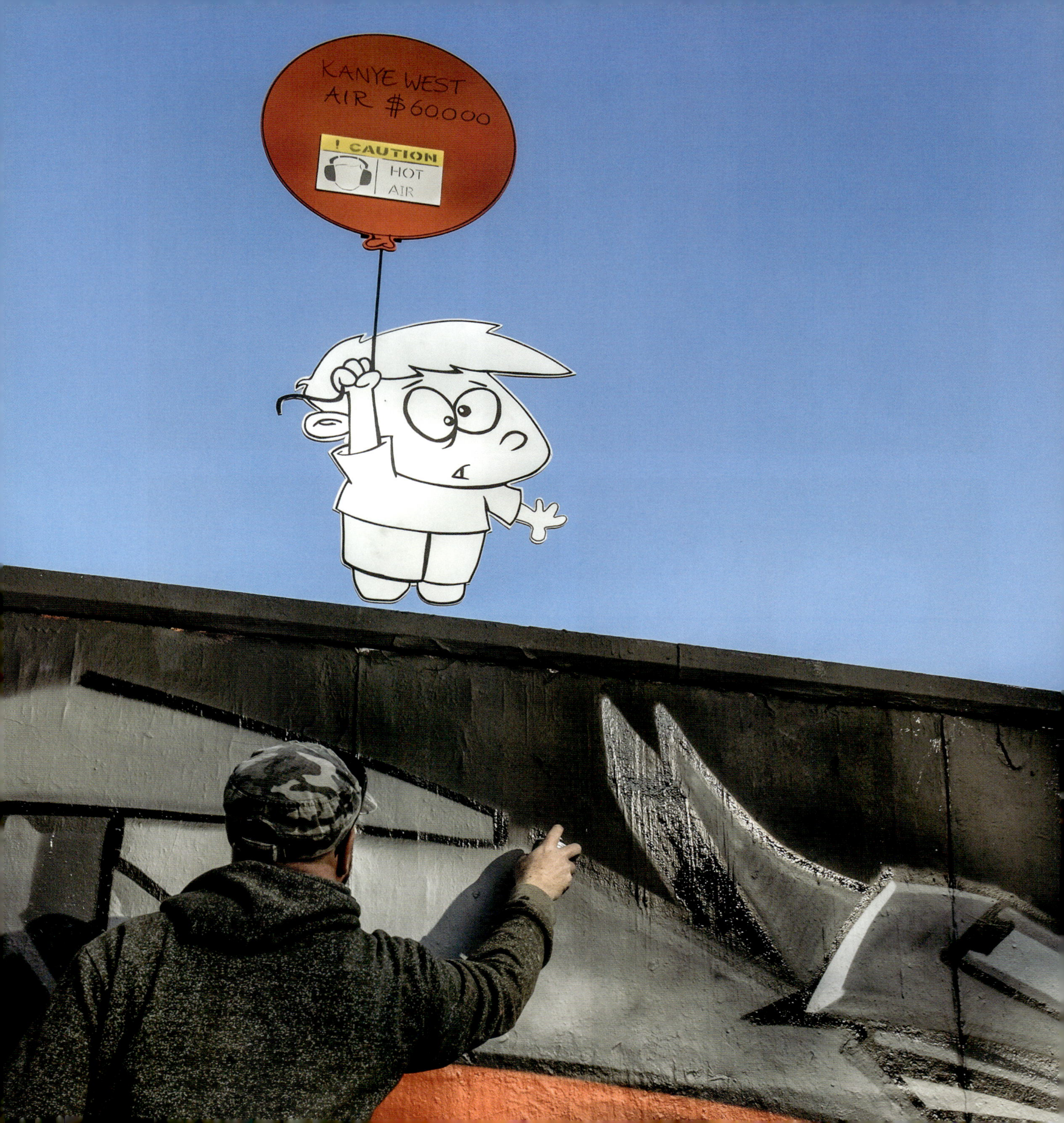

KANYE WEST
AIR $60000
! CAUTION
HOT
AIR

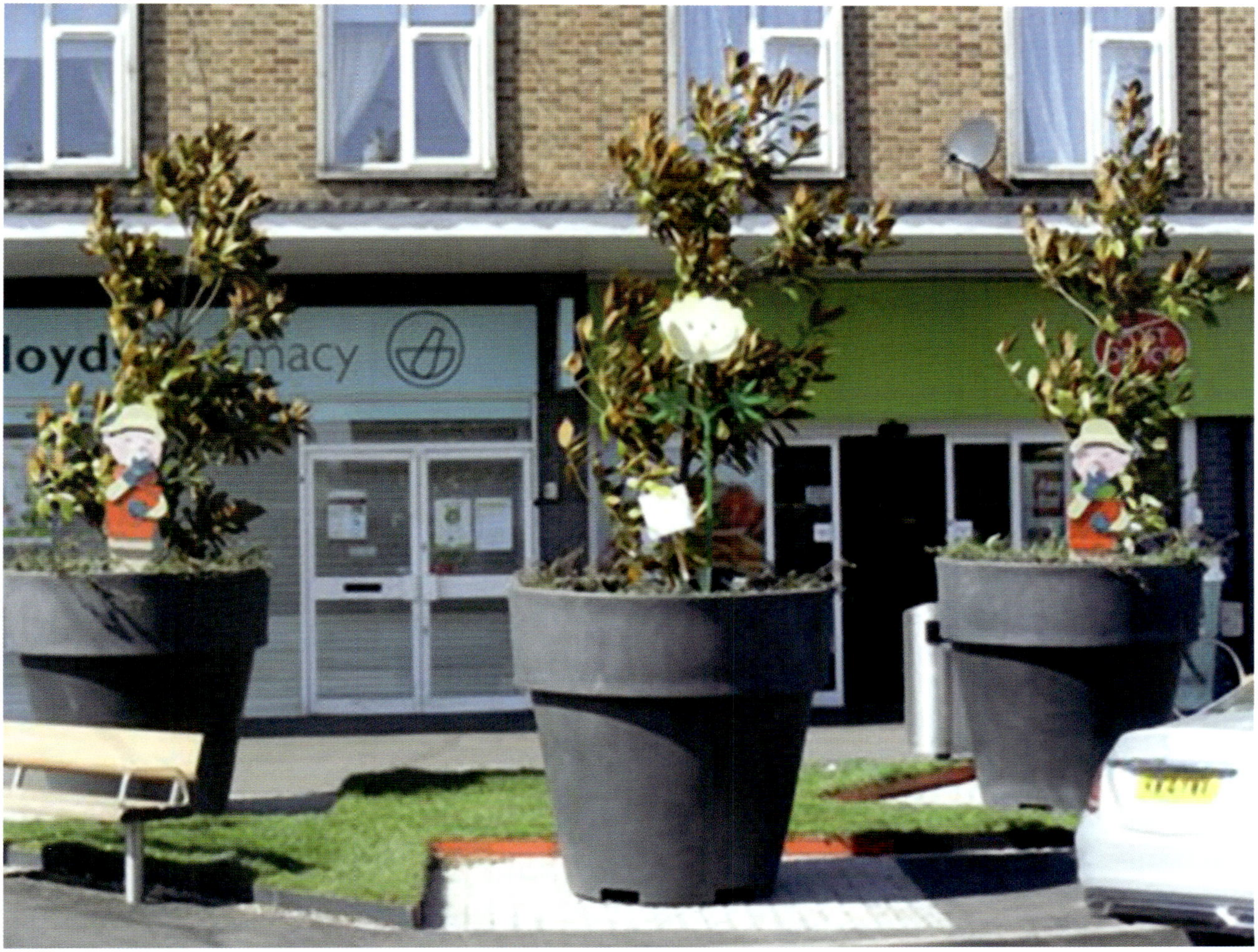

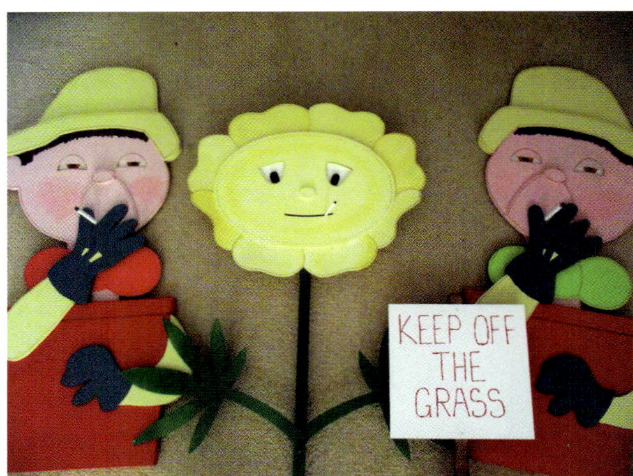

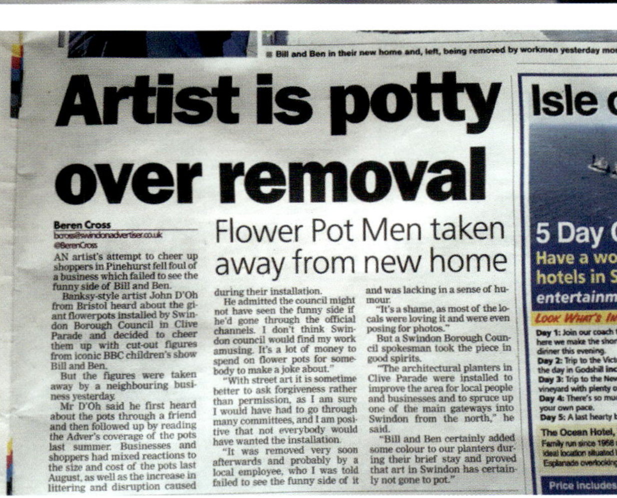

Bill and Ben in their new home and, left, being removed by workmen yesterda

Artist is potty over removal

Flower Pot Men taken away from new home

Beren Cross
bcross@swindonadvertiser.co.uk
@BerenCross

AN artist's attempt to cheer up shoppers in Pinehurst fell foul of a business which failed to see the funny side of Bill and Ben.

Banksy-style artist John D'Oh from Bristol heard about the giant flowerpots installed by Swindon Borough Council in Clive Parade and decided to cheer them up with cut-out figures from iconic BBC children's show Bill and Ben.

But the figures were taken away by a neighbouring business yesterday.

Mr D'Oh said he first heard about the pots through a friend and then followed up by reading the Adver's coverage of the pots last summer. Businesses and shoppers had mixed reactions to the size and cost of the pots last August, as well as the increase in littering and disruption caused during their installation.

He admitted the council might not have seen the funny side if he'd gone through the official channels. I don't think Swindon council would find my work amusing. It's a lot of money to spend on flower pots for somebody to make a joke about."

"With street art it is sometime better to ask forgiveness rather than permission, as I am sure I would have had to go through many committees, and I am positive that not everybody would have wanted the installation.

"It was removed very soon afterwards and probably by a local employee, who I was told failed to see the funny side of it and was lacking in a sense of humour.

"It's a shame, as most of the locals were loving it and were even posing for photos."

But a Swindon Borough Council spokesman took the piece in good spirits.

"The architectural planters in Clive Parade were installed to improve the area for local people and businesses and to spruce up one of the main gateways into Swindon from the north," he said.

"Bill and Ben certainly added some colour to our planters during their brief stay and proved that art in Swindon has certainly not gone to pot."

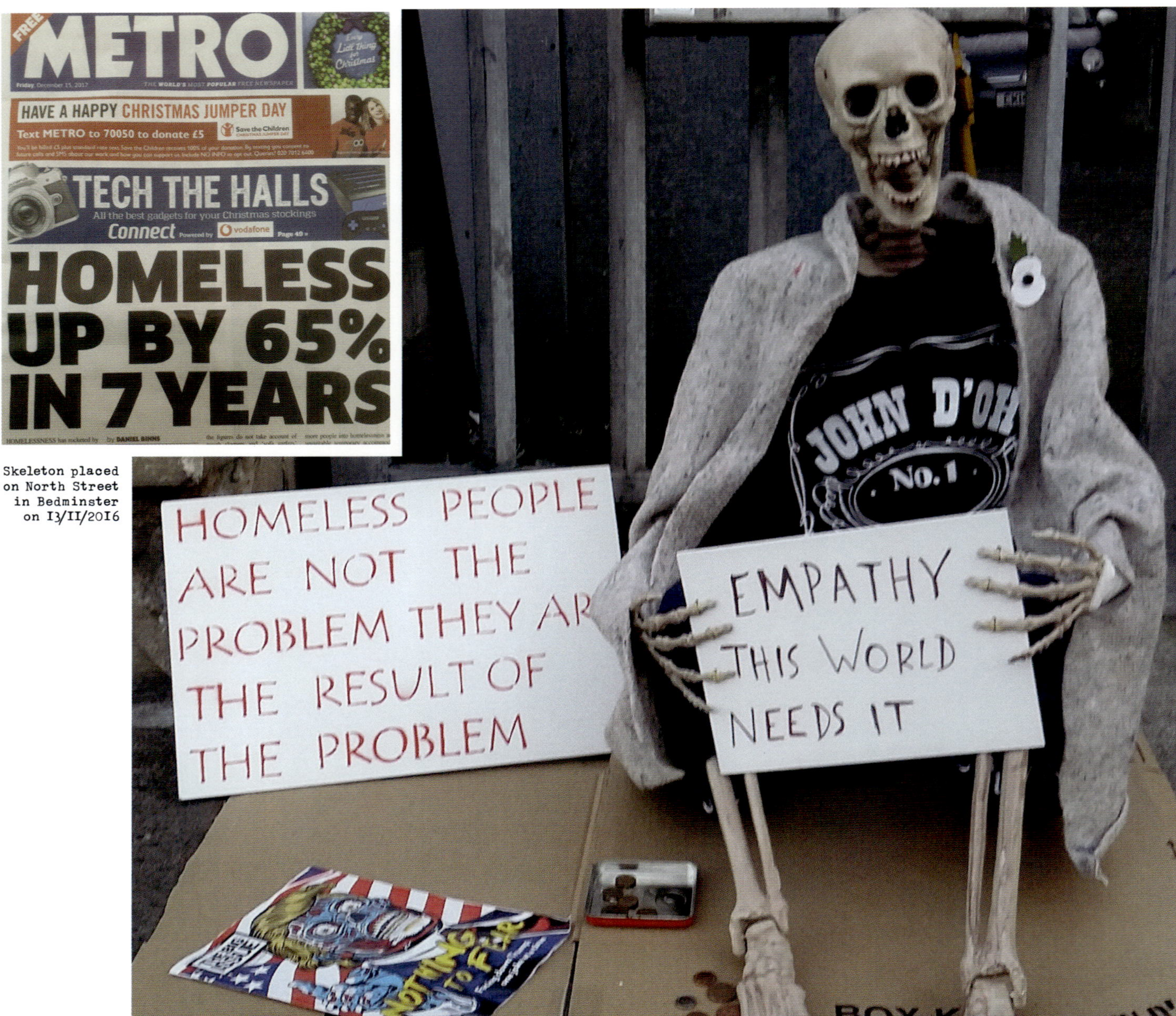

Skeleton placed
on North Street
in Bedminster
on 13/11/2016

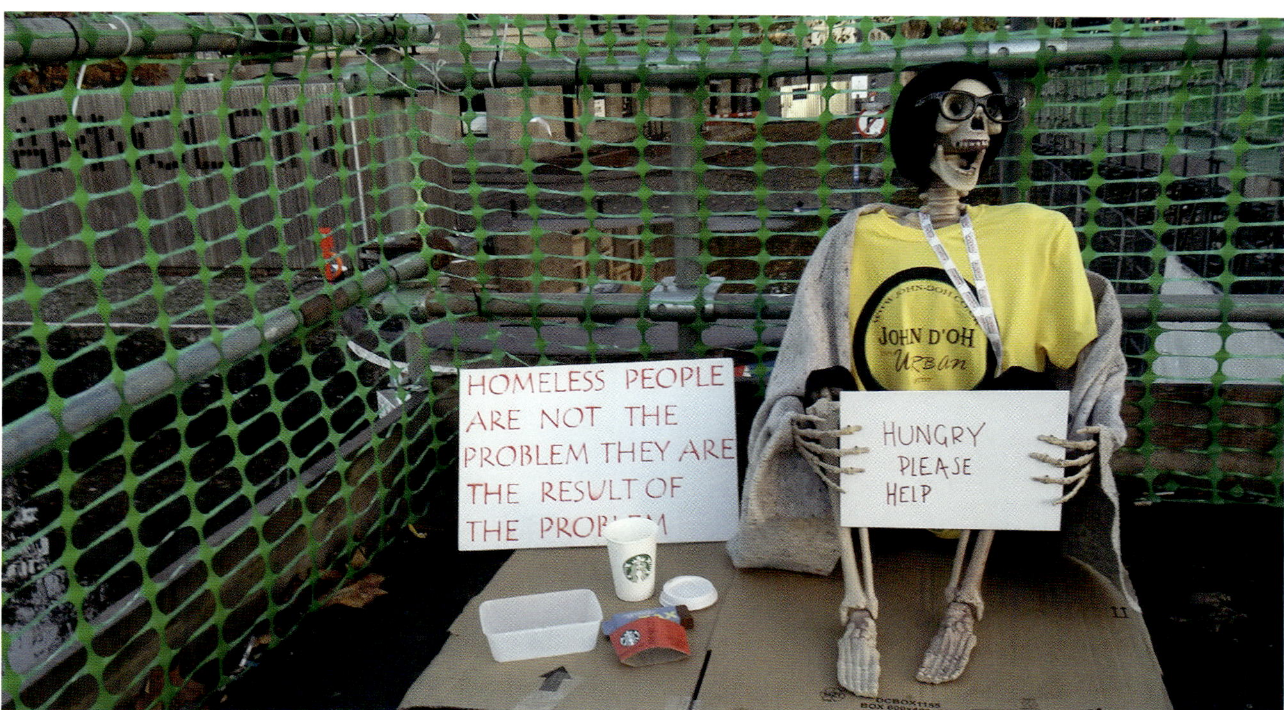

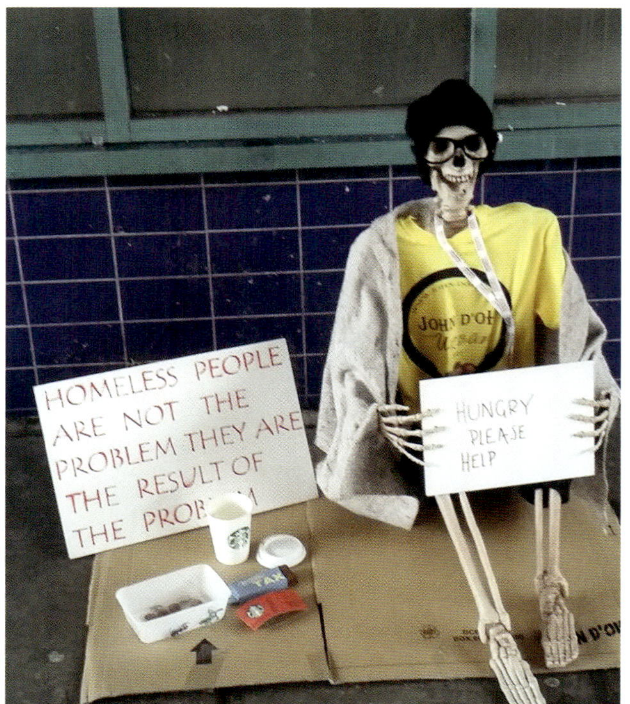

HOMELESS SKELETONS

"Like slavery and apartheid, poverty is not natural," said Nelson Mandela. "It is man-made and it can be overcome and eradicated by the actions of human beings." With the rising number of homeless people sleeping rough on the streets, it is sad to see the only government initiative is to install 'defensive architecture'. This may sound like something used to protect people against terrorists or violent criminals, but is actually the technical term to describe things such as homeless spikes and anti-homeless benches.

Instead of trying to solve the problem at the causal or systemic level, local authorities try to address the symptomatic and visual consequences of misgovernment by moving the increasing number of homeless out of sight. In fact, such techniques can be seen as a way of dehumanising the homeless, with the spikes used to prevent people sleeping in doorways or under shelters being comparable to the pigeon spikes used as a kind

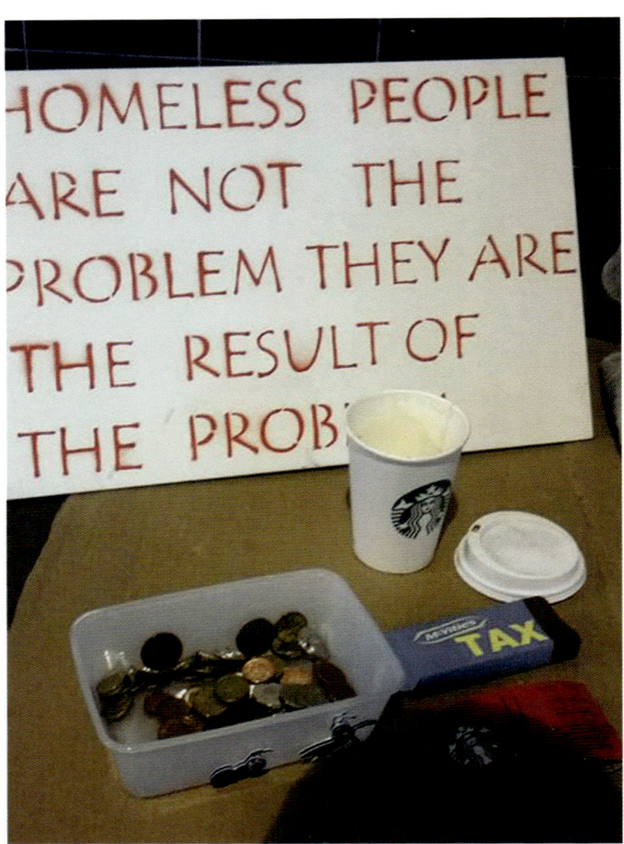

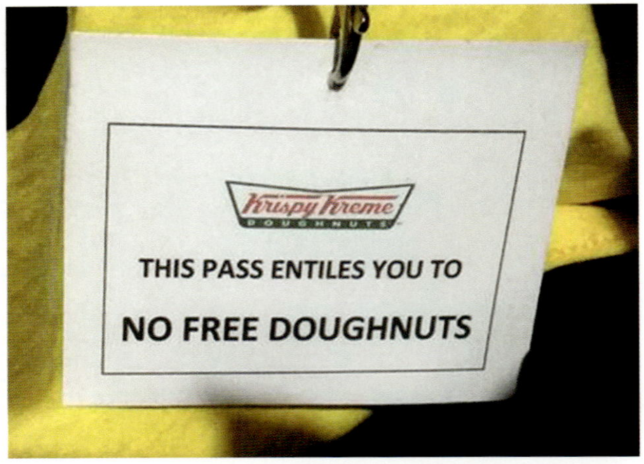

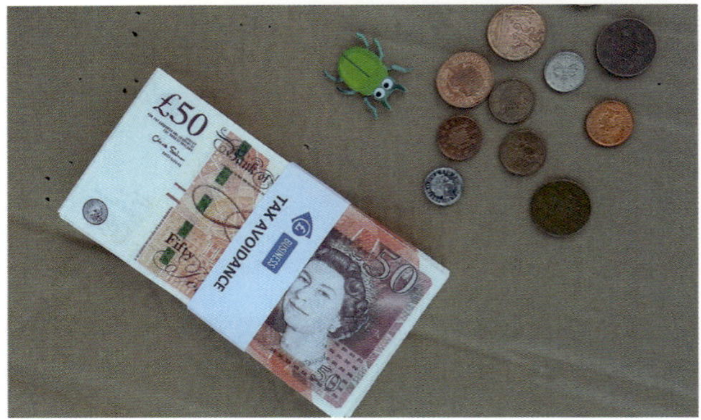

of pest control. With the budget for mental health and social care being increasingly cut and housing or rental costs soaring across the country, the government is adding to the problem or simply allowing it to intensify. It is a common sight to see people walking straight past the begging homeless with an overly expensive cup of Starbucks coffee in their hands. If companies like Starbucks paid the proper amount of tax instead of using loopholes and offshore accounts or if people spent less on unnecessary luxuries and more on charitable causes, society could be improved relatively quickly.

This is why I have used a range of branded items or big wedges of cash as props to comment on the financial or behavioural actions of some large companies. A Starbucks cup refers to how the company reportedly paid just £8.6m in corporation tax in the UK over the previous 14 years and then nothing in the final four years, despite sales of £400m that year alone.

The Krispy Kreme pass entitling you "to NO free donuts" referred to a scandal in which the company was shown to bin thousands of unsold products which many critics and newspapers felt should have been given to the homeless. I placed the original one in London when I attended an event at the Westbank Gallery but decided not to leave him in London due to a risk of a £5,000 fine for flytipping, although perhaps such a scandal might have helped comment on how homeless human beings are being treated as social detritus by the majority of people. Instead I took my chances in Bristol, where I put three skeletons in various locations around the city.

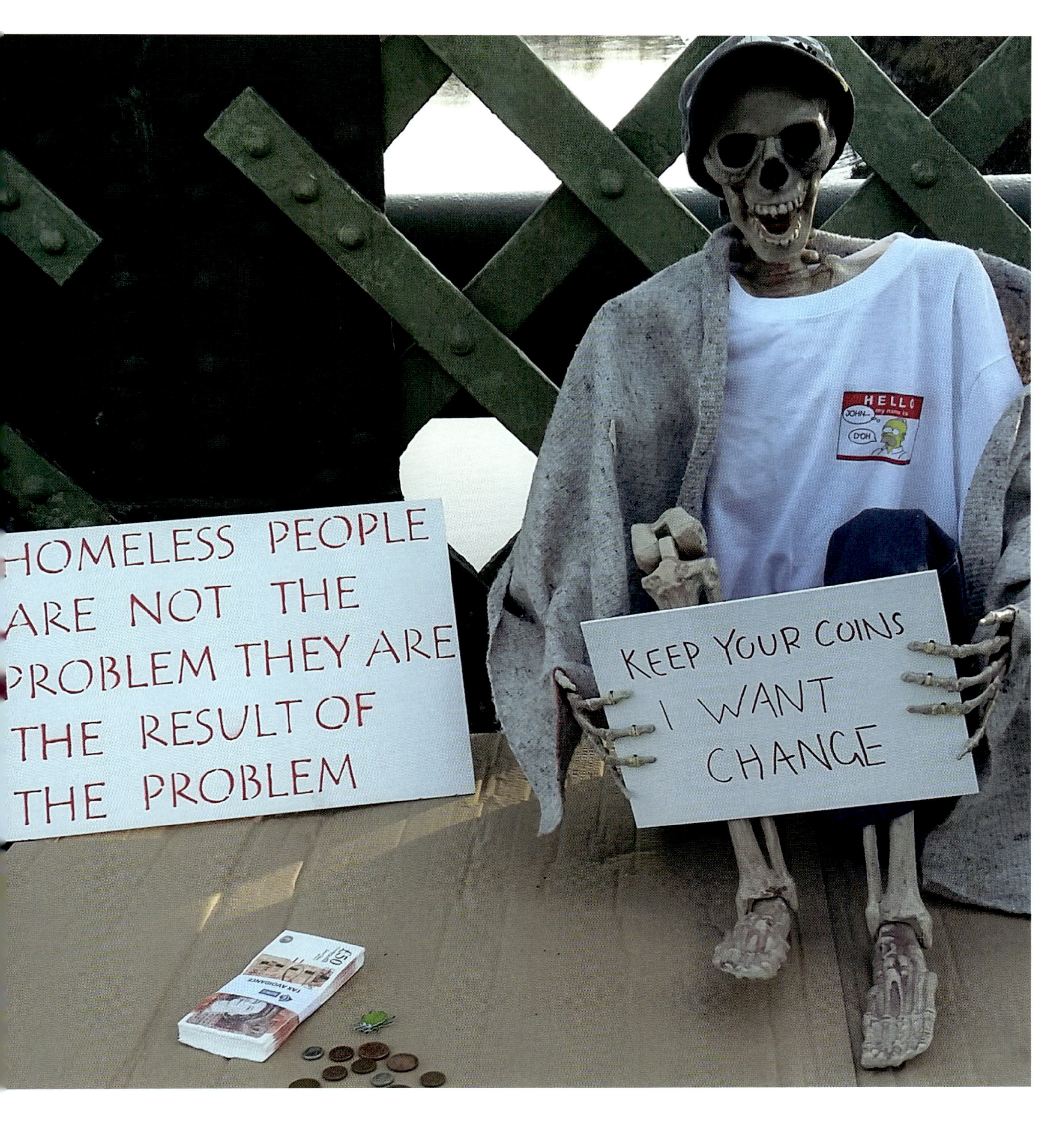

HOMELESS PEOPLE ARE NOT THE PROBLEM THEY ARE THE RESULT OF THE PROBLEM
KEEP YOUR COINS I WANT CHANGE
HELLO my name is
JOHN...
D'OH

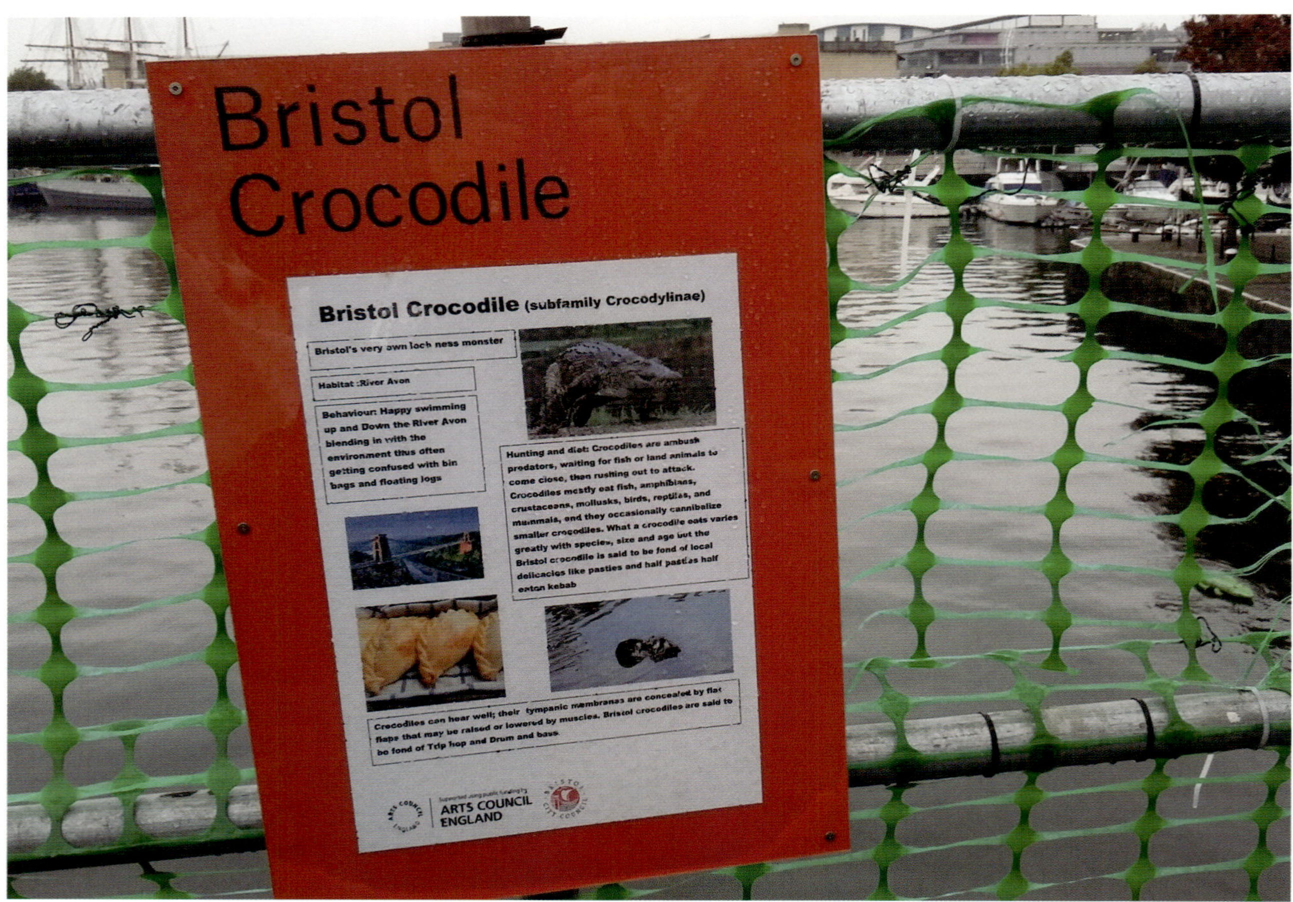

BRISTOL CROCODILE

In this age of post-truth and conspiracy politics, it is not surprising that from 2014 onwards headlines in major national newspapers repeatedly appeared with reports on sightings, photographs and video footage about a wild, mysterious crocodile swimming in Bristol waterways. In response to the media hysteria, I decided to do what the *Bristol Observer* called "a jokey art installation" and placed an inflatable green crocodile in the water between the Arnolfini and M Shed, with mock-up museum-style information boards attached around the Harbourside and Prince Street Bridge. These signs offered commuters pseudo-biological information about the animal, emphasising its local and urban characteristics, such as enjoying delicacies such as "half-eaten kebab" and being attracted to the sounds of "trip-hop and drum and bass". Instead of eye-witnesses mistaking pollution and rubbish for an animal, as they had been accused of, my signs declared that "getting confused with bin bags" was a camouflage tactic that the animal used to blend in with its "natural" environment.

It is perhaps not surprising that the reported sightings of the so-called 'Bristol Crocodile' occurred during Bristol's year as the European Green Capital, when there was a city-wide focus on sustainable living and the Green Party replaced the Liberal Democrats as the third largest party on Bristol City Council. Often, these sightings of incongruous animals or strange monsters in Western, urban locations reflect a modern environmental anxiety, guiltily repopulating the citified world with animals who have apparently resisted man-made extinctions or nostalgically returning the world to a wild, magical or more natural state, albeit from the comfort of home and without scientific expertise. So it seemed appropriate to use a plastic, inflatable beach toy for my so-called "croc shock for commuters", as this imaginary animal can be seen as a shameful fantasy of and a guilty response to our romantically touristic and self-consciously exploitative relationship to nature in the contemporary world.

Placing my floating art between two contemporary museums with posters claiming ironically that my crocodile was "supported by the Arts Council of England and Bristol City Council" was a jocular critique of how funds for environmentally-focused businesses and arts were suddenly being prioritised as part of the Green Capital award. However, in a case of life imitating art, it was announced four months later in March 2017 that the Creative Seed Fund of Bristol City Council would give a £3,000 grant to an art project that aimed to create a life-sized model of the elusive Bristol Crocodile. People across the city would come together to manufacture the legendary beast out of wire, papier-mâché and crochet, with the completed animal going on display at locations around the city docks.

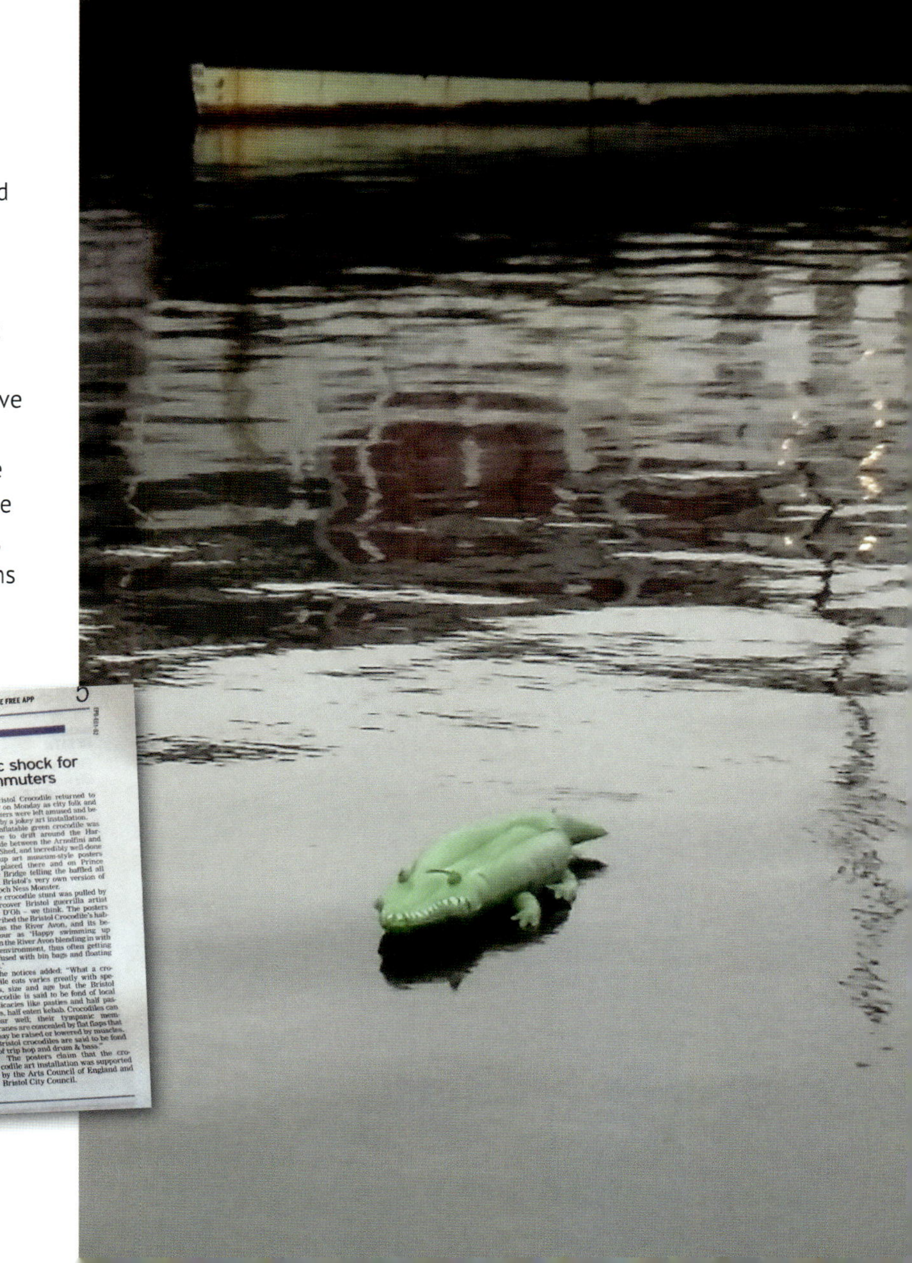

Tuesday, October 25, 2016

GET THE BRISTOL POST ON IPAD, IPHONE AND ANDROID   DOWNLOAD THE FREE APP

ART

Croc shock for commuters

THE Bristol Crocodile returned to the city on Monday as city folk and commuters were left amused and bemused by a jokey art installation.

An inflatable green crocodile was set free to drift around the Harbourside between the Arnolfini and the M Shed, and incredibly well-done mock-up art museum-style posters were placed there and on Prince Street Bridge telling the baffled all about Bristol's very own version of the Loch Ness Monster.

The crocodile stunt was pulled by undercover Bristol guerrilla artist John D'Oh – we think. The posters described the Bristol Crocodile's habitat as the River Avon, and its behaviour as "Happy swimming up down the River Avon blending in with the environment, thus often getting confused with bin bags and floating logs."

The notices added: "What a crocodile eats varies greatly with species, size and age but the Bristol crocodile is said to be fond of local delicacies like pasties and half pasties, half eaten kebab. Crocodiles can hear well, their tympanic membranes are concealed by flat flaps that may be raised or lowered by muscles. Bristol crocodiles are said to be fond of trip hop and drum & bass."

The posters claim that the crocodile art installation was supported by the Arts Council of England and Bristol City Council.

● The Bristol Crocodile art installation by John D'oh

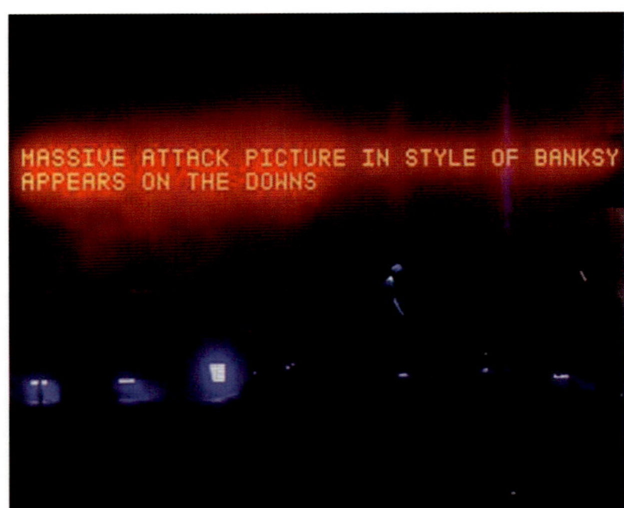

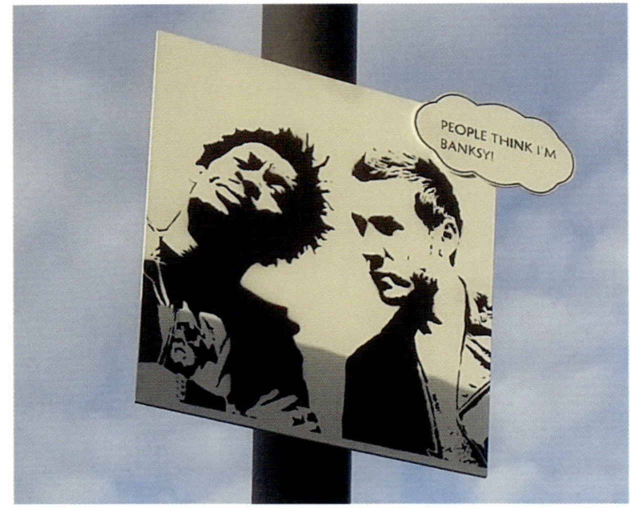

MASSIVE ATTACK AND PEOPLE THINK I'M BANKSY

(Installed on 02/09/2016 at the Clifton Downs)

This one was a really quick turnaround – even for me. News broke that Robert '3D' Del Naja, an artist, musician and founding member of the band Massive Attack, was allegedly Banksy. It was claimed that a man called Craig Williams had gone through Massive Attack tour dates and correlated them to the locations and times when Banksy artwork appeared. Naturally, it became global news overnight and the fake news industry went into overdrive. All this controversy occurred just a couple of days before the band was scheduled to play their first Bristol gig in 12 years in September 2016. So, being both a Bristolian and a Massive Attack fan, I decided to have a bit of fun with the article.

I wanted to get something up near the venue but I knew it wasn't going to be easy, especially when a festival like that is basically a massive field without many spaces to paint on. Adapting to the situation, I thought I would use lampposts. People use the visibility provided by street lighting to make their way safely home, making lampposts focal points during the evening or night and therefore useful, prominent locations to put up artwork. I made wooden plaques saying "People Think I'm Banksy" and attached them with cable ties as high up on the street lights as I could get. The artwork seemed very popular and was featured in the *Bristol Post* and people where getting their photos taken underneath them even in the rain.

I was lucky enough to attend the Massive Attack concert and have VIP access. The concert was spectacular and then, to my surprise, in big red lights 'MASSIVE ATTACK PICTURE IN THE STYLE OF BANKSY APPEARS ON THE DOWNS' appears on the stage as part of the performance. I think that is the closest I have ever come to having my name in lights. I was stood in the pouring rain, absolutely soaked and completely anonymous, but smiling from ear to ear knowing that I was the person who did that.

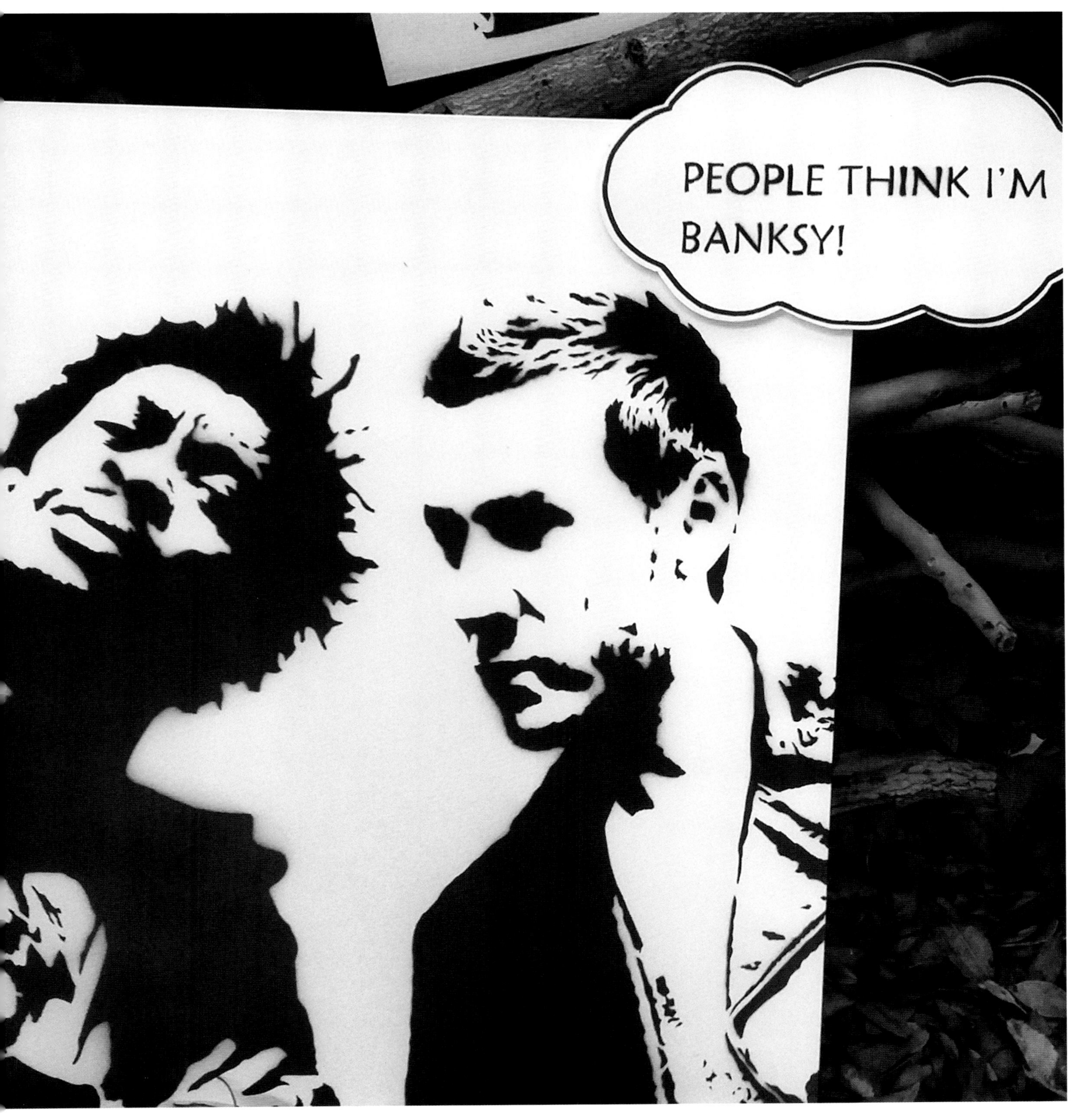

PEOPLE THINK I'M BANKSY!

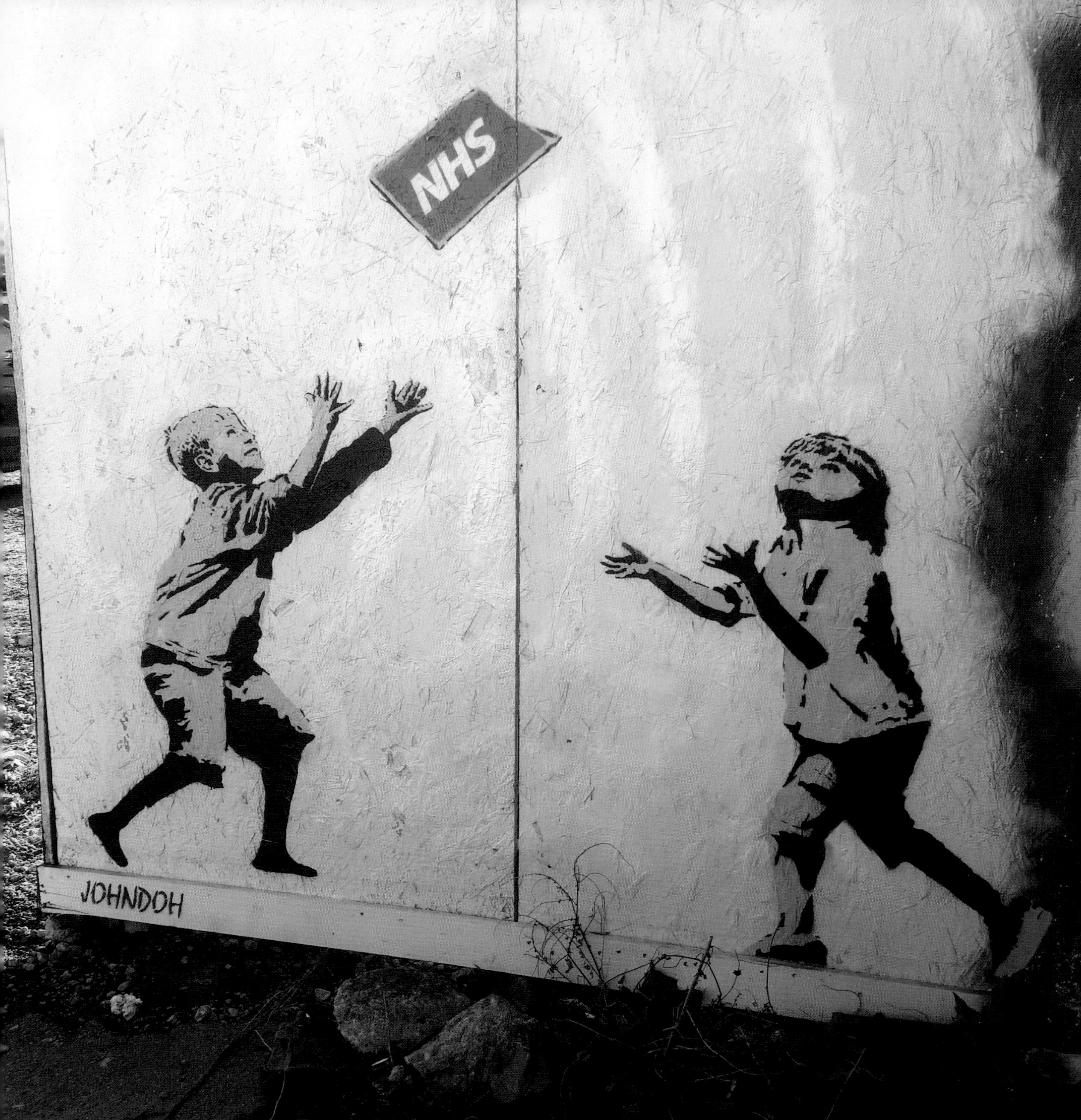

NHS
JOHNDOH

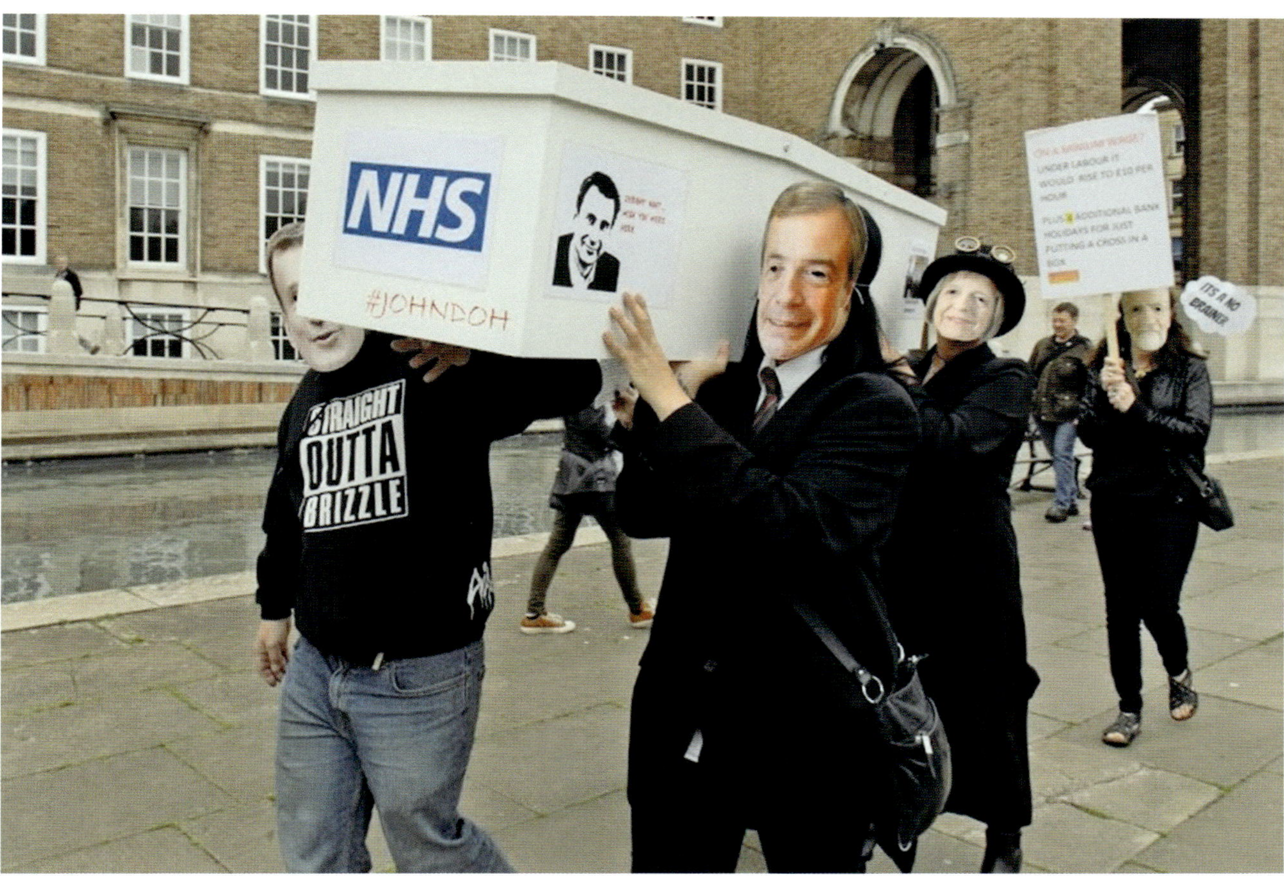

THE NATIONAL HEALTH SERVICE

The National Health Service is something you will see frequently come up in my art because it is something I feel very strongly and passionately about. This includes pieces of installation art, such as the skeleton placed in Thornbury in response to what the *Thornbury Gazette* called "unthinkable" measures and cuts planned to services in South Gloucestershire. In fact, the local paper described my conscious-raising piece as "a visual protest against the plans" where "concerns have been raised over the potential for selling off assets". But I have also occasionally used performance art and protest theatre, like when I organised a group of friends to wear masks of well-known political figures and carry a self-built 'NHS' coffin during a protest march, in order to raise awareness and gather support for what has previously been called 'one of the greatest achievements of civilisation', the NHS.

I just find it increasingly difficult watching the National Health Service fail through a lack of investment and through the large contracts being given out to people who are profit-orientated. One well-known individual getting increasingly involved in the NHS is Richard Branson, whose Virgin Trains East Coast contract was terminated three years early and could potentially cost taxpayers hundreds of millions pounds. Consequently, I find it highly worrying and suspicious

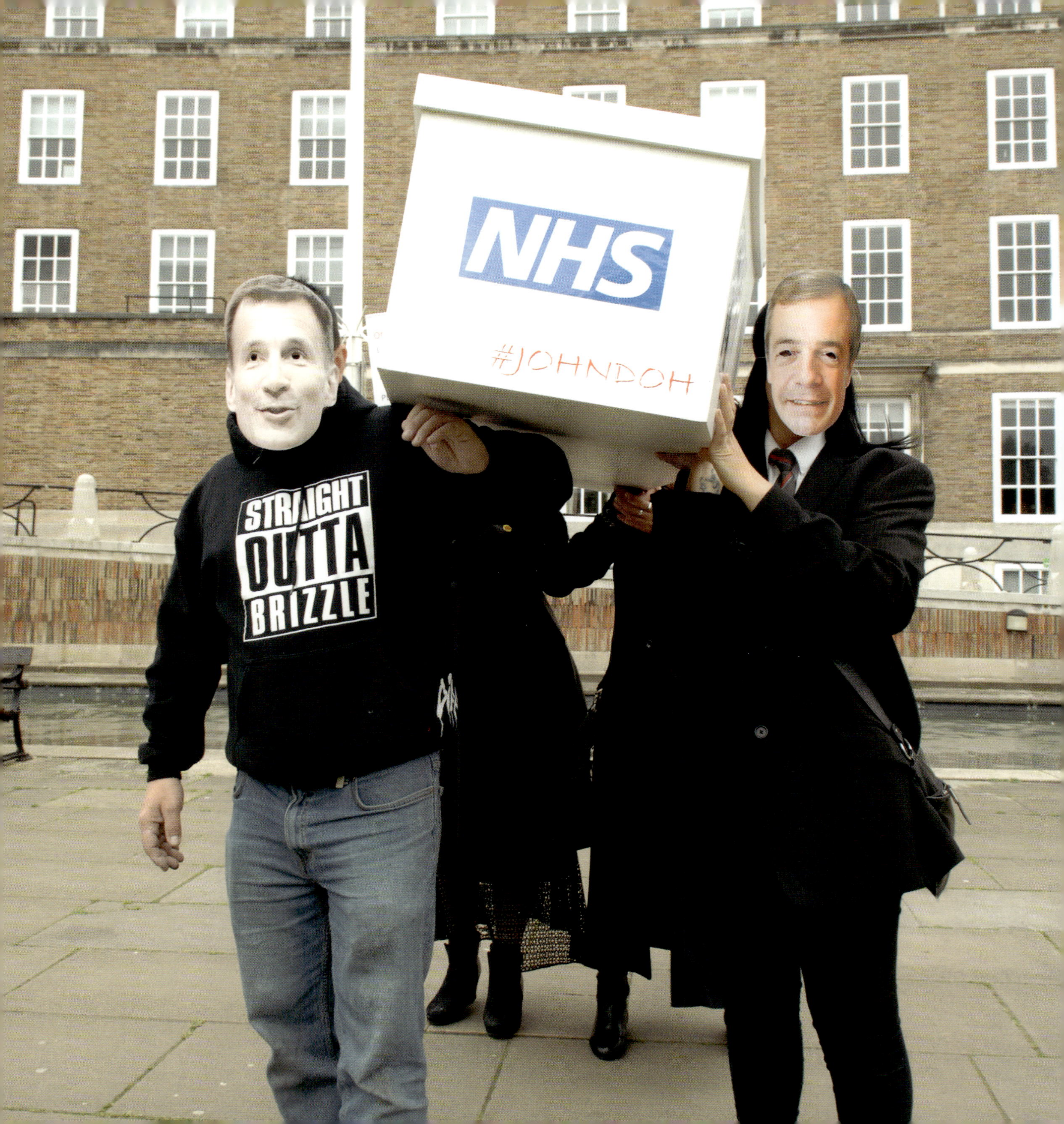

NHS
#JOHNDOH
STRAIGHT
OUTTA
BRIZZLE

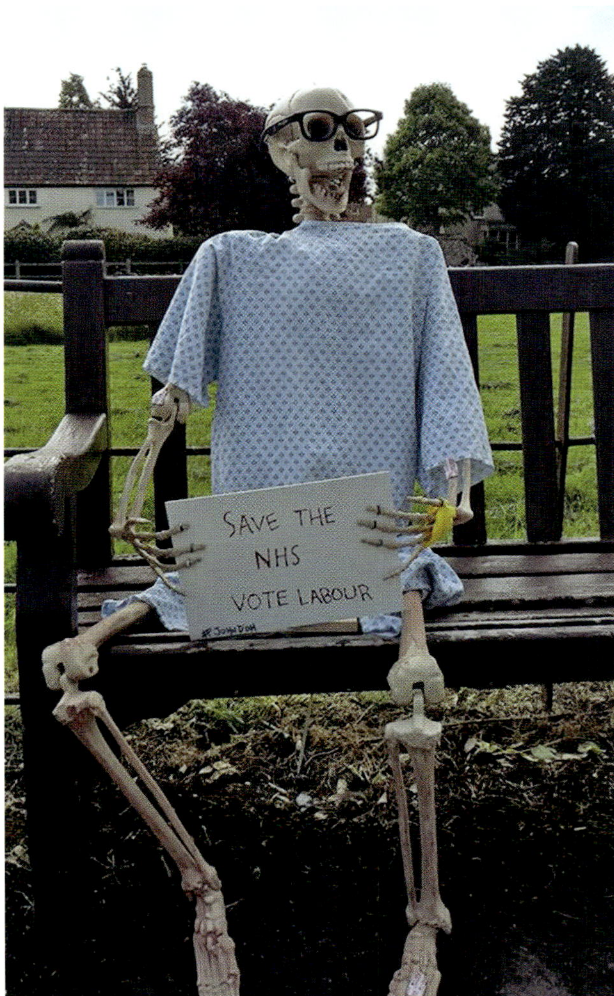

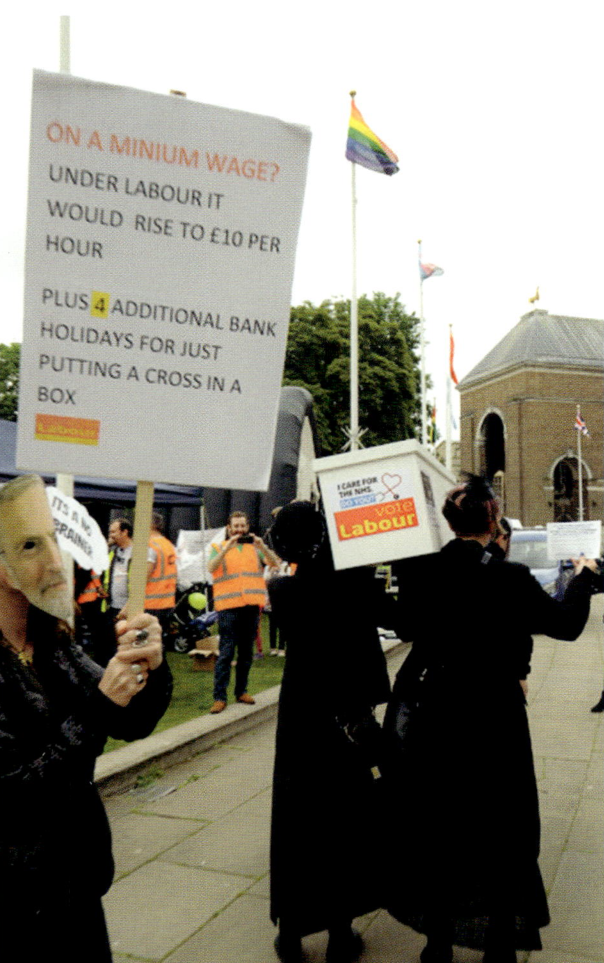

That page:
College Green
in Bristol

This page:
Skeleton on
a Bench in
Thornbury,
Bristol

that Virgin Care is now being rewarded £1bn of NHS contracts. Surprisingly, hardly any of our newspapers picked up on it. Instead, it was all sneaked in the back door while we read about the antics of Donald Trump during the American election. The NHS was created out of the ideal that good healthcare should be available to all, regardless of wealth, yet we are now heading away from this goal as we head towards a US-style insurance system.

To top it all off, the man in charge is Jeremy Hunt. Or, perhaps it would be more accurate to call him a figurehead, as "in charge" makes him sound competent. Appointed as Health Secretary back in 2012, he has continued to run the service into the ground. During Theresa May's cabinet reshuffle there was a lot of rumour and expectation that he was going to be demoted from the position, but, to everybody's disbelief, he got promoted to Secretary of State for Health… AND Social Care. It helps if you are going to cause so much damage nationally to have one of the safest local constituencies. Unsurprisingly, you might see him pop up from time to time in a lot of my work.

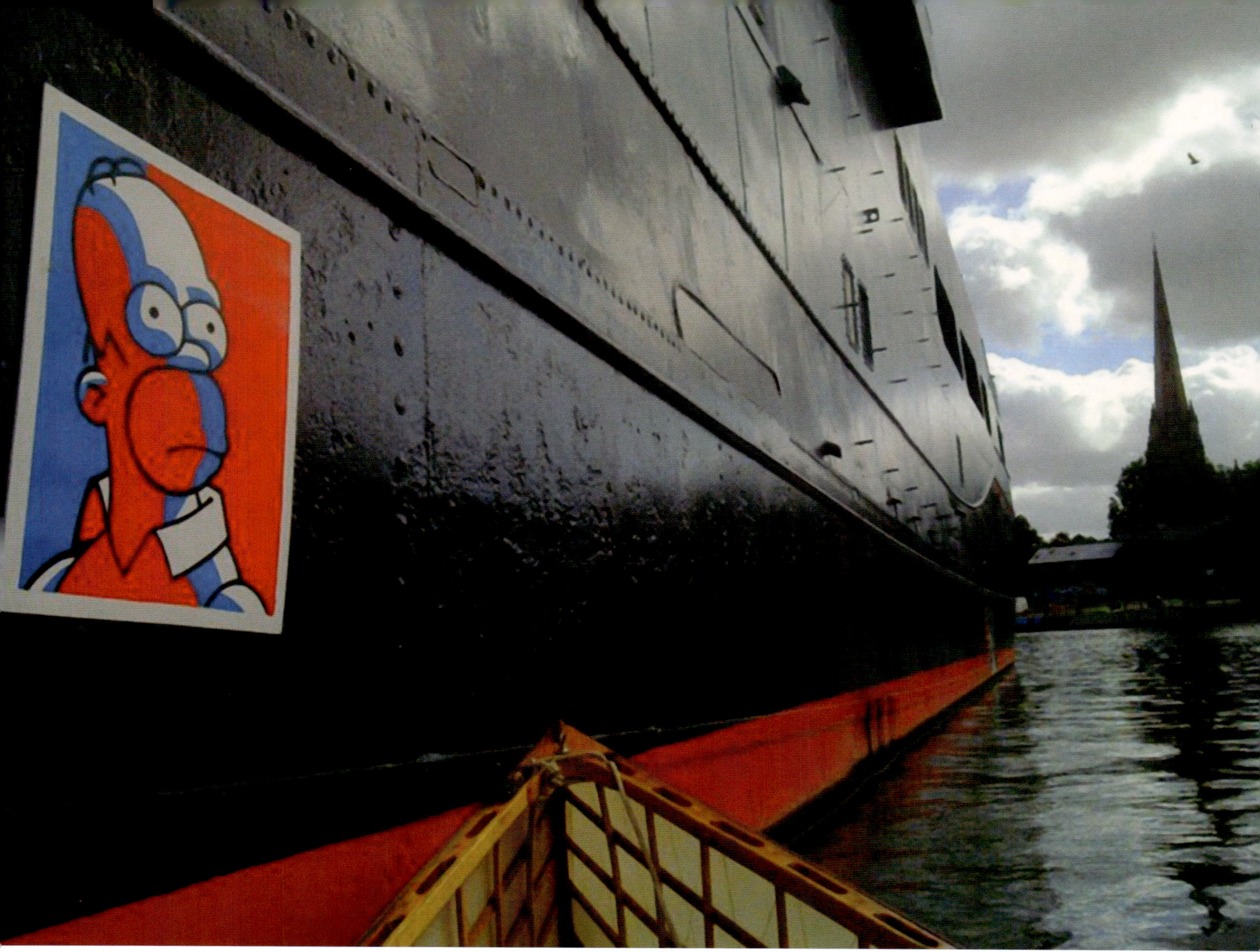

THEKLA

The Thekla is a well-known cargo ship which was brought to Bristol by novelist Ki Longfellow and has been a part of the Bristol Docks since 1983.

Banksy first tagged the Thekla in 2003 which was painted over by the harbourmaster according to the artist. This upset the club and they threatened to sue.

Banksy later went back and replaced it with the *Grim Reaper*. In 2014 the ship went into Abel's Shipyard in Albion Dockside for maintenance and whilst it was in there the *Reaper* was cut out of its steel hull. Years of deterioration meant that the piece required conservation and it was moved to a new home at M Shed museum,

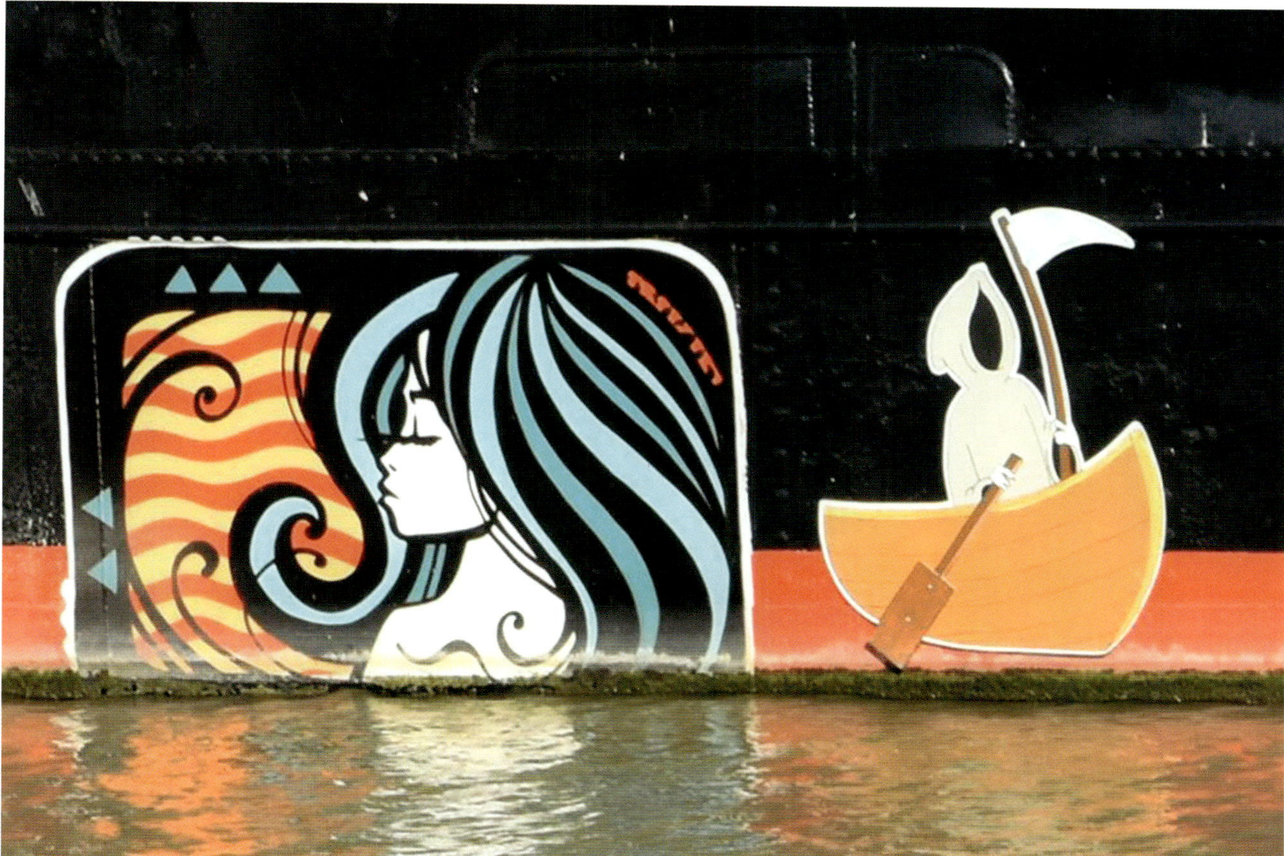

Not Quite Banksy, the Reaper I attached to the Thekla using high-powered magnets

where it is on display for free to the general public. While it was in dry dock fellow Bristol graffiti artist Inkie painted some art where the *Reaper* had been and the ship was then returned to the docks.

As I missed the original, I thought it would be fun to have a go at putting the *Reaper* back on the ship. So I painted a cut-out in my own personal style and, not wanting to damage the newly refurbished ship, attached high powered magnets to the back of the artwork hoping it would stick to its hull.

What I can say is that since 2003 the docks have become a hive of activity with rowing clubs, tour boats and the harbourmaster making it a bit of a challenge, especially when you don't own a river-worthy boat.

While waiting for the right opportunity, I had a drink with friends in the pub opposite. I am pretty sure they were all eager to see me fall in. Having waited until the water activities had slowed down, I ran down the jetty with a small inflatable boat and the artwork, which was near enough the same size as the inflatable. As you can imagine, this made rowing a bit of a challenge. A rat bid me farewell as it ran along a mooring rope of a nearby boat and I rowed as steady and as quickly as I could whilst still hearing the laughing from the pub and hoping not to lose an oar. The artwork stuck to the hull like a limpet mine with a big clunk and it stayed there for I think it was around 12 months before coming off in a storm. But it was later fished out of the dock and I believe hung inside the Thekla.

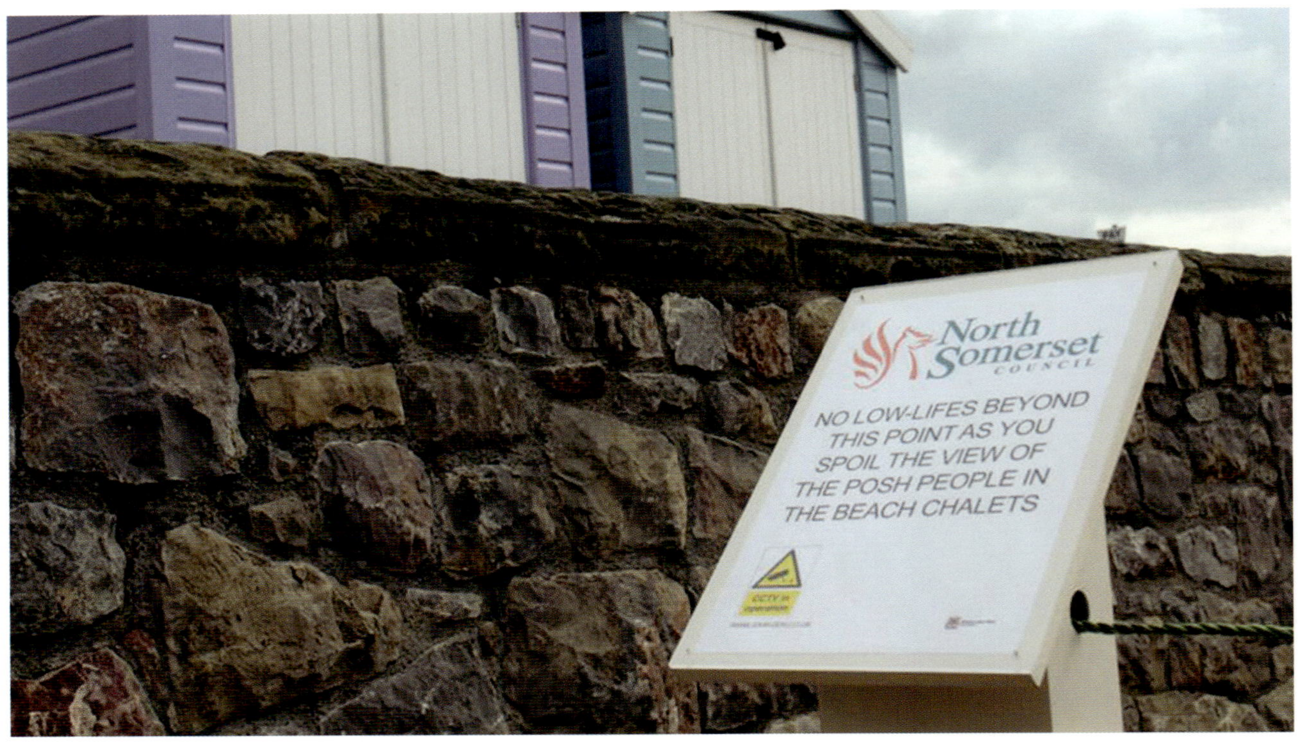

"NO LOW-LIFES" IN WESTON-SUPER-MARE

The original plans by North Somerset Council in 2015 to build 100 huts along the seafront of Weston-super-Mare were abandoned after public consultation and instead 24 huts were constructed. Humorously, the Council broke its own planning codes by making them 20 per cent too big and had to apply for retroactive permission. A row broke out in Weston-super-Mare after signs appeared asking people not to use the promenade in front of the new beach huts. The signs declared: "The promenade in front of these beach huts is reserved for beach hut users. Please respect their privacy." Apparently, the signs were put up after several near-misses with cyclists and passers-by being rude and intrusive to the owners of the huts. Locals argued that it was demeaning to be forced to walk behind the privately-owned huts and lose their publicly shared sea view. In response to this, I created a satirical public notice out of recycled goods, emblazoned with official paraphernalia such as the North Somerset Council logo and a "CCTV in operation", saying "NO LOW-LIFES BEYOND THIS POINT AS YOU WILL SPOIL THE VIEW OF THE POSH PEOPLE IN THE BEACH CHALETS".

The artwork only took around an hour to build and just minutes to install. The piece soon disappeared and the Council claimed not to have taken it away, so it was perhaps taken by art collectors who kept a keen eye out for any street art in the area after the Dismaland exhibition. Not only did I want to satirise this privatisation of the public and environmental commons by those with financial superiority, I also wanted to criticise how the local authority was overtly siding with moneyed outsiders rather than the local residents who live there and pay their salaries. The issue has become increasingly confrontational, with the beach hut renters being driven away by having their furniture thrown onto

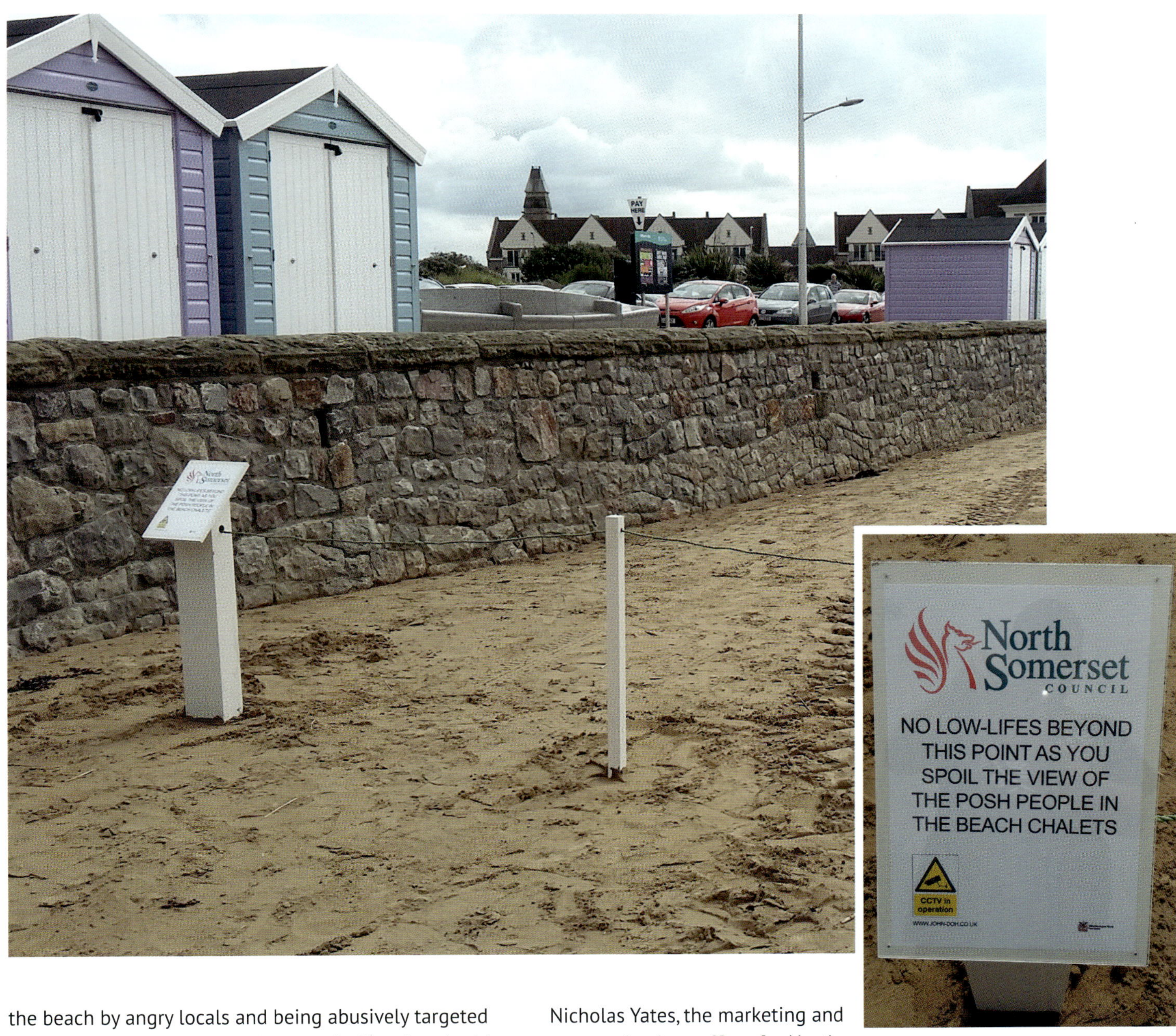

the beach by angry locals and being abusively targeted online by those opposed to the so-called 'garden sheds'. This is why my political art is often a bit humorous, jocular or silly – it is a way of raising issues or criticising people at fault in a way that makes people laugh, smile and think without encouraging aggression, violence and unnecessary confrontation. This is perhaps why Nicholas Yates, the marketing and communications officer for North Somerset Council praised my work in the *Bristol Post* for its "commentary" and for being "quite amusing". Art helps raise awareness, create discussion and changes minds without the need to resort to violence.

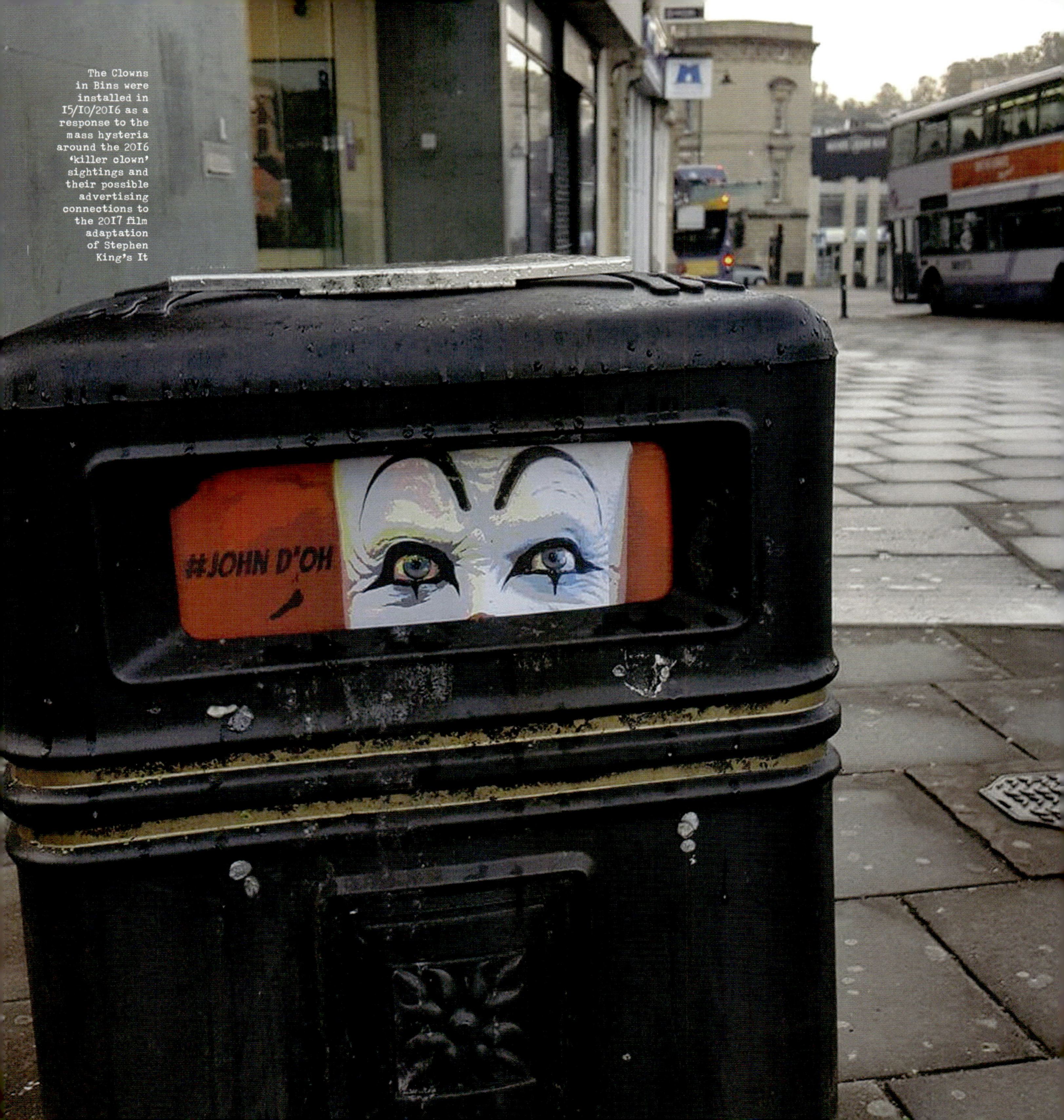

The Clowns in Bins were installed in 15/10/2016 as a response to the mass hysteria around the 2016 'killer clown' sightings and their possible advertising connections to the 2017 film adaptation of Stephen King's It

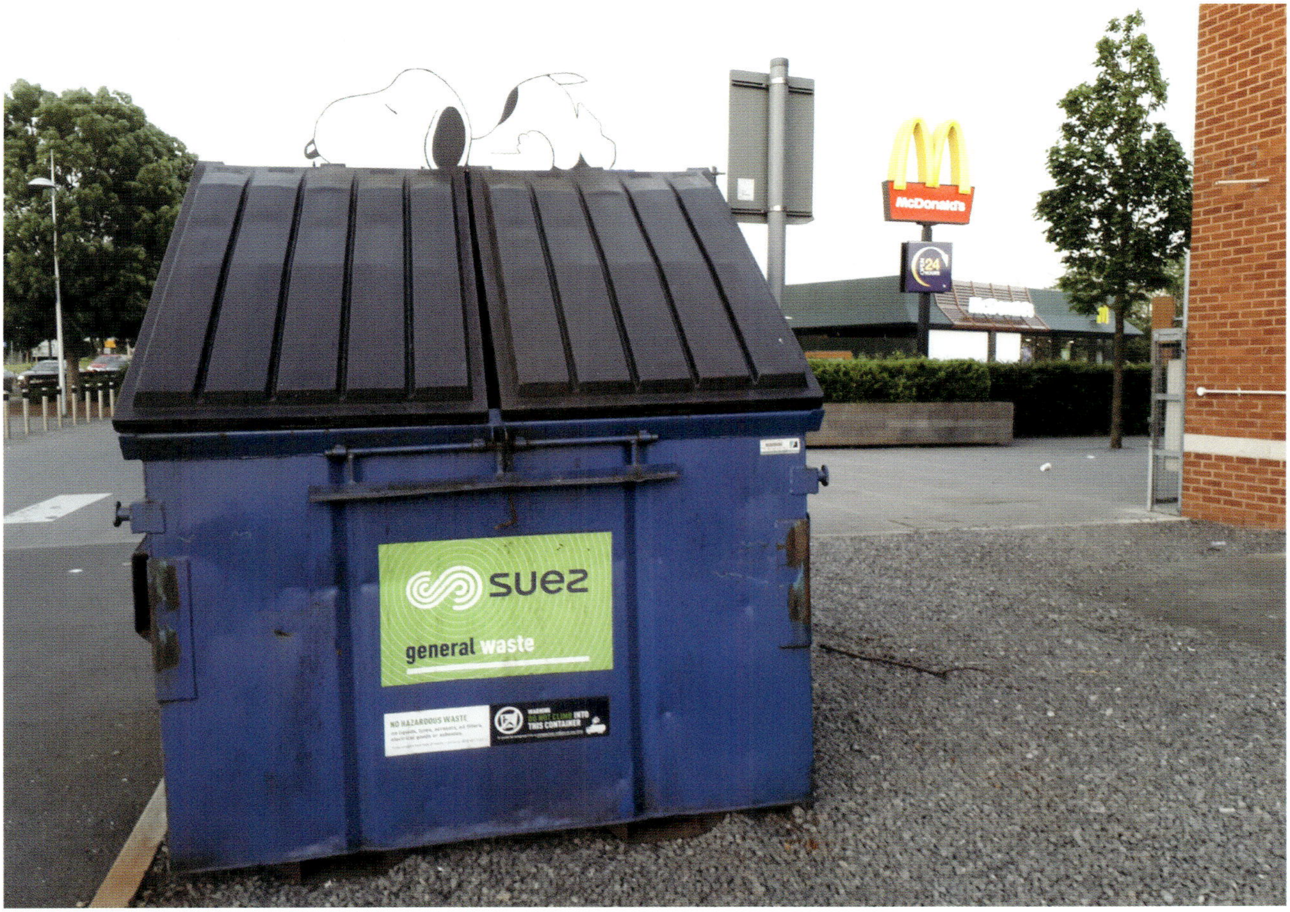

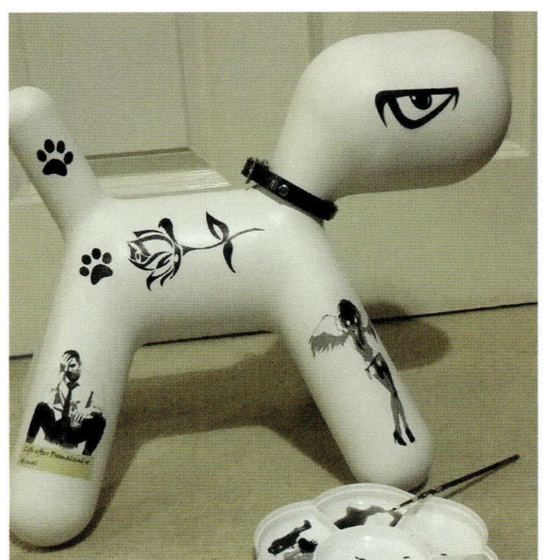
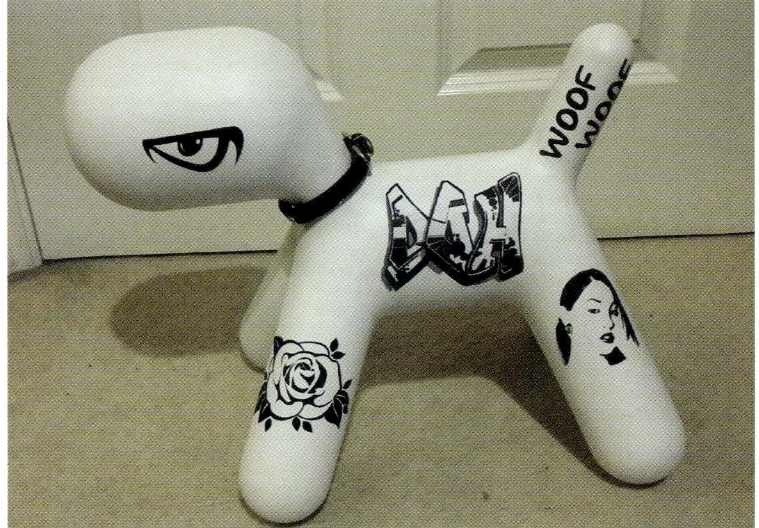
WOOF
WOOF

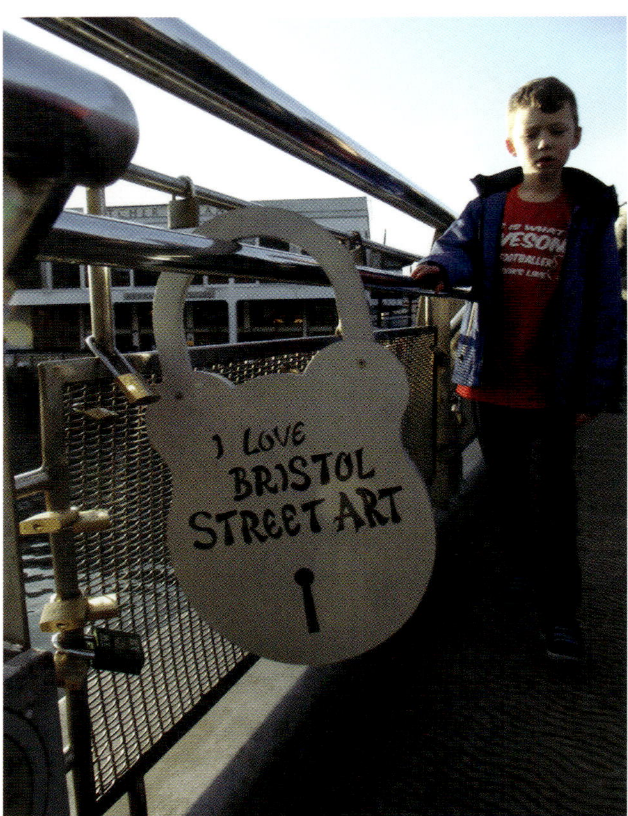

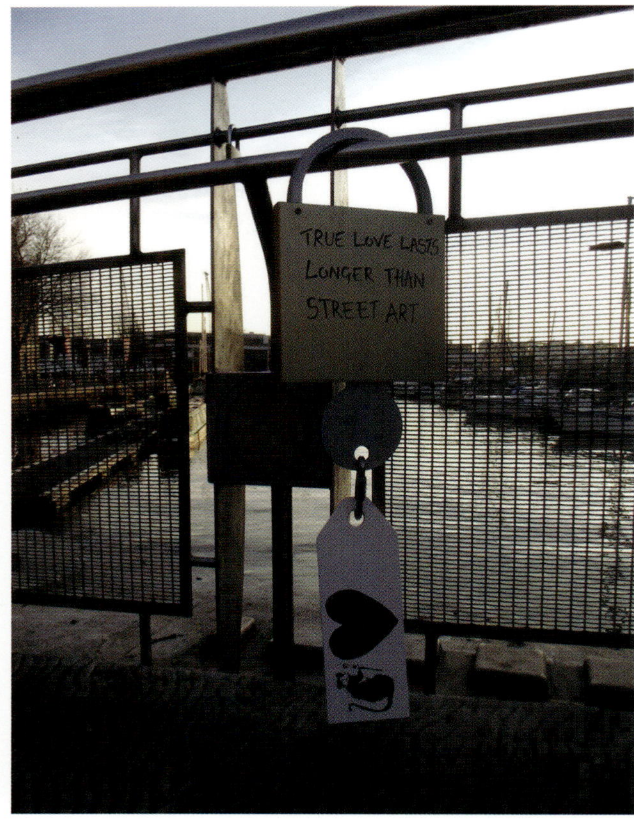

VALENTINE'S DAY

Love Locks

I love my city. Bristol is a vibrant, diverse metropolis with a lot of exciting and interesting events constantly happening. It has a fantastic music and arts scene and is home to some of the most famous graffiti and street artists in the world. Since 2014, I have been doing something humorous for Valentine's Day. It all started with some large padlocks I attached to Pero's Bridge, a local landmark that had gradually accumulated hundreds of small "love locks" over the years. This caused a bit of a stir. A "love lock" is a padlock, sometimes inscribed with a message, which couples affix to a bridge, monument or similar public structure to symbolize their "unbreakable" commitment to each other. In the last two decades, love locks have become more and more common at different locations worldwide. For some authorities, these romantic destinations have been embraced as tourist attractions and used for charity or other fundraising projects. For other authorities, however, the locks are treated as litter, vandalism or a safety hazard. The protective railings on some bridges have been damaged and even fallen off under the weight of all the attached locks. Others complain that historical, ancient and traditionally beautiful bridges are now adorned with modern, metallic and mass-produced padlocks that ruin the aesthetic and can cost quite a bit to remove. I placed quite a few oversized love locks on the bridge but shortly afterward the elected Mayor at the time George Ferguson called for the removal of all the locks because he considered them to be "a menace" that could impair

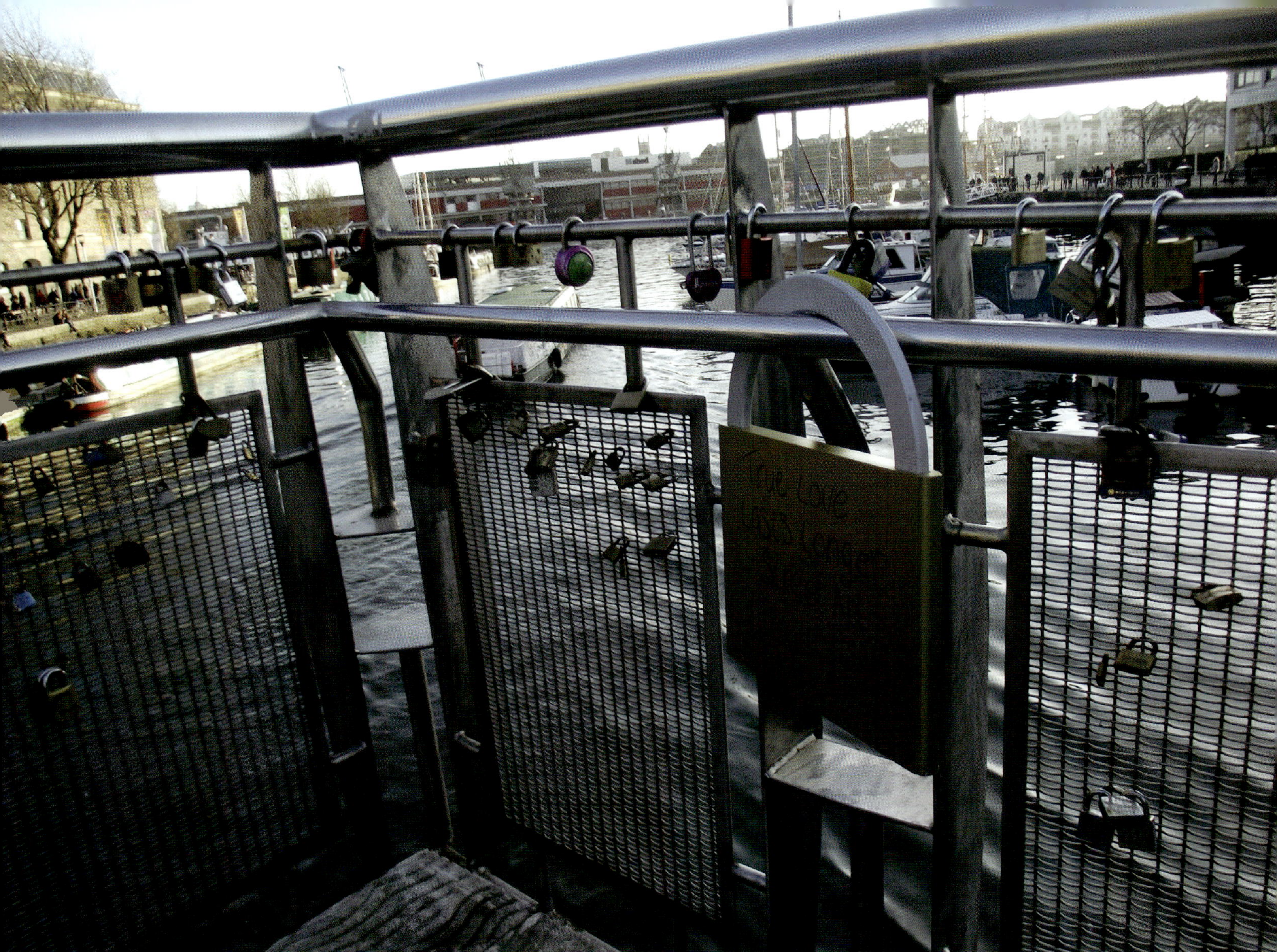

the bridge's operational function when it lifts. I recall that he also found them ugly and detracting from the architecture. It was featured in the *Bristol Post* and the locks were starting to be removed with bolt-cutters, but a public backlash meant that the locks were all allowed to stay. I was invited to go on the *Radio Bristol* Morning Show with Sacha Bigwood but, being an anonymous street artist, I had to decline. By writing "True love lasts longer than street art" on the lock I wanted to highlight the hypocritical disparity between the constant removal of street art and the public acceptance of attaching locks to a bridge forever.

Moreover, by making the locks comically huge, I aimed to show how these outward gestures of romantic attachment are, like graffiti, essentially individualistic in nature; a personal declaration of private feeling that colonises the public space.

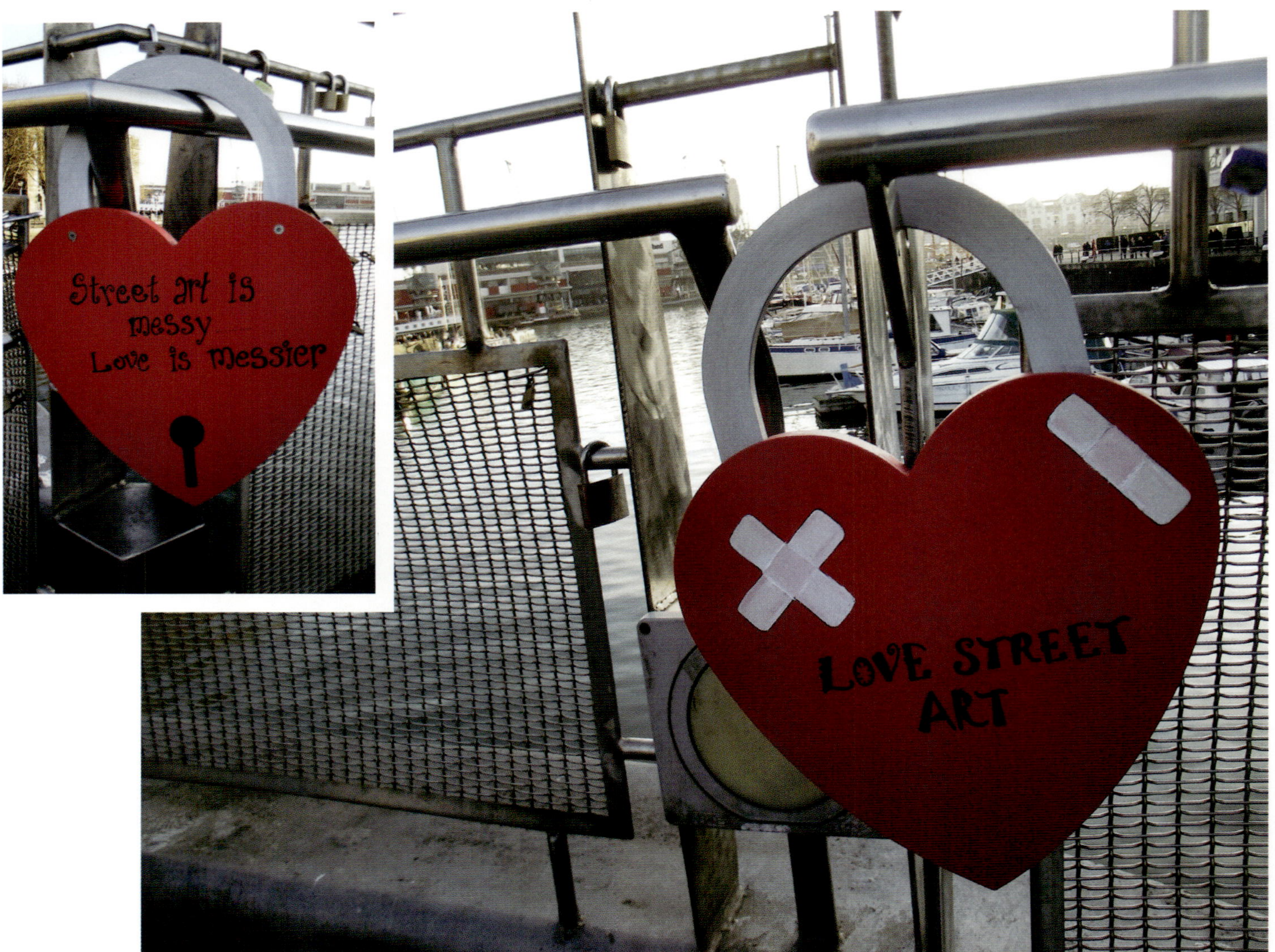

Love Hearts

I placed these large, colourful imitations of Love Heart sweets on lampposts around Bedminster, St. Wergburgh's and Brick Lane in London. However, I replaced the phrases that you find on the original confectionary with my own little slogans and comments. One remained in Brick Lane for well over a year. The "hug-a-hoodie" expression was part of David Cameron's attempt to shift the Conservatives' image on crime from punitive to rehabilitative, rhetoric which was later contradicted by his "Broken Britain" campaign. By using a mass-produced and sentimental sweet, I intended to demonstrate how spurious this political catchphrase was.

Skeletons

I placed a male skeleton on a bench outside Habitat and a female skeleton on the top of Park Street, both holding boards saying "waiting for love". It probably was one of

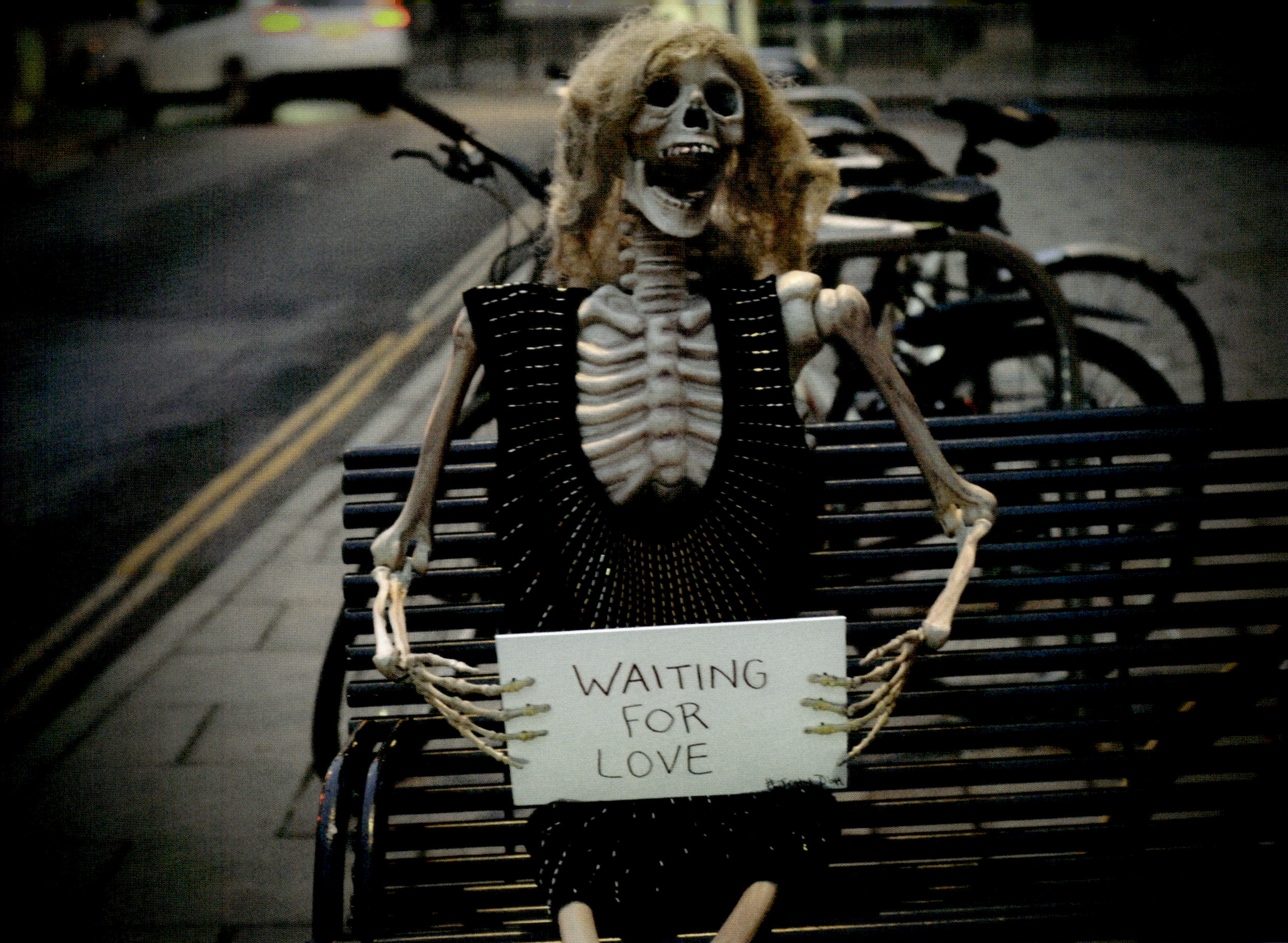

my most successful stunts so far and was featured in a couple of newspapers. It featured heavily on social media, with people queuing up to have their photos taken and interacting with them. Apparently, I heard that students eventually removed both the skeletons and reunited them together on another bench in a local park.

Where is the love?
I had planned to do so much more on Valentine's Day 2018, but it rained solidly all day. I painted a piece about homelessness in the Bristol Bearpit, to highlight the fact that the number of homeless people in the city has risen by a shocking 128 per cent over the past three years. After so much negativity appearing in the newspapers, portraying the homeless as gangs and professional beggars, I wanted to spread a little love on Valentine's Day to all our fellow citizens.

Love Notice
Board. Bristol
Bearpit
Valentine's
Day 2018. Just
a collection
of paste ups
I produced to
raise a smile

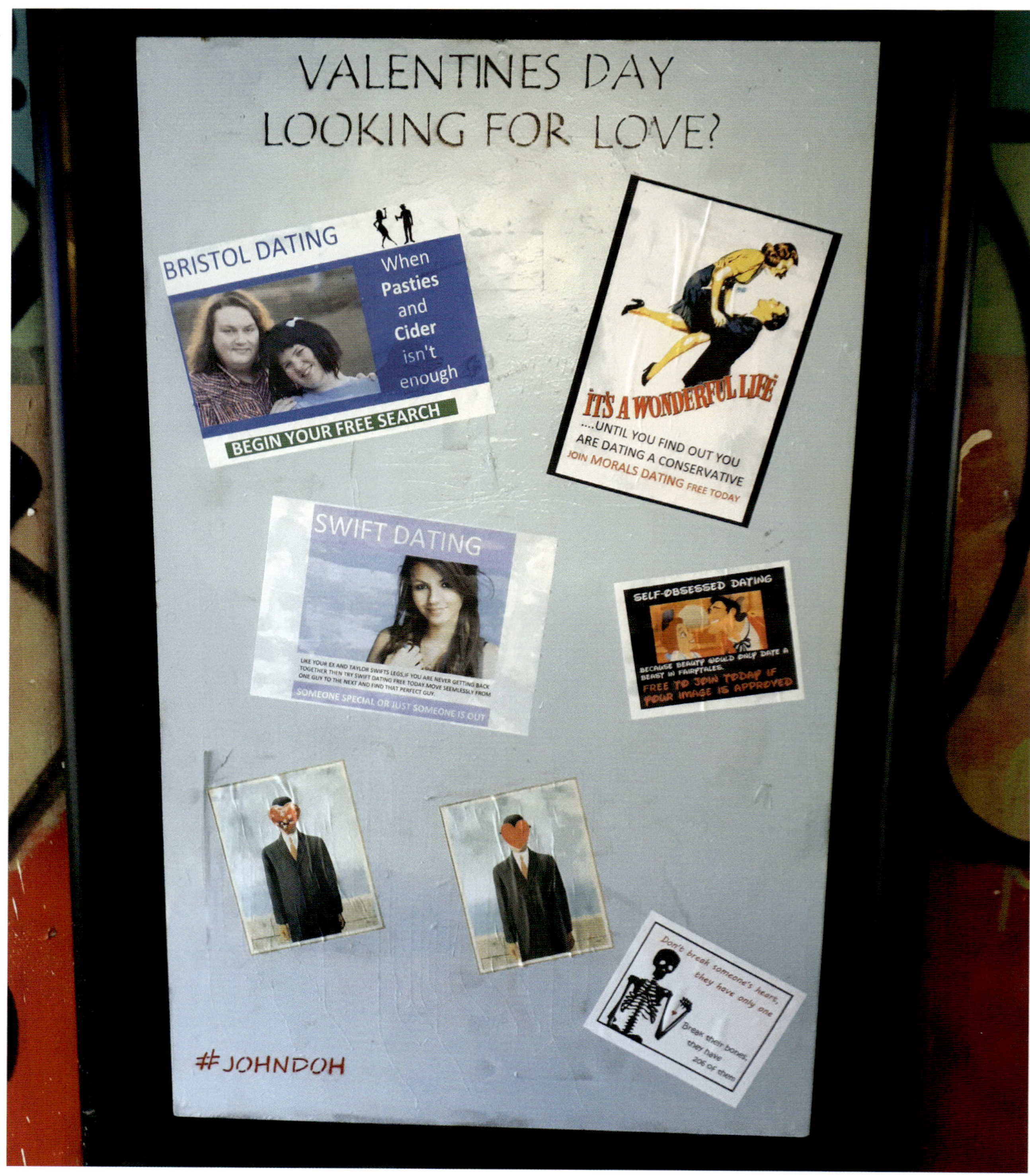

VALENTINES DAY
LOOKING FOR LOVE?

BRISTOL DATING
When
Pasties
and
Cider
isn't
enough
BEGIN YOUR FREE SEARCH

IT'S A WONDERFUL LIFE
....UNTIL YOU FIND OUT YOU
ARE DATING A CONSERVATIVE
JOIN MORALS DATING FREE TODAY

SWIFT DATING
LIKE YOUR EX AND TAYLOR SWIFTS LEGS,IF YOU ARE NEVER GETTING BACK
TOGETHER THEN TRY SWIFT DATING FREE TODAY,MOVE SEEMLESSLY FROM
ONE GUY TO THE NEXT AND FIND THAT PERFECT GUY.
SOMEONE SPECIAL OR JUST SOMEONE IS OUT

SELF-OBSESSED DATING
BECAUSE BEAUTY WOULD ONLY DATE A
BEAST IN FAIRYTALES.
FREE TO JOIN TODAY IF
YOUR IMAGE IS APPROVED

Don't break someone's heart,
they have only one
Break their bones,
they have
206 of them

#JOHNDOH

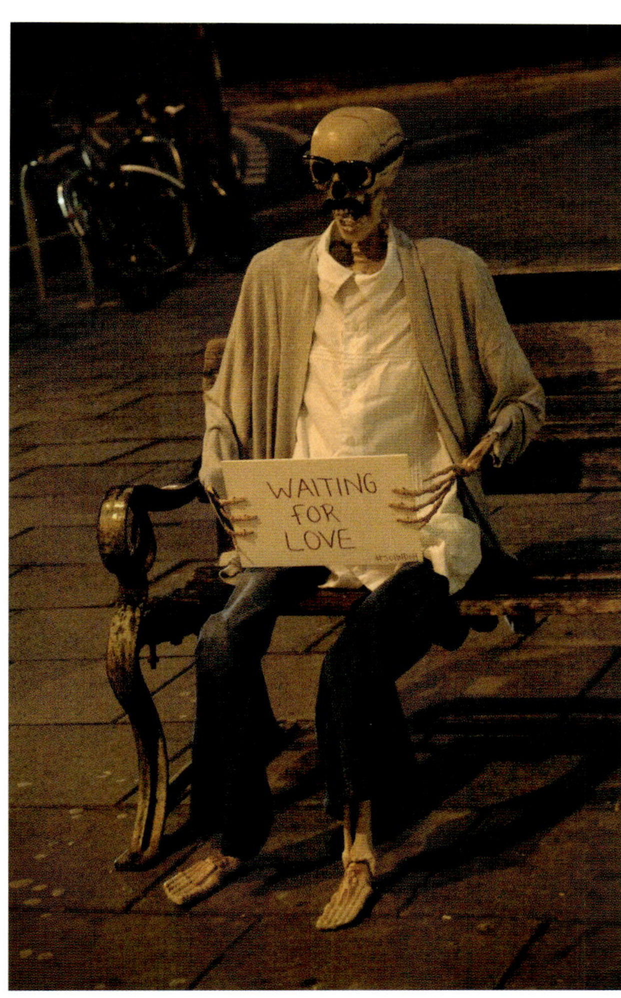

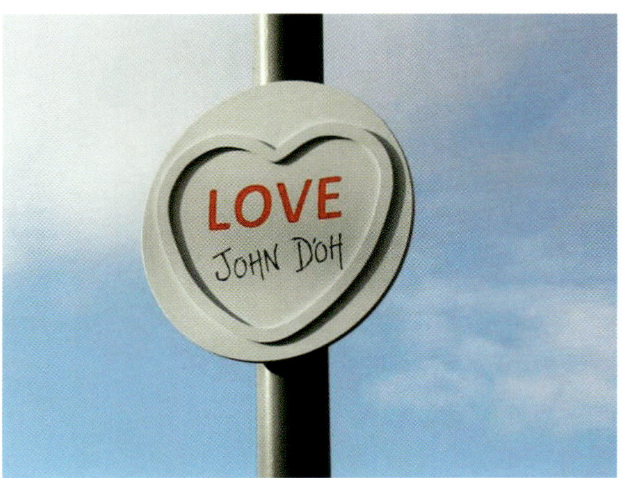

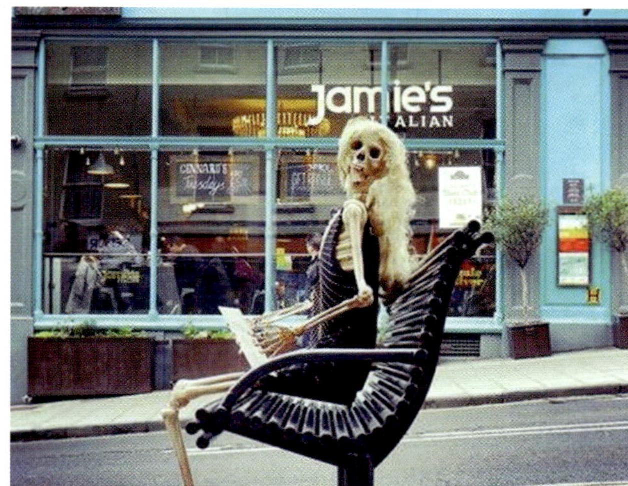

Valentine's Day 2017 Male Skeleton installation. Positioned outside the old Habitat building in Clifton Bristol. People were queuing to have their photos taken sitting next to the skeletons (featured prominently on social media and in various newspapers)

Female skeleton installed at the top of Park Street 2017

Love hearts attached to lamp posts in Bedminster, St Werburgh's (Farm pub) and Brick Lane in London for Valentine's Day 2016

Spreading Love to the Homeless. Valentine's Day 2018: A quote from Theresa May said "Homeless does not mean homeless" as she desperately tried to play down the rising number of homeless as the numbers sored and individuals were found dead on our streets during one of the coldest winters for years

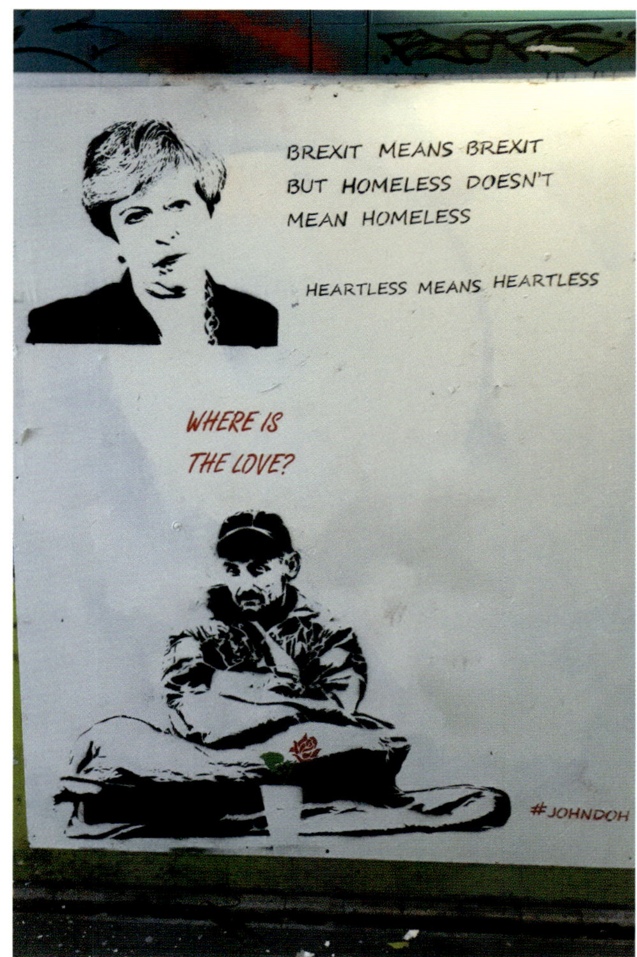

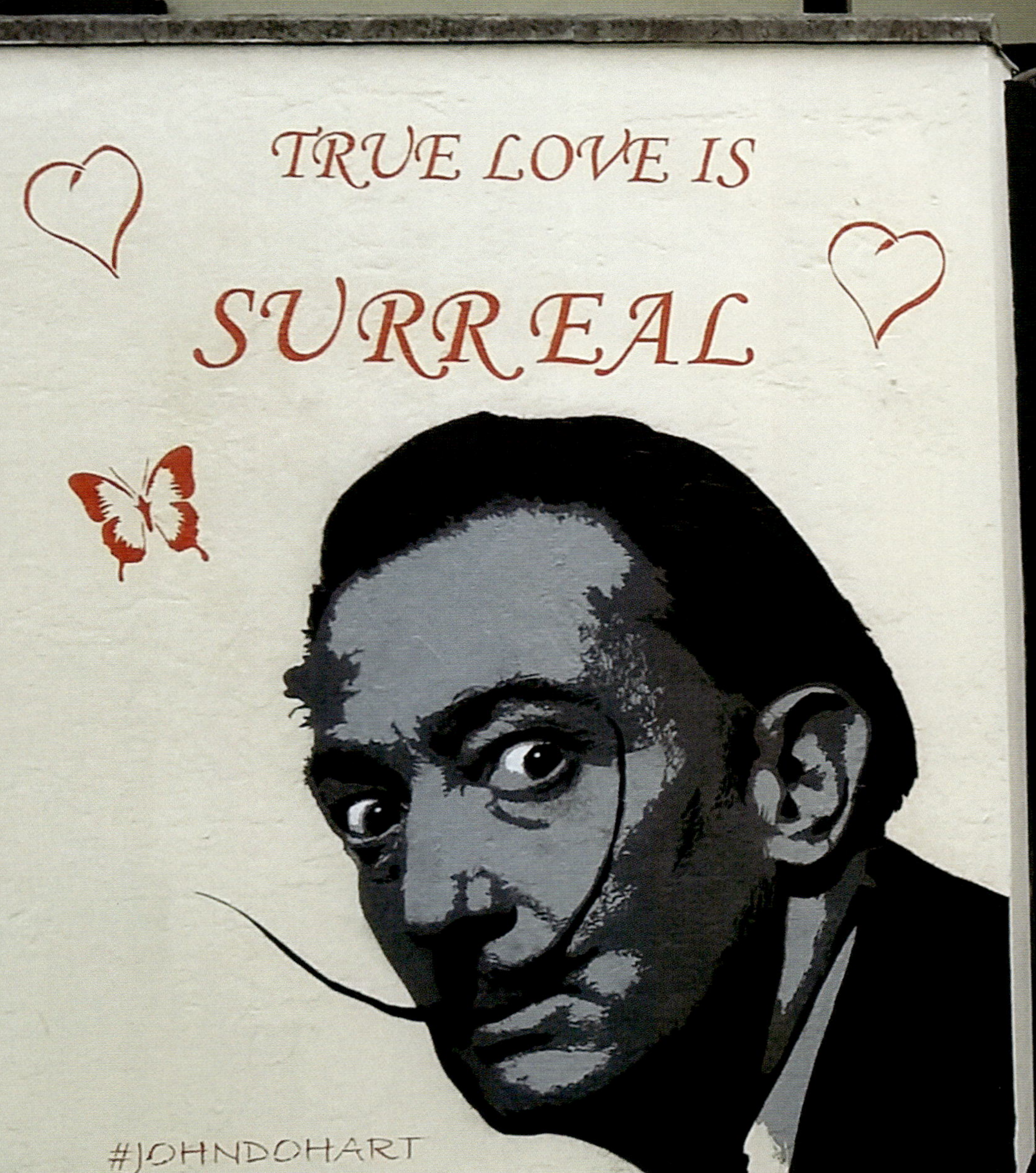

TRUE LOVE IS
SURREAL
#JOHNDOHART

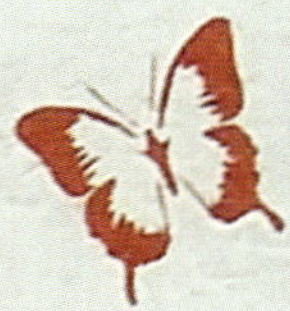

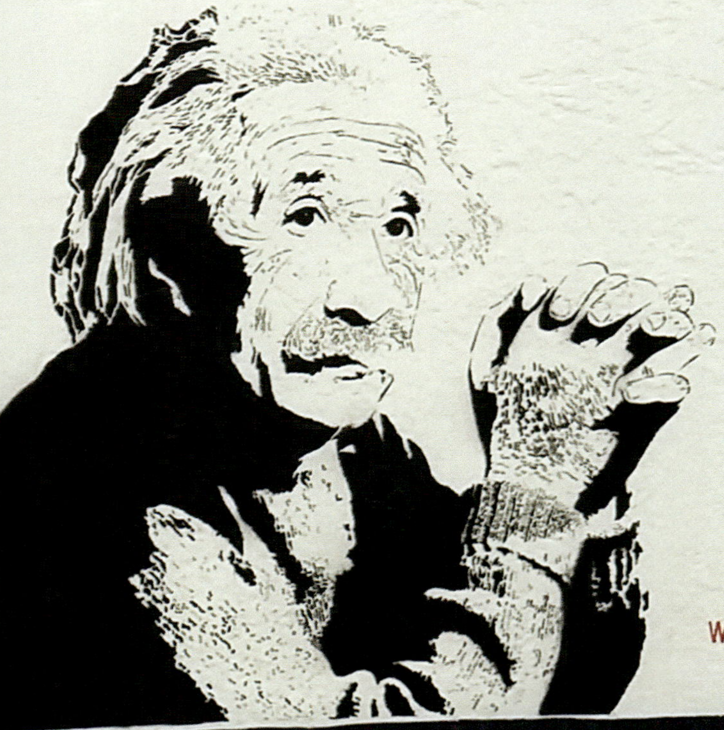
THERE IS NO EQUATION
FOR LOVE
√JOHN
D'OH
www.john-doh.co.uk

Conclusion

History is littered with many embarrassing and incorrect attempts by artists, critics and commentators to summarise, canonise and prophesise the artistic output, trends and personalities of their time.

Contemporary street art is no longer seen primarily as a criminal or iconoclastic act, instead graffiti is increasingly accepted, commercialised and legitimised as part of mainstream popular culture. From popular brands to politicians, the style of urban art has been used and appropriated in order to generate and profit from an aura of reckless individuality and authenticity. In looking around at the current urban art scene, the growing usage of trompe l'oeil, anamorphosis and forced perspective by street artists in order to create detailed and misleading three-dimensional imagery seems to suggest that graffiti is in a kind of "baroque phase", perhaps due to its ever-increasing popularity and social media use. In the past, the otherwise flat and enclosed interior space of a baroque church was opened up by illusionistic paintings of a heavenly sky or fictional dome on its ceiling in order to show how art, ritual and spirituality could transcend our mundane, earthly existence by inspiring awe in churchgoers. The elaborate set-pieces created by contemporary three-dimensional street artists also attempts to surprise its viewers, perhaps temporarily stirring them out of their anonymous commute or conformist shopping and causing them to rethink their preconceptions about how "open" or "free" our cityscapes really are. This can be seen, for example, in the misleading and interactive artwork of individuals such as Odeith, Leon Keer and Edgar Müller. Critics of the baroque claimed that it was an excessively sentimental, ornamental or amoral style. Likewise, critics of contemporary street art dislike these large optical illusions for apparently being concerned more with delighting viewers with theatrical spectacle or emotion rather than challenging them with political, social and moral ideas. In fact, the installation of large, prefabricated and mixed-material artworks is also on the rise; when I started my artistic "career" I was one of the first to use this process, but now, even just in Bristol, there are dozens. While this playful and often selfie-friendly artwork seems to be more and more popular with the public, in the same way that the extravagant mannerism of the baroque gave way to a neoclassicism that focused on rationality, morality and classicism, perhaps the future of street art will be reactionary and result in a more austere, overtly moral and self-consciously cultural kind of imagery?

In reaction to globalisation, environmental concerns and work-life imbalances, urban designers from many countries are returning to traditional and classical styles of architecture in order to reaffirm a sense of national identity and city planners are embracing a new pedestrianism which promotes walkable neighbourhoods with green spaces, safe streets and easily-accessible infrastructure. The most well-known example in the United Kingdom is the experimental new town of Poundbury in Dorset. These theatrically old-fashioned places have architectural details or iconography that may seem superfluous and without function in these commercial and utilitarian times, but they express to the passerby a shared sense of community, civility and aesthetic enjoyment. While this opposition to suburban sprawl, anonymous cosmopolitanism and mindless consumerism shares similarities with the artistic and anti-capitalist functions of street art, this "New Urbanism" is in opposition to many of the social, economic and cultural changes that have fostered, promoted and legitimised street art. Indeed, any tagging, stencils or spray paint would be seen, even more so than usual, not as a way of personalising and reclaiming the cityscape, but as a narcissistic attack on the common space and shared environment.

As technology continues to develop, we can already see artists adapting and innovating to find new ways to create art. Carlo Ratti's 'Paint By Drone' system uses the flying robots to recreate any artwork submitted to its mobile app on a multi-storey building or other inaccessible surface. But, as we have seen, graffiti and urban art can often be appropriate for commercial and political reasons. Previously, drones have been heavily associated with inaccurate unmanned warfare or sneaking drugs into prisons, so transforming drones into instruments of art and individualism may be seen as part of a wider attempt to rehabilitate the public image of the potentially disruptive technology, which also includes using drones in documentaries on archaeology and history. Drones, like street art, often access areas normally considered out of reach or off-limits for members of the public, including private residences and government sites. And, like graffiti on another individual's wall, a drone hovering over a person's garden or an airport may be a form of self-expression that also violates certain privacy laws, property rights and even safety legislation. Arguably, then, the ongoing debate about the legality and self-expression of street art intertwines with and mirrors the issues about violent content, fake information and free speech on the internet and other contemporary technologies.

What originally started out as a bit of schoolboy fun or perhaps even vandalism has evolved throughout the course of my life into a more focused, methodical and pre-planned approach to art with an emphasis on making a meaningful statement about the times we live in. My personal journey is proof that you don't need to paint something huge and flashy in order to make a difference – even a small stencil painted at the right time and in the right place can make people think, laugh or become outraged to great social effect. In fact, in a landscape crammed with advertising billboards and neon signs that often borrow the imagery of urban art in order to seem subversive, pre-empt anti-consumerist criticism and increase sales, making a localistic, personal or low-key artwork may be the only true challenge to impersonal consumerism in our anonymous public spaces.

In many ways, however, my street art still maintains elements of the practical joke. Whether it is rowing around Bristol Harbour on a dingy or almost falling down a large hill of dirt, the process of creating or installing the artworks has elements of buffoonery or prankishness. Unlike the self-importance of an art gallery or museum, these light-hearted actions or silly images subvert the functionality, seriousness and oppressiveness of the commercialised and anonymous urban space, raising awareness and bringing people together through laughter and humour.

As I have become more well-known due to my controversial and humorous pieces in the local and national news, painting anonymously has become more of a challenge. I have even had the ironic honour of giving a talk at the Parson Street Primary School in Bristol as part of the "well-known Bristolians" week they were hosting. Some may question the morality and educational purpose of teaching or talking to children about street art or vandalism, but the inherent challenges that street art proposes as an aesthetic form cause us to reflect on the differences between the public and private spheres, between anonymity and identity and between artistic expression and personal responsibility to others. To quote Salvador Dali: "Those who do not want to imitate anything, produce nothing." And in the street art scene, nearly everything is imitated, dissected and recreated for the better, furthering debate and creating a shared culture. Surely, if street art can inspire, encourage and provoke such important ideas in the next generation, then it is a worthwhile endeavour to teach it. In response to stories about declining literacy rates among children and their overexposure to the internet or social media, encouraging children to think creatively and actively engage in the world may help them to develop the useful skills and social attitudes necessary in twenty-first century Britain.

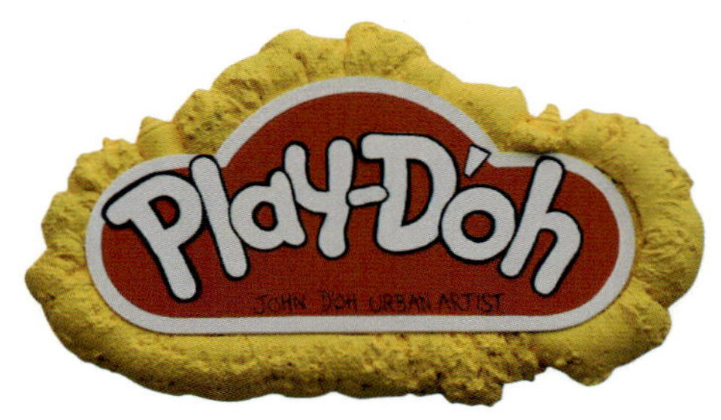
Play-Doh
JOHN DOH URBAN ARTIST